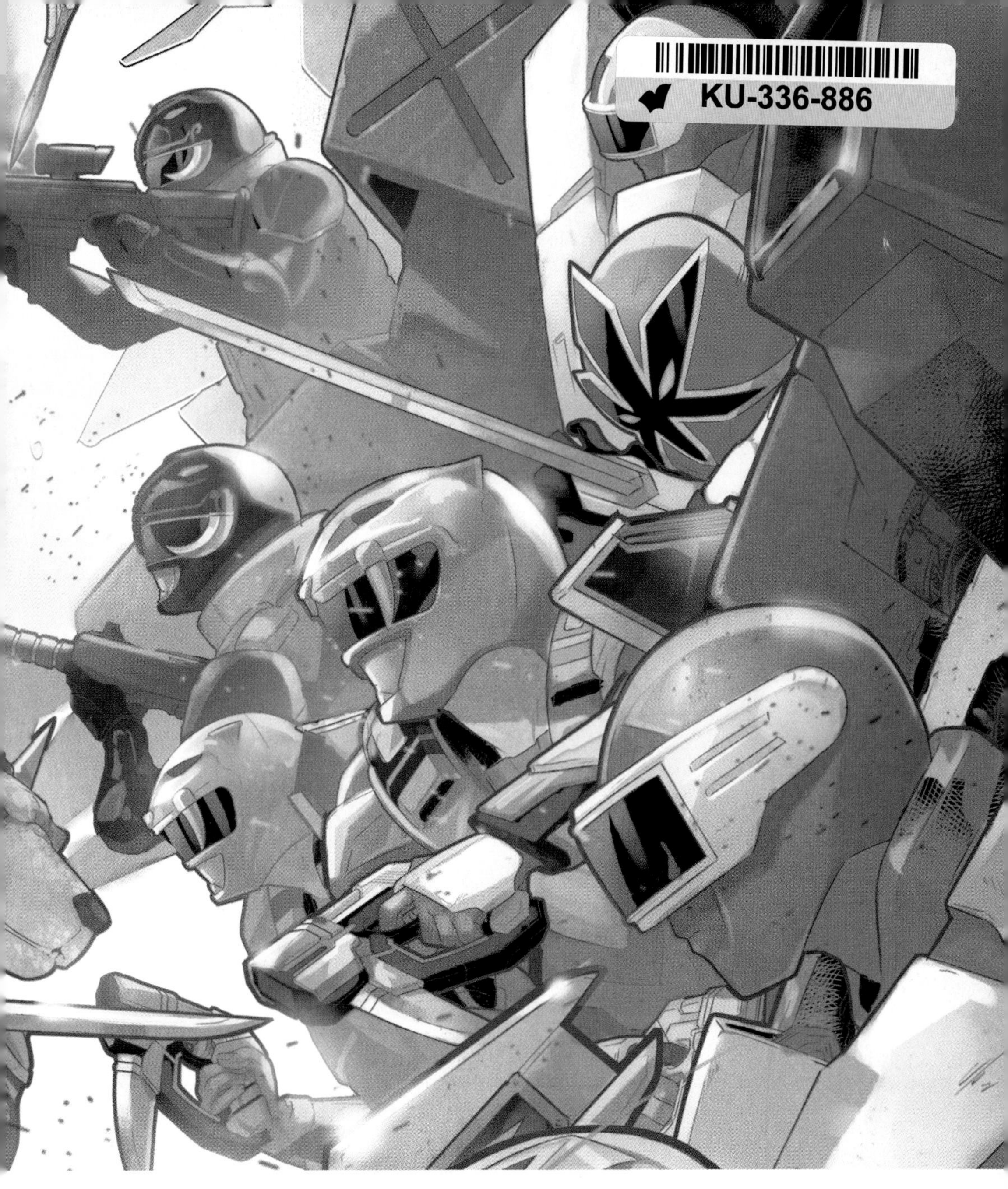

WRITTEN BY
KYLE HIGGINS

ILLUSTRATED BY
DANIELE DI NICUOLO
WITH INK ASSISTANCE BY
SIMONA DI GIANFELICE

COLORS BY
WALTER BAIAMONTE

LETTERS BY
ED DUKESHIRE

COVER BY
JAMAL CAMPBELL

SERIES DESIGNER
SCOTT NEWMAN

COLLECTION DESIGNER
JILLIAN CRAB

SERIES ASSISTANT EDITOR
MICHAEL MOCCIO

COLLECTION ASSISTANT EDITOR
GWEN WALLER

EDITOR
DAFNA PLEBAN

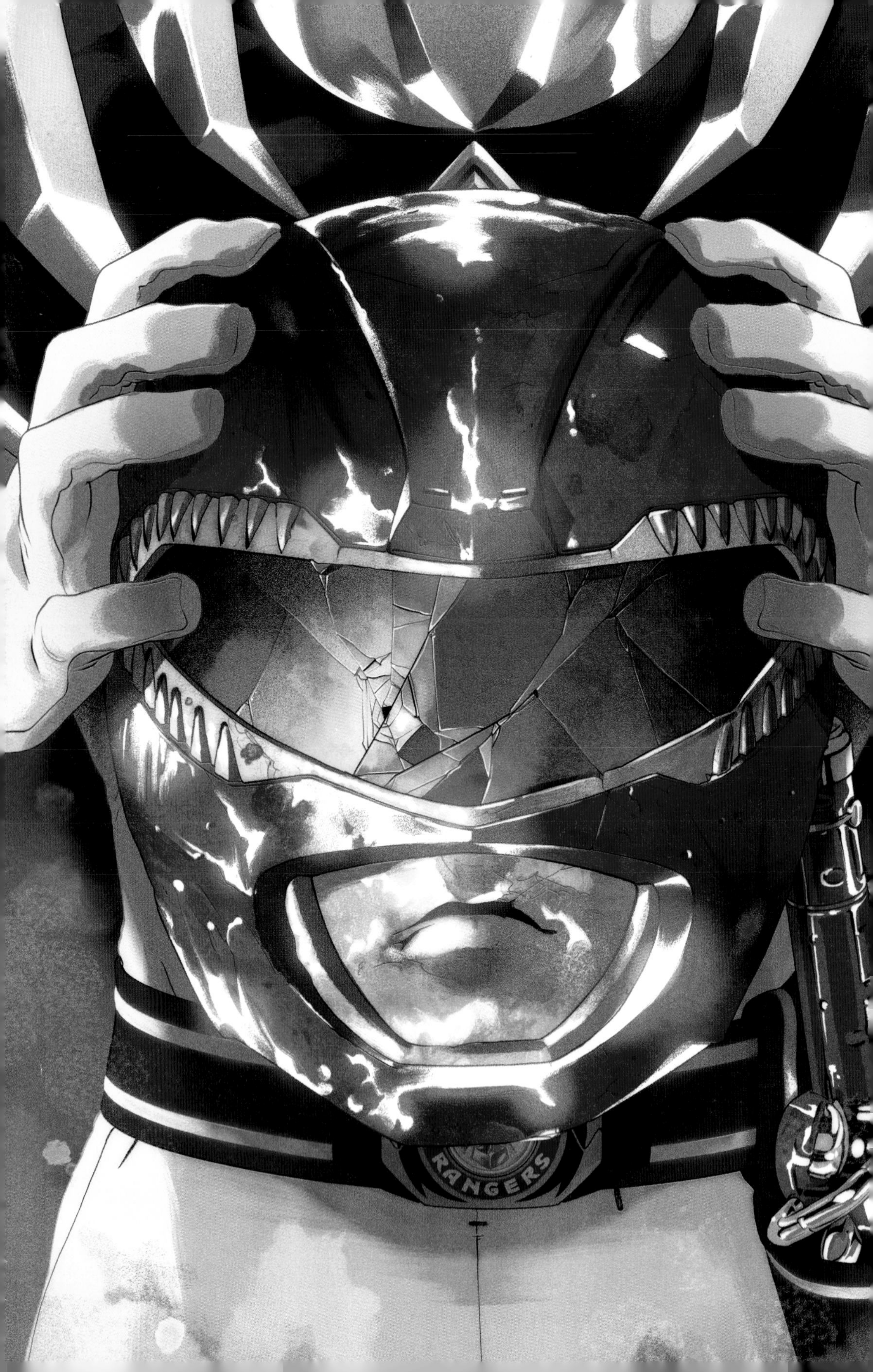
RANGERS

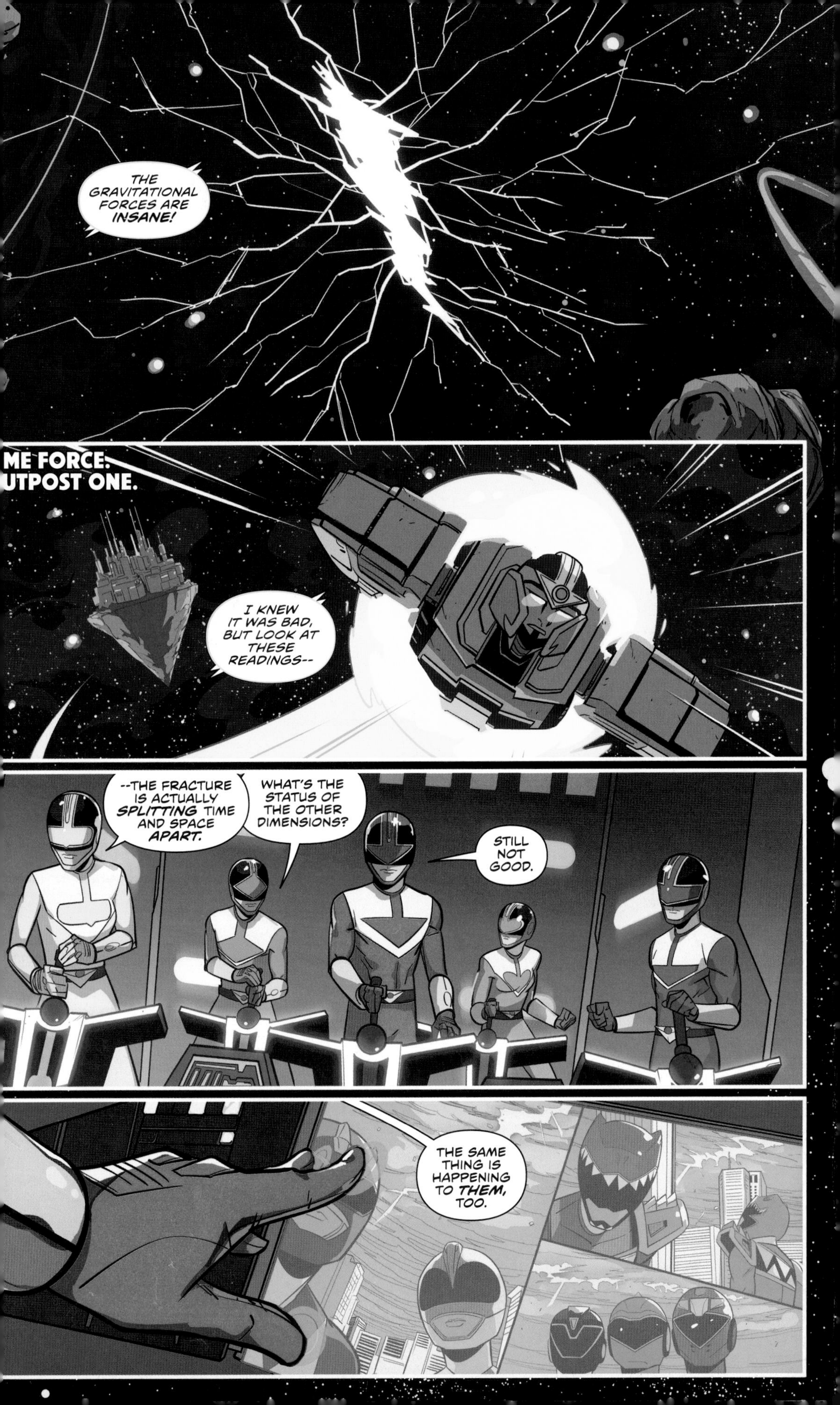

THE GRAVITATIONAL FORCES ARE INSANE!
ME FORCE: UTPOST ONE.
I KNEW IT WAS BAD, BUT LOOK AT THESE READINGS--
--THE FRACTURE IS ACTUALLY SPLITTING TIME AND SPACE APART.
WHAT'S THE STATUS OF THE OTHER DIMENSIONS?
STILL NOT GOOD.
THE SAME THING IS HAPPENING TO THEM, TOO.

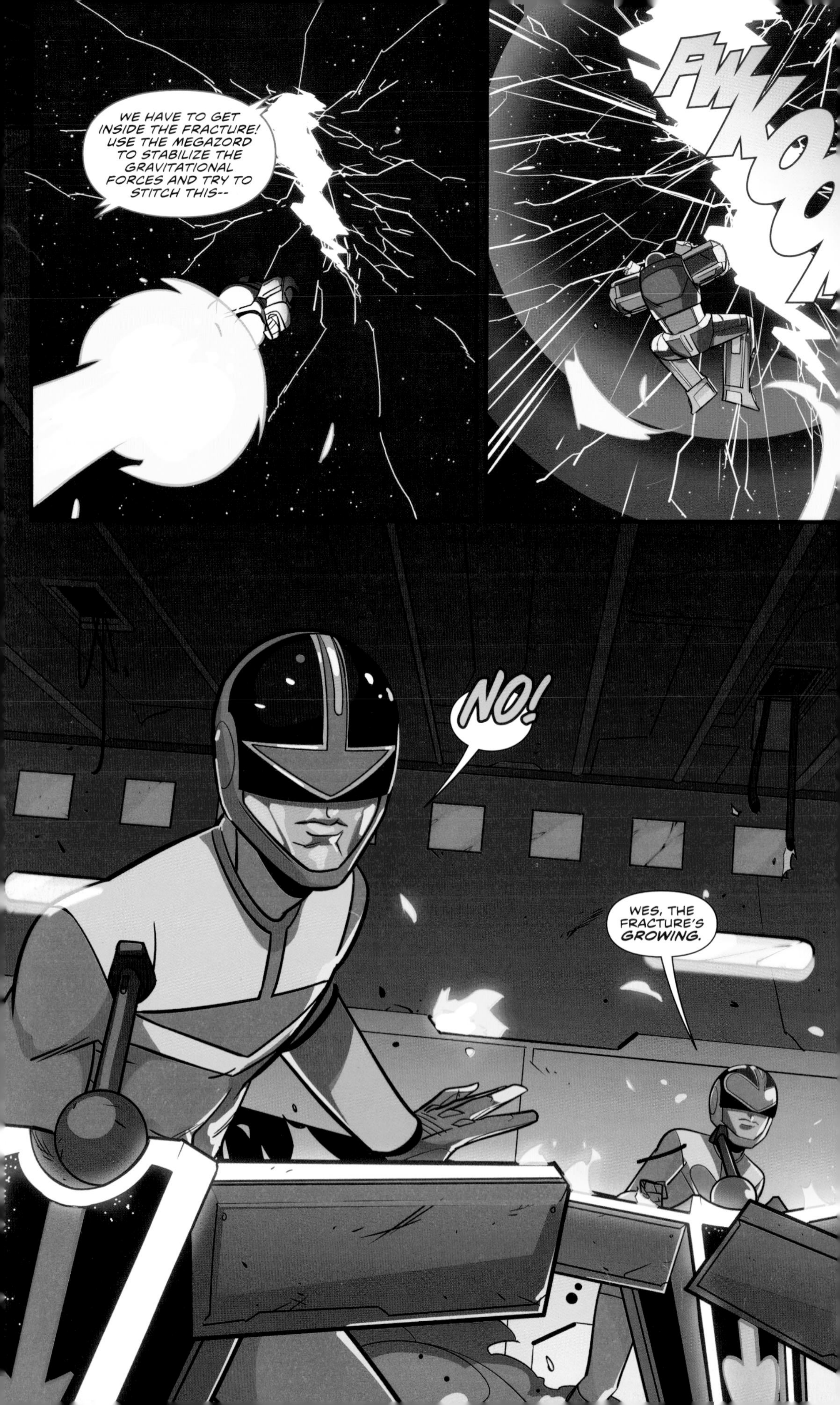
WE HAVE TO GET INSIDE THE FRACTURE! USE THE MEGAZORD TO STABILIZE THE GRAVITATIONAL FORCES AND TRY TO STITCH THIS--
FWKOO
NO!
WES, THE FRACTURE'S GROWING.

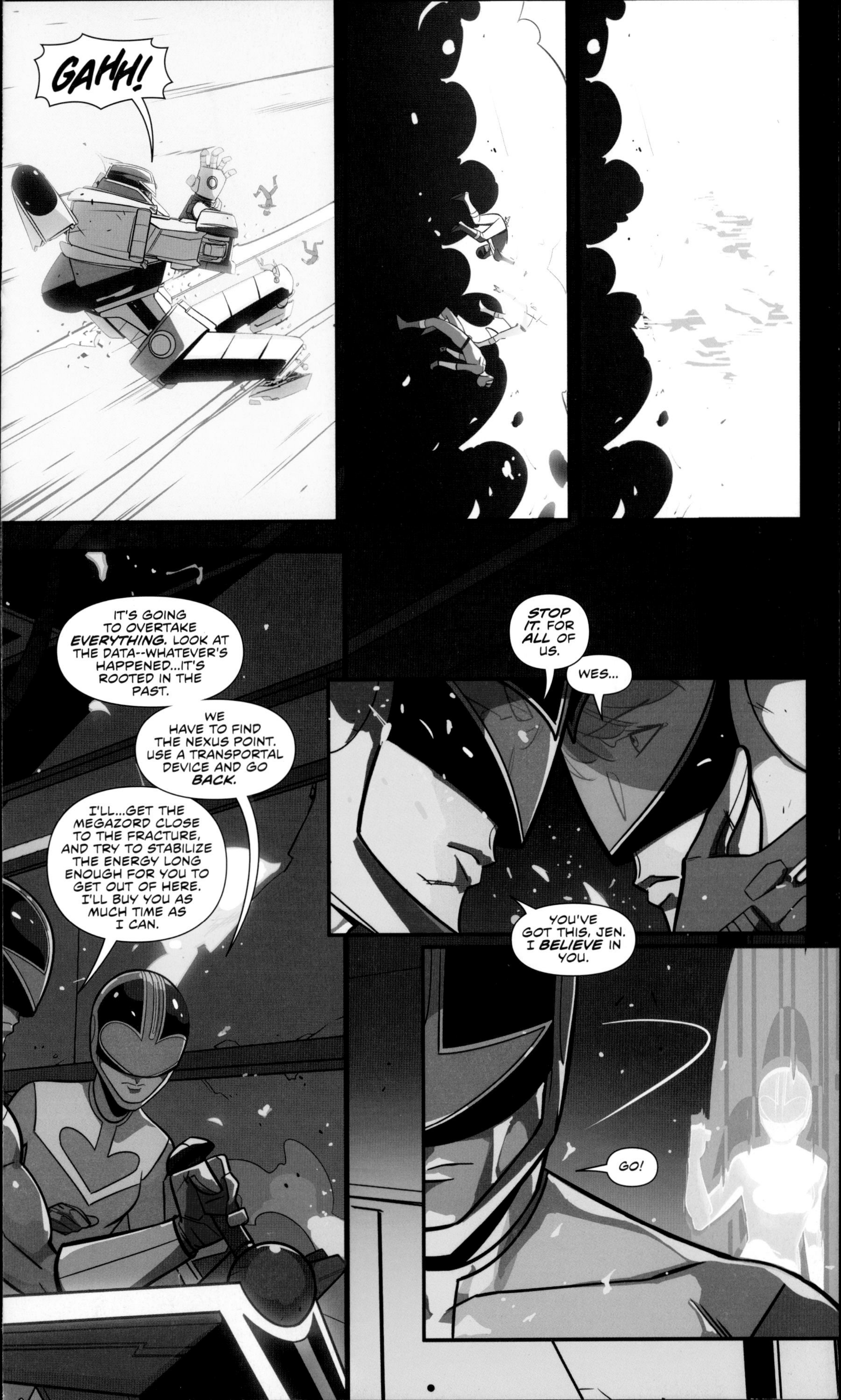
GAHH!
IT'S GOING TO OVERTAKE EVERYTHING. LOOK AT THE DATA--WHATEVER'S HAPPENED...IT'S ROOTED IN THE PAST.
WE HAVE TO FIND THE NEXUS POINT. USE A TRANSPORTAL DEVICE AND GO BACK.
I'LL...GET THE MEGAZORD CLOSE TO THE FRACTURE, AND TRY TO STABILIZE THE ENERGY LONG ENOUGH FOR YOU TO GET OUT OF HERE. I'LL BUY YOU AS MUCH TIME AS I CAN.
STOP IT. FOR ALL OF US.
WES...
YOU'VE GOT THIS, JEN. I BELIEVE IN YOU.
GO!

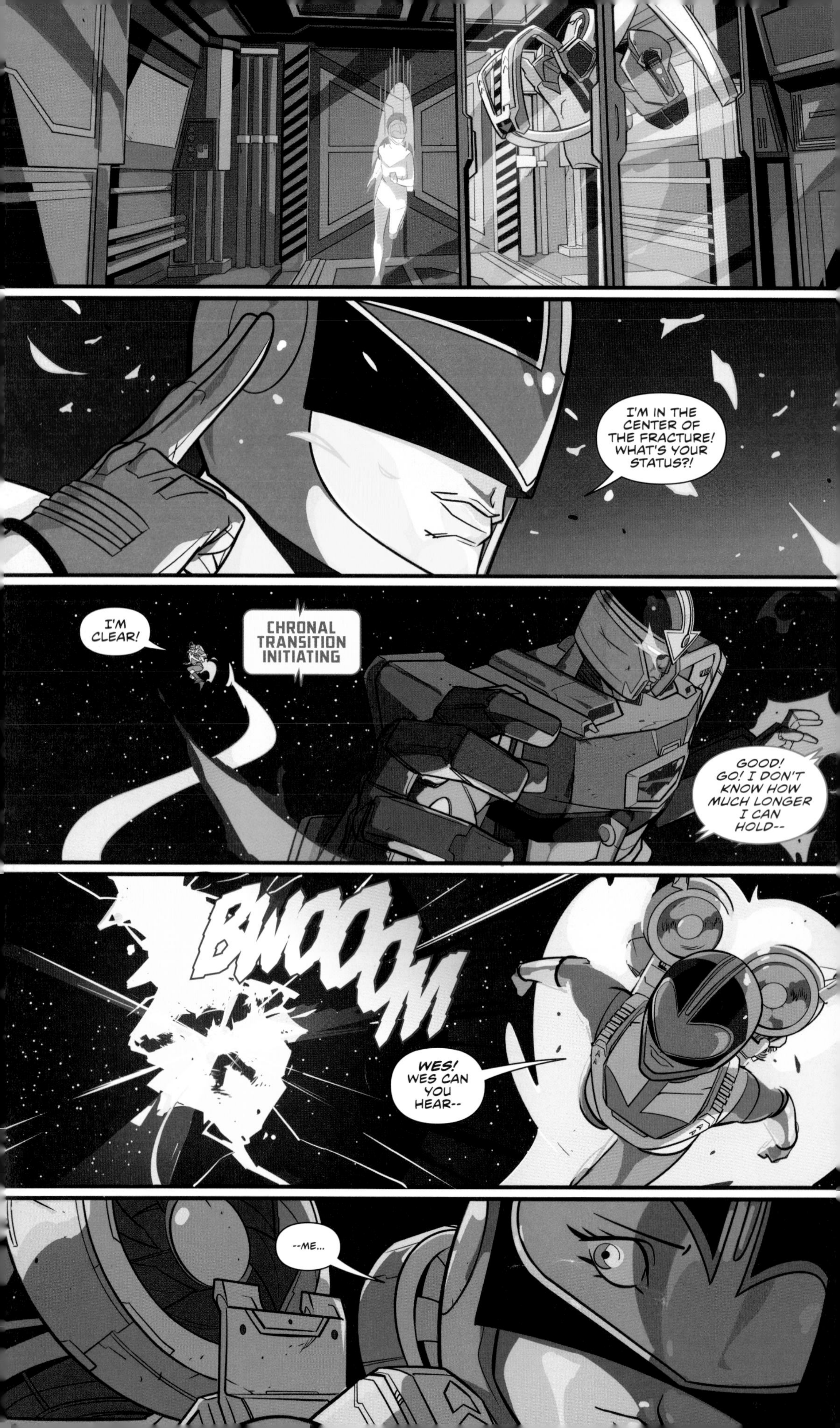
I'M IN THE CENTER OF THE FRACTURE! WHAT'S YOUR STATUS?!
I'M CLEAR!
CHRONAL TRANSITION INITIATING
GOOD! GO! I DON'T KNOW HOW MUCH LONGER I CAN HOLD--
BWOOOM
WES! WES CAN YOU HEAR--
--ME...

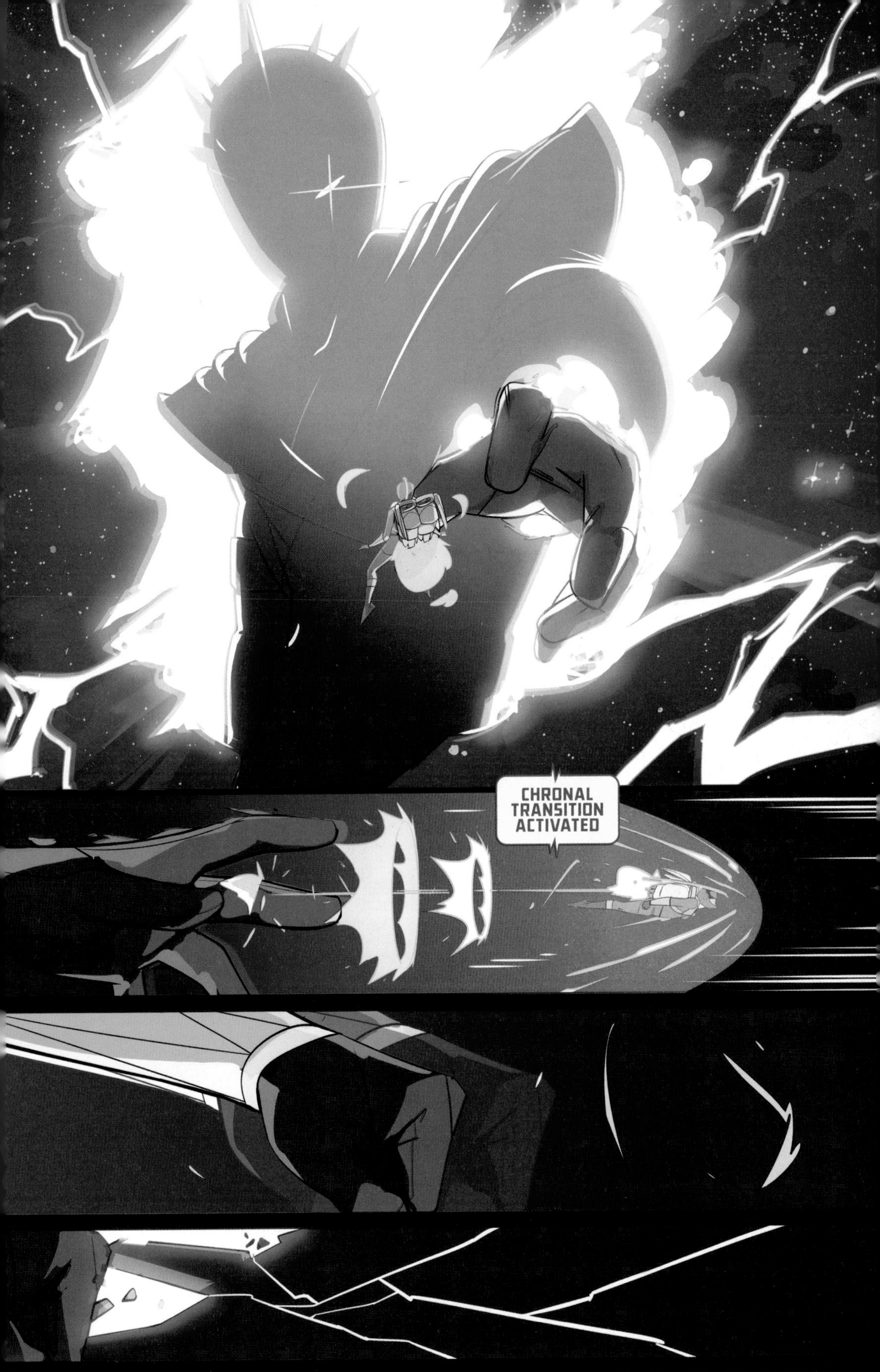
CHRONAL TRANSITION ACTIVATED

SHATTERED GRID

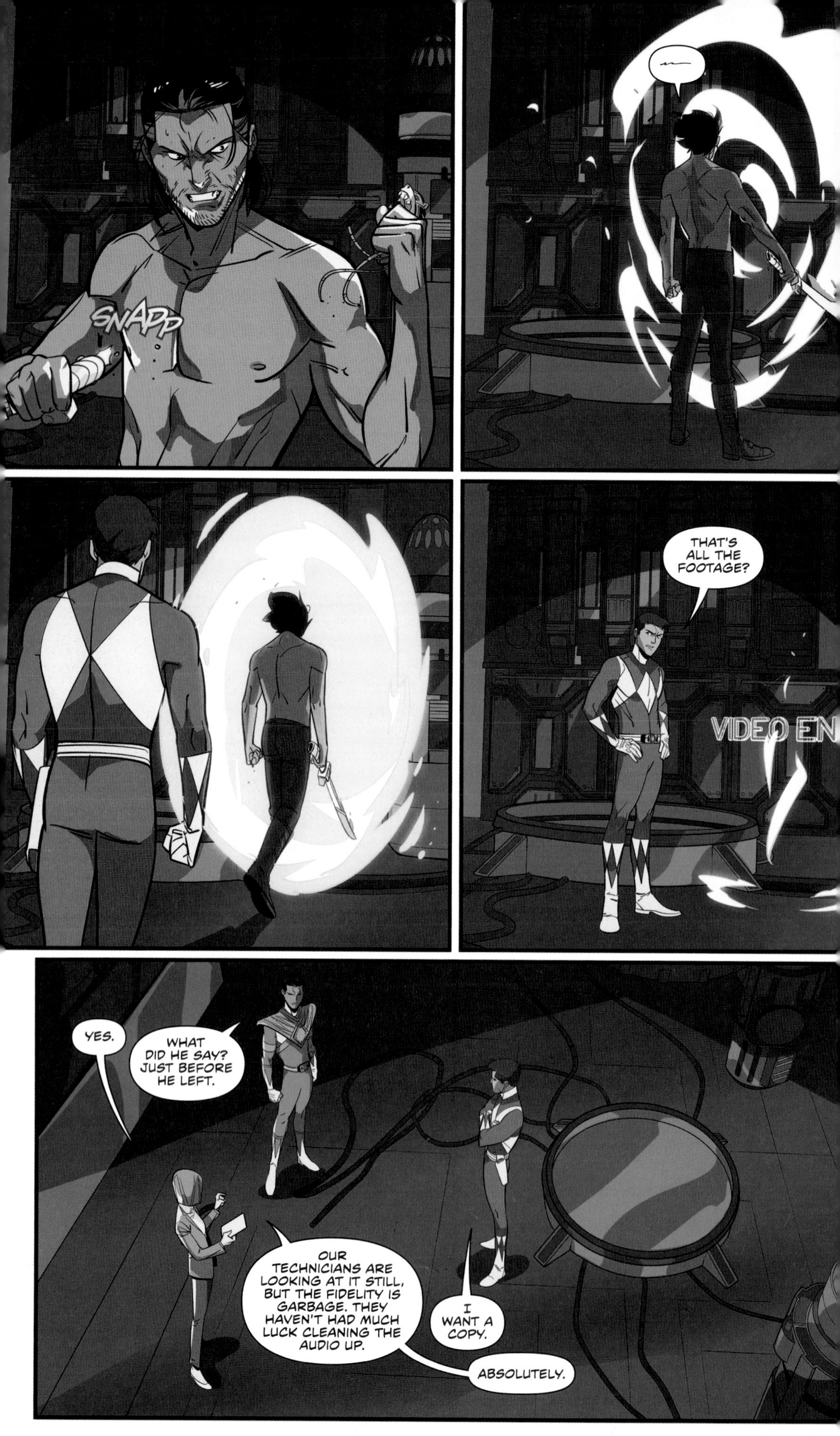
SNAPP
...
THAT'S ALL THE FOOTAGE?
VIDEO EN
YES.
WHAT DID HE SAY? JUST BEFORE HE LEFT.
OUR TECHNICIANS ARE LOOKING AT IT STILL, BUT THE FIDELITY IS GARBAGE. THEY HAVEN'T HAD MUCH LUCK CLEANING THE AUDIO UP.
I WANT A COPY.
ABSOLUTELY.

WHAT DO YOU THINK?

I'M...TRYING TO GET MY HEAD AROUND ALL THIS. SABA...I MEAN...WE DIDN'T KNOW HIM THAT WELL, BUT... HE *SAVED* ME AND BILLY. AND NOW...

I KNOW. IT'S... A LOT TO PROCESS.

ANY WAY PROMETHEA CAN HELP, WE'RE HAPPY TO--

NO.

"NO?"

YOU TOOK DRAKKON PRISONER, *KEPT* HIM FROM US, AND THEN ON *TOP* OF ALL THAT...LET HIM ESCAPE.

I'M SORRY WE WEREN'T BETTER PREPARED FOR A *TELEPORTING SABER*.

EXACTLY. IF YOU'D BEEN HONEST WITH US FROM THE START, WE MIGHT HAVE BEEN ABLE TO DO SOMETHING ABOUT THIS. *TOGETHER*.

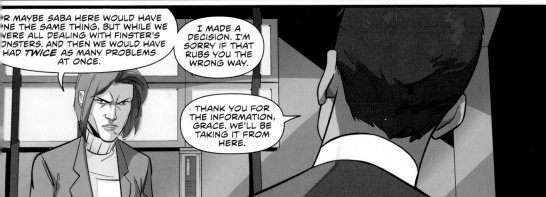

R MAYBE SABA HERE WOULD HAVE NE THE SAME THING, BUT WHILE WE ERE ALL DEALING WITH FINSTER'S NSTERS. AND THEN WE WOULD HAVE HAD *TWICE* AS MANY PROBLEMS AT ONCE.

I MADE A DECISION. I'M SORRY IF THAT RUBS YOU THE WRONG WAY.

THANK YOU FOR THE INFORMATION, GRACE. WE'LL BE TAKING IT FROM HERE.

ALL RIGHT THEN. IF THAT'S WHAT YOU THINK IS BEST.

THERE IS...*ONE* OTHER THING YOU SHOULD KNOW THOUGH. BEFORE DRAKKON LEFT OUR FACILITY COMPLETELY...

...HE *TOOK* SOMETHING WITH HIM.

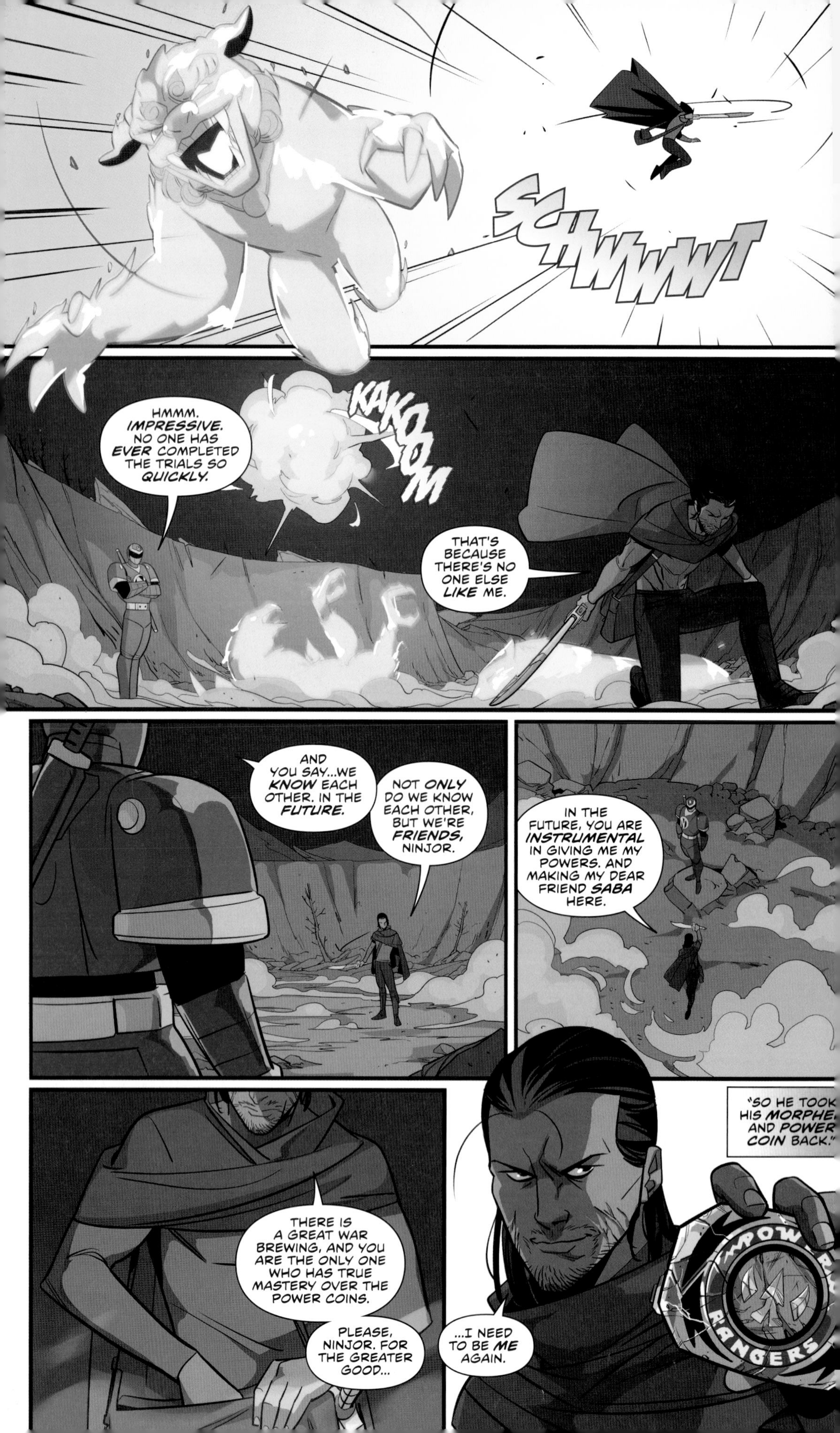
SCHWWWT
KAKOOM
HMMM. IMPRESSIVE. NO ONE HAS EVER COMPLETED THE TRIALS SO QUICKLY.
THAT'S BECAUSE THERE'S NO ONE ELSE LIKE ME.
AND YOU SAY...WE KNOW EACH OTHER. IN THE FUTURE.
NOT ONLY DO WE KNOW EACH OTHER, BUT WE'RE FRIENDS, NINJOR.
IN THE FUTURE, YOU ARE INSTRUMENTAL IN GIVING ME MY POWERS. AND MAKING MY DEAR FRIEND SABA HERE.
THERE IS A GREAT WAR BREWING, AND YOU ARE THE ONLY ONE WHO HAS TRUE MASTERY OVER THE POWER COINS.
PLEASE, NINJOR. FOR THE GREATER GOOD...
...I NEED TO BE ME AGAIN.
RANGERS

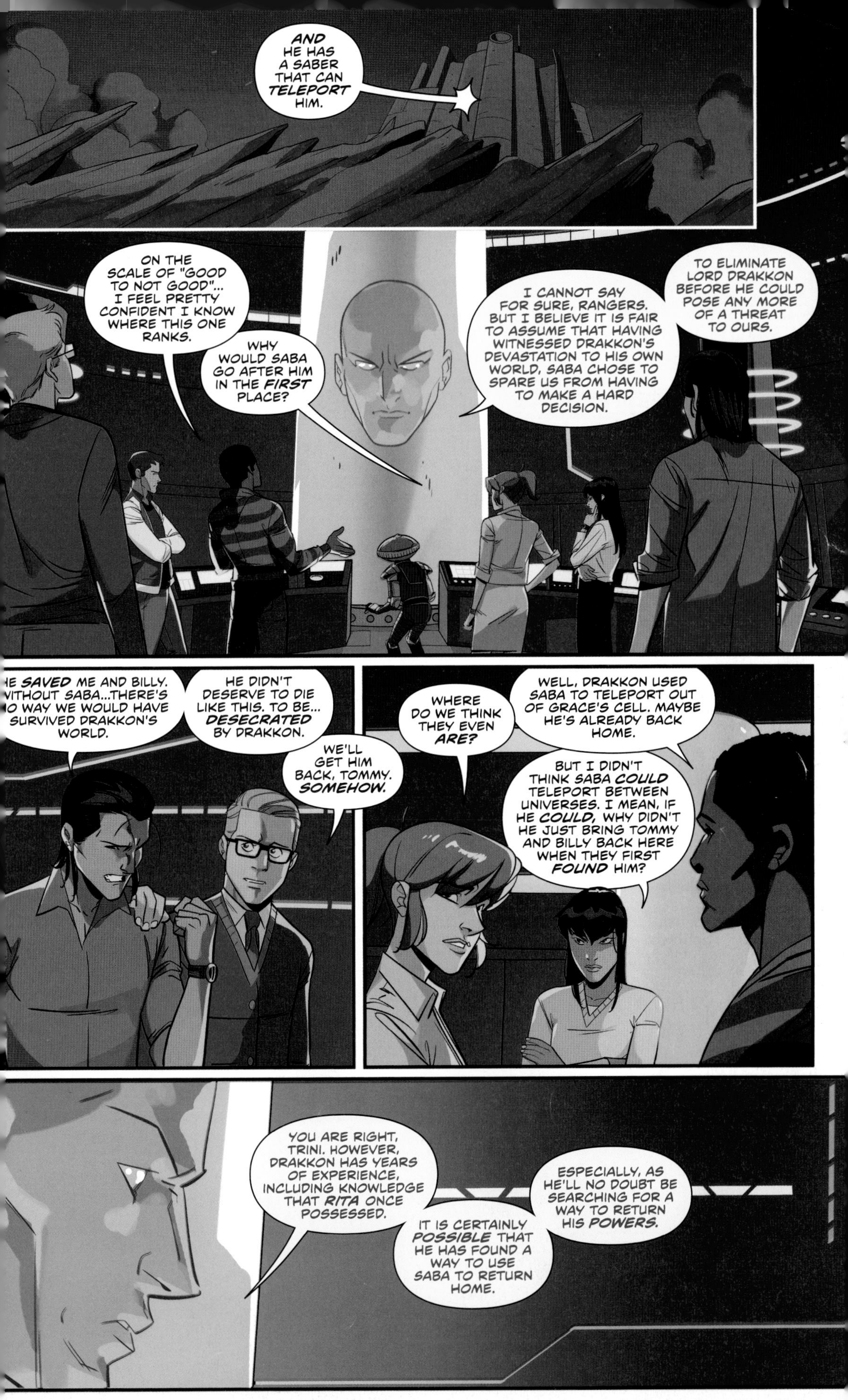
AND HE HAS A SABER THAT CAN TELEPORT HIM.
ON THE SCALE OF "GOOD TO NOT GOOD"... I FEEL PRETTY CONFIDENT I KNOW WHERE THIS ONE RANKS.
WHY WOULD SABA GO AFTER HIM IN THE FIRST PLACE?
I CANNOT SAY FOR SURE, RANGERS. BUT I BELIEVE IT IS FAIR TO ASSUME THAT HAVING WITNESSED DRAKKON'S DEVASTATION TO HIS OWN WORLD, SABA CHOSE TO SPARE US FROM HAVING TO MAKE A HARD DECISION.
TO ELIMINATE LORD DRAKKON BEFORE HE COULD POSE ANY MORE OF A THREAT TO OURS.
HE SAVED ME AND BILLY. WITHOUT SABA...THERE'S NO WAY WE WOULD HAVE SURVIVED DRAKKON'S WORLD.
HE DIDN'T DESERVE TO DIE LIKE THIS. TO BE... DESECRATED BY DRAKKON.
WE'LL GET HIM BACK, TOMMY. SOMEHOW.
WHERE DO WE THINK THEY EVEN ARE?
WELL, DRAKKON USED SABA TO TELEPORT OUT OF GRACE'S CELL. MAYBE HE'S ALREADY BACK HOME.
BUT I DIDN'T THINK SABA COULD TELEPORT BETWEEN UNIVERSES. I MEAN, IF HE COULD, WHY DIDN'T HE JUST BRING TOMMY AND BILLY BACK HERE WHEN THEY FIRST FOUND HIM?
YOU ARE RIGHT, TRINI. HOWEVER, DRAKKON HAS YEARS OF EXPERIENCE, INCLUDING KNOWLEDGE THAT RITA ONCE POSSESSED.
IT IS CERTAINLY POSSIBLE THAT HE HAS FOUND A WAY TO USE SABA TO RETURN HOME.
ESPECIALLY, AS HE'LL NO DOUBT BE SEARCHING FOR A WAY TO RETURN HIS POWERS.

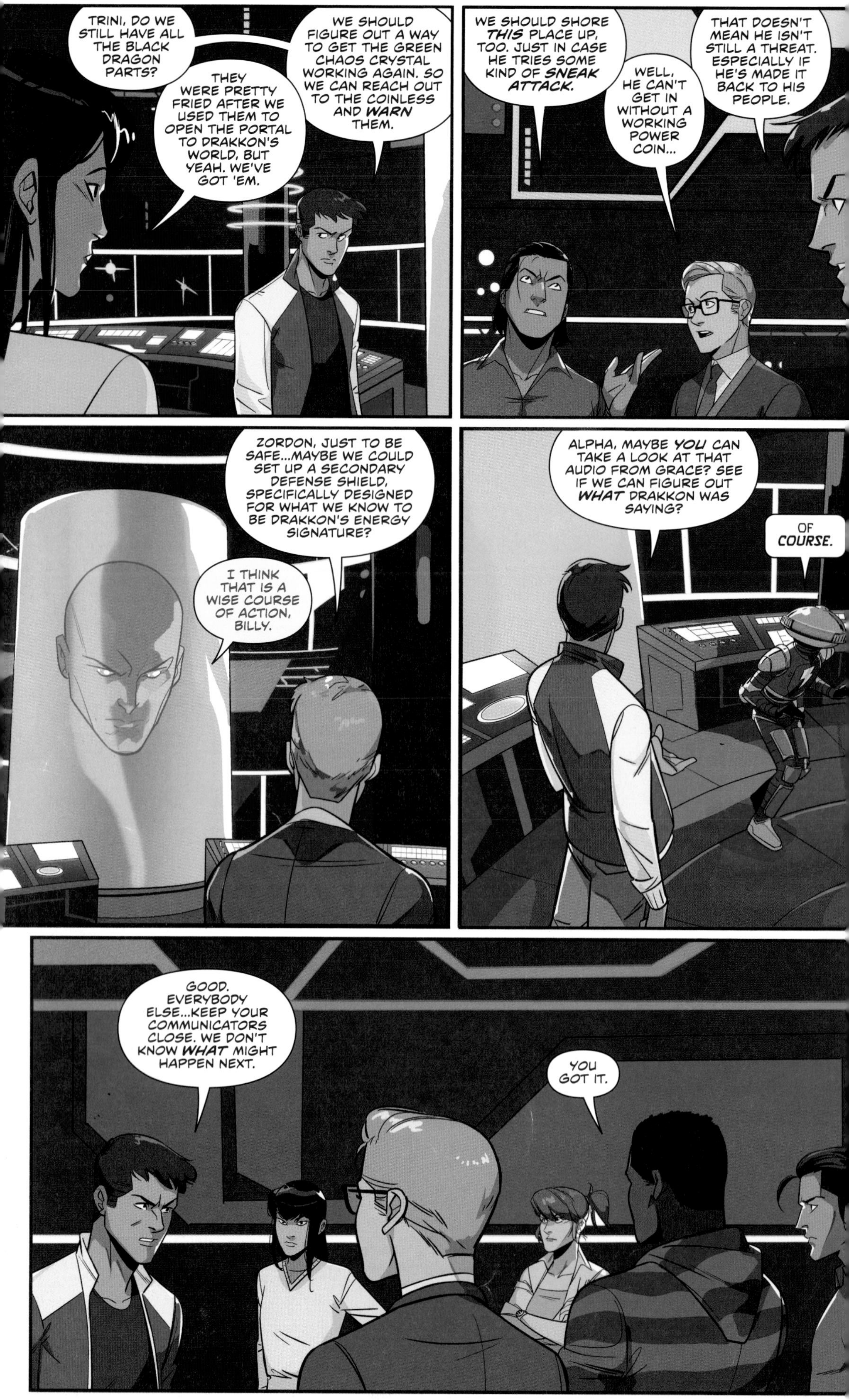
TRINI, DO WE STILL HAVE ALL THE BLACK DRAGON PARTS?
THEY WERE PRETTY FRIED AFTER WE USED THEM TO OPEN THE PORTAL TO DRAKKON'S WORLD, BUT YEAH. WE'VE GOT 'EM.
WE SHOULD FIGURE OUT A WAY TO GET THE GREEN CHAOS CRYSTAL WORKING AGAIN. SO WE CAN REACH OUT TO THE COINLESS AND *WARN* THEM.
WE SHOULD SHORE *THIS* PLACE UP, TOO. JUST IN CASE HE TRIES SOME KIND OF *SNEAK ATTACK.*
WELL, HE CAN'T GET IN WITHOUT A WORKING POWER COIN...
THAT DOESN'T MEAN HE ISN'T STILL A THREAT. ESPECIALLY IF HE'S MADE IT BACK TO HIS PEOPLE.
ZORDON, JUST TO BE SAFE...MAYBE WE COULD SET UP A SECONDARY DEFENSE SHIELD, SPECIFICALLY DESIGNED FOR WHAT WE KNOW TO BE DRAKKON'S ENERGY SIGNATURE?
I THINK THAT IS A WISE COURSE OF ACTION, BILLY.
ALPHA, MAYBE *YOU* CAN TAKE A LOOK AT THAT AUDIO FROM GRACE? SEE IF WE CAN FIGURE OUT *WHAT* DRAKKON WAS SAYING?
OF *COURSE.*
GOOD. EVERYBODY ELSE...KEEP YOUR COMMUNICATORS CLOSE. WE DON'T KNOW *WHAT* MIGHT HAPPEN NEXT.
YOU GOT IT.

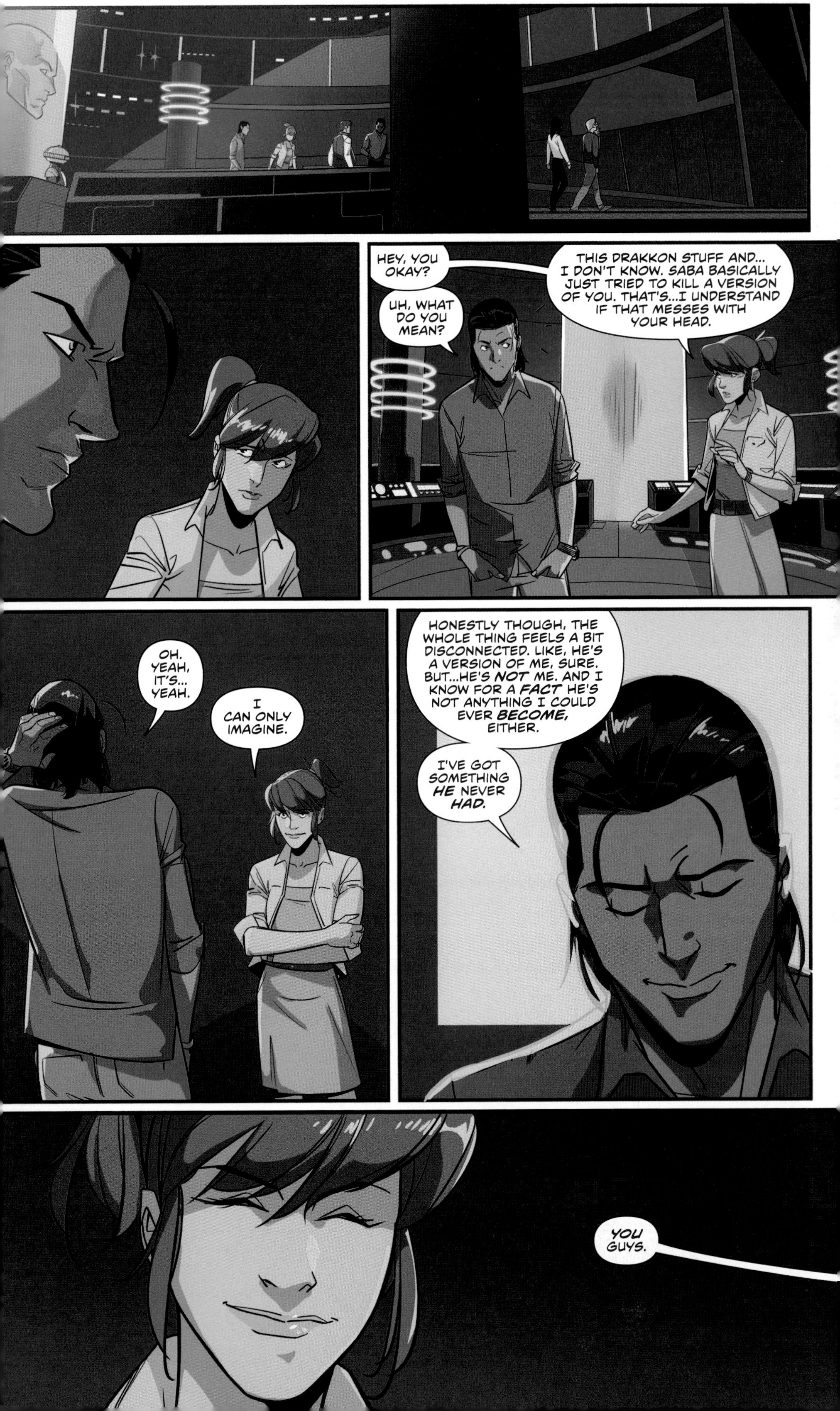
HEY, YOU OKAY?
UH, WHAT DO YOU MEAN?
THIS DRAKKON STUFF AND... I DON'T KNOW. SABA BASICALLY JUST TRIED TO KILL A VERSION OF YOU. THAT'S...I UNDERSTAND IF THAT MESSES WITH YOUR HEAD.
OH. YEAH, IT'S... YEAH.
I CAN ONLY IMAGINE.
HONESTLY THOUGH, THE WHOLE THING FEELS A BIT DISCONNECTED. LIKE, HE'S A VERSION OF ME, SURE. BUT...HE'S NOT ME. AND I KNOW FOR A FACT HE'S NOT ANYTHING I COULD EVER BECOME, EITHER.
I'VE GOT SOMETHING HE NEVER HAD.
YOU GUYS.

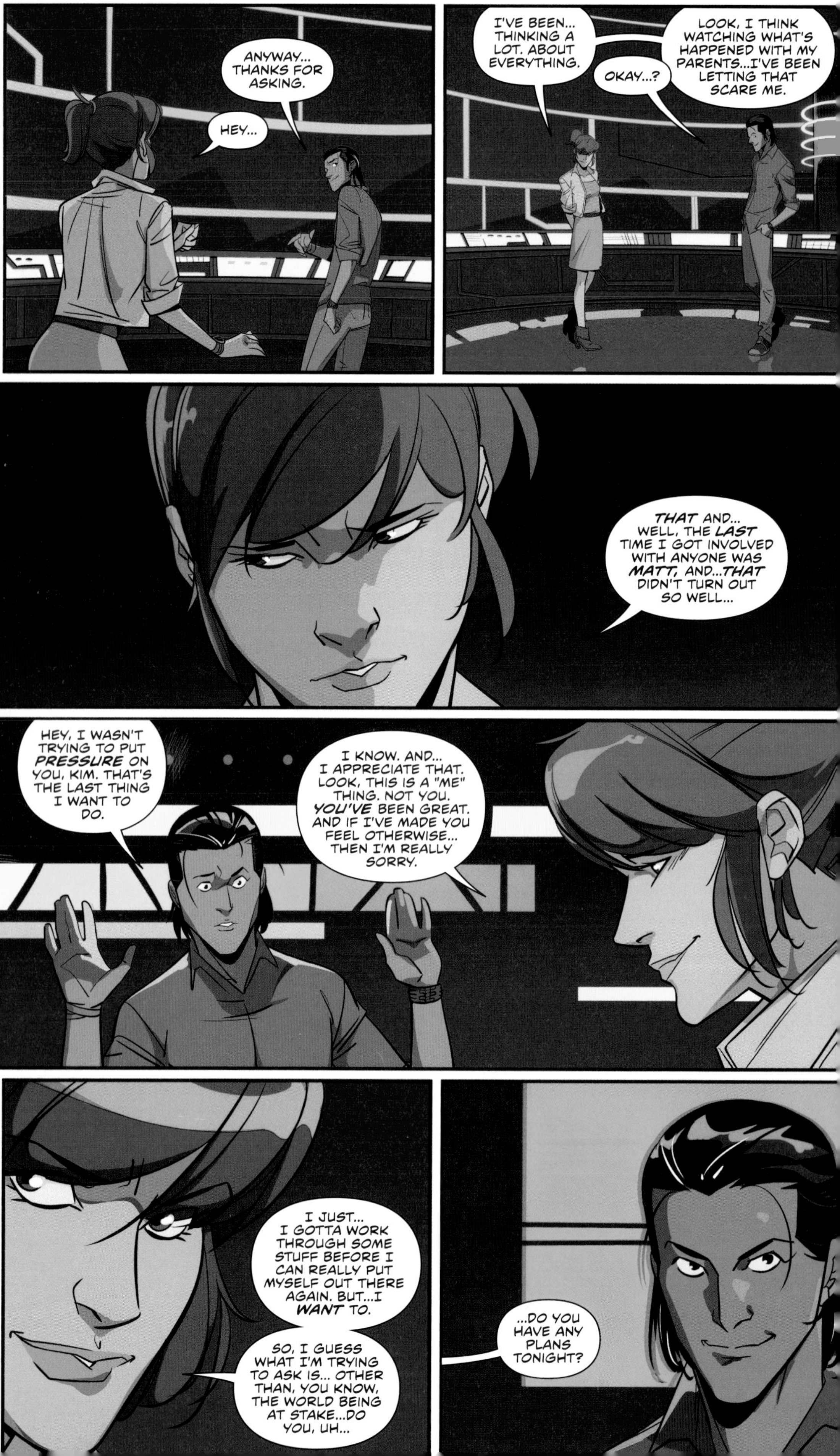
ANYWAY... THANKS FOR ASKING.
HEY...
I'VE BEEN... THINKING A LOT. ABOUT EVERYTHING.
OKAY...?
LOOK, I THINK WATCHING WHAT'S HAPPENED WITH MY PARENTS...I'VE BEEN LETTING THAT SCARE ME.
THAT AND... WELL, THE *LAST* TIME I GOT INVOLVED WITH ANYONE WAS *MATT,* AND...*THAT* DIDN'T TURN OUT SO WELL...
HEY, I WASN'T TRYING TO PUT *PRESSURE* ON YOU, KIM. THAT'S THE LAST THING I WANT TO DO.
I KNOW. AND... I APPRECIATE THAT. LOOK, THIS IS A "ME" THING. NOT YOU. *YOU'VE* BEEN GREAT. AND IF I'VE MADE YOU FEEL OTHERWISE... THEN I'M REALLY SORRY.
I JUST... I GOTTA WORK THROUGH SOME STUFF BEFORE I CAN REALLY PUT MYSELF OUT THERE AGAIN. BUT...I *WANT* TO.
SO, I GUESS WHAT I'M TRYING TO ASK IS... OTHER THAN, YOU KNOW, THE WORLD BEING AT STAKE...DO YOU, UH...
...DO YOU HAVE ANY PLANS TONIGHT?

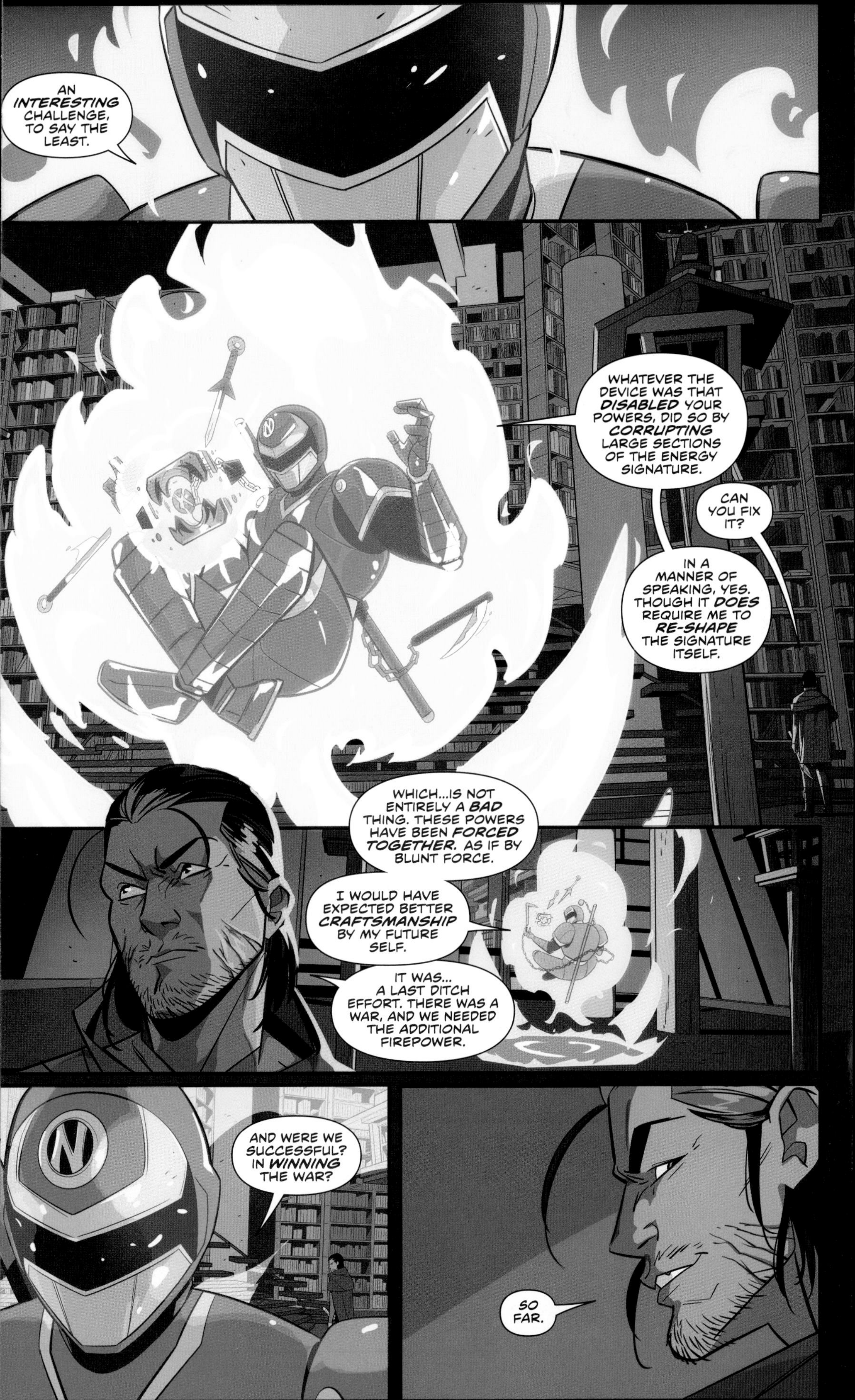
AN *INTERESTING* CHALLENGE, TO SAY THE LEAST.
WHATEVER THE DEVICE WAS THAT *DISABLED* YOUR POWERS, DID SO BY *CORRUPTING* LARGE SECTIONS OF THE ENERGY SIGNATURE.
CAN YOU FIX IT?
IN A MANNER OF SPEAKING, YES. THOUGH IT *DOES* REQUIRE ME TO *RE-SHAPE* THE SIGNATURE ITSELF.
WHICH...IS NOT ENTIRELY A *BAD* THING. THESE POWERS HAVE BEEN *FORCED TOGETHER.* AS IF BY BLUNT FORCE.
I WOULD HAVE EXPECTED BETTER *CRAFTSMANSHIP* BY MY FUTURE SELF.
IT WAS... A LAST DITCH EFFORT. THERE WAS A WAR, AND WE NEEDED THE ADDITIONAL FIREPOWER.
AND WERE WE SUCCESSFUL? IN *WINNING* THE WAR?
SO FAR.

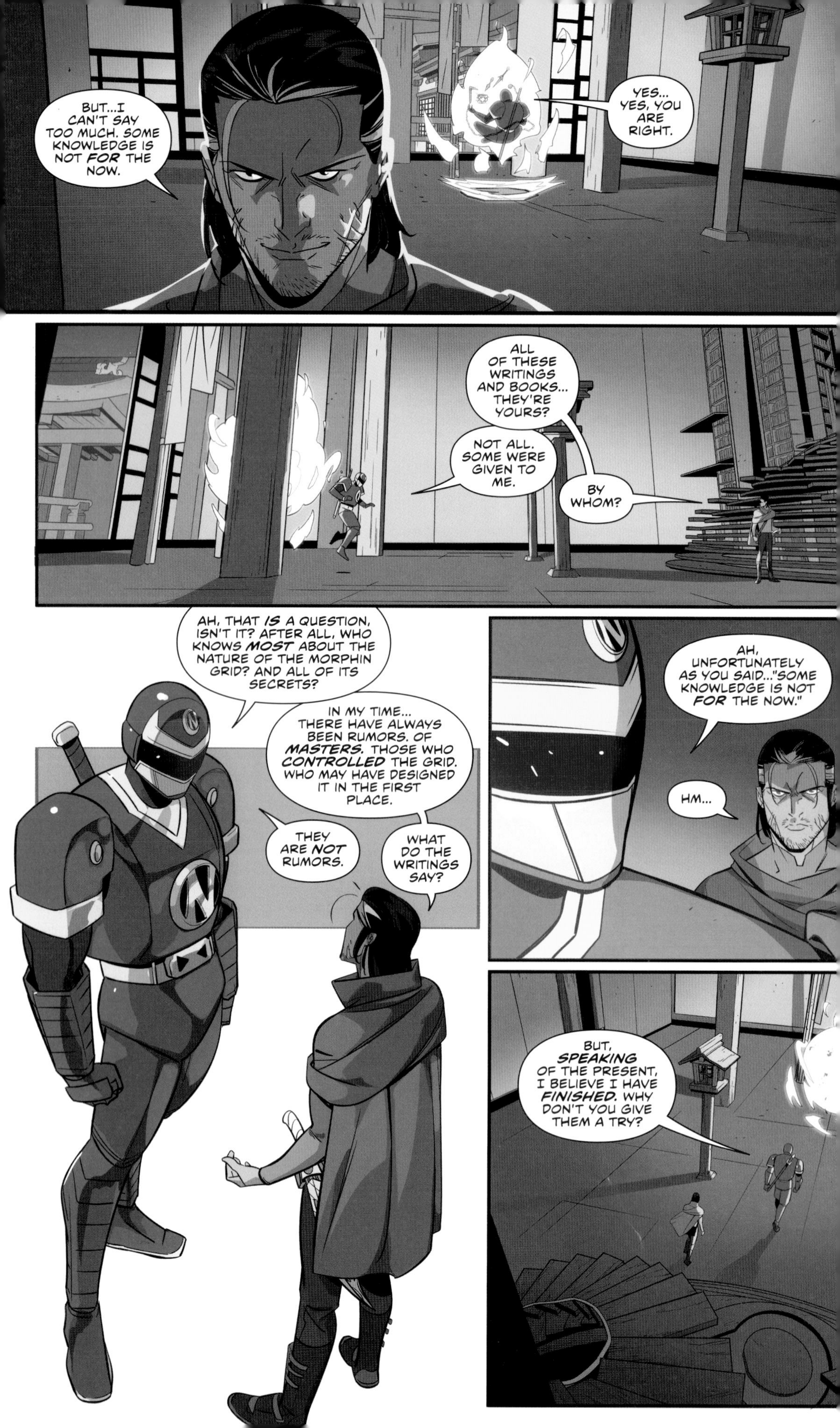
BUT...I CAN'T SAY TOO MUCH. SOME KNOWLEDGE IS NOT *FOR* THE NOW.
YES... YES, YOU ARE RIGHT.
ALL OF THESE WRITINGS AND BOOKS... THEY'RE YOURS?
NOT ALL. SOME WERE GIVEN TO ME.
BY WHOM?
AH, THAT *IS* A QUESTION, ISN'T IT? AFTER ALL, WHO KNOWS *MOST* ABOUT THE NATURE OF THE MORPHIN GRID? AND ALL OF ITS SECRETS?
IN MY TIME... THERE HAVE ALWAYS BEEN RUMORS. OF *MASTERS.* THOSE WHO *CONTROLLED* THE GRID. WHO MAY HAVE DESIGNED IT IN THE FIRST PLACE.
THEY ARE *NOT* RUMORS.
WHAT DO THE WRITINGS SAY?
AH, UNFORTUNATELY AS YOU SAID..."SOME KNOWLEDGE IS NOT *FOR* THE NOW."
HM...
BUT, *SPEAKING* OF THE PRESENT, I BELIEVE I HAVE *FINISHED.* WHY DON'T YOU GIVE THEM A TRY?

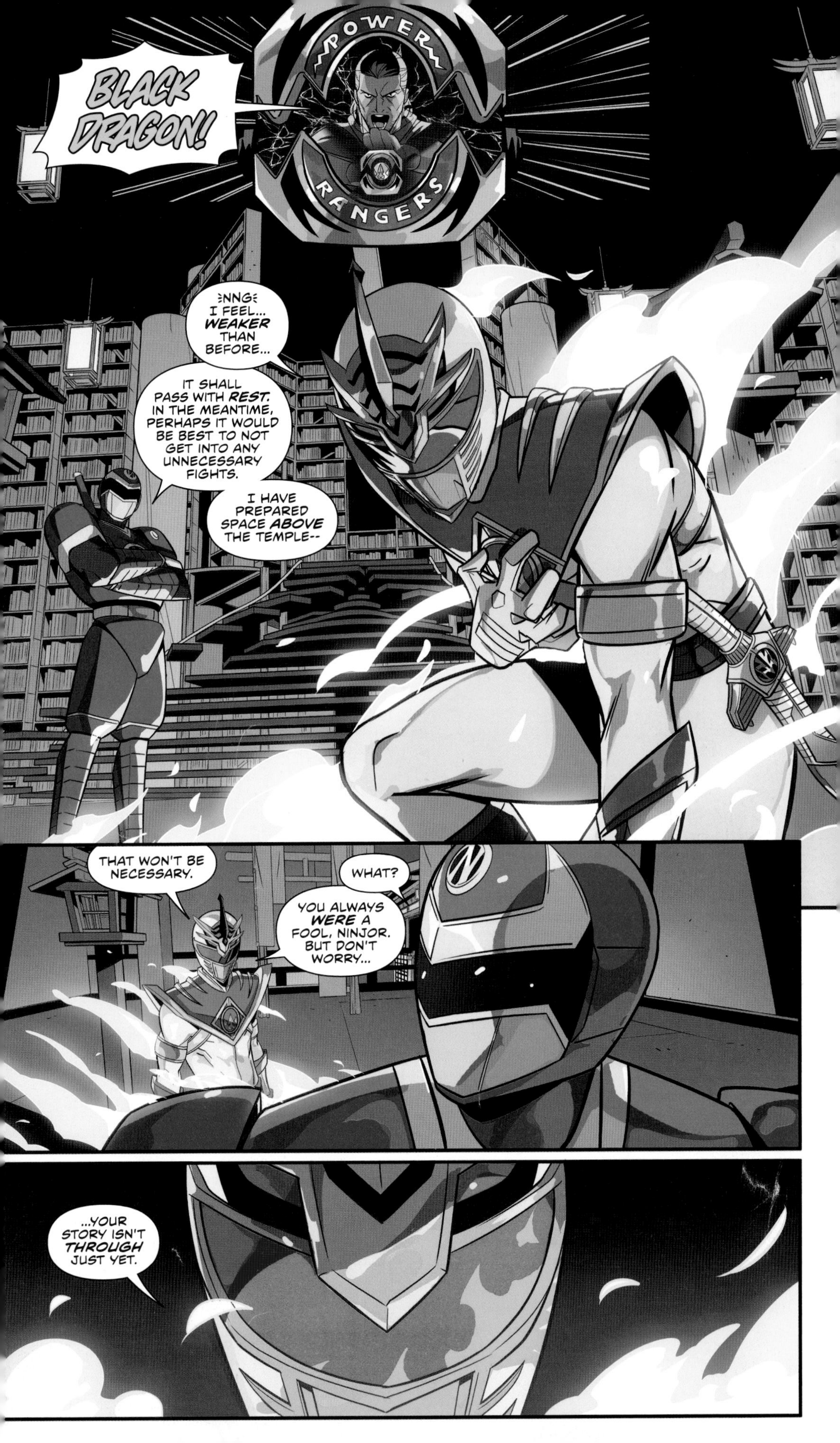

POWER RANGERS
BLACK DRAGON!
NNG I FEEL... WEAKER THAN BEFORE...
IT SHALL PASS WITH REST. IN THE MEANTIME, PERHAPS IT WOULD BE BEST TO NOT GET INTO ANY UNNECESSARY FIGHTS.
I HAVE PREPARED SPACE ABOVE THE TEMPLE--
THAT WON'T BE NECESSARY.
WHAT?
YOU ALWAYS WERE A FOOL, NINJOR. BUT DON'T WORRY...
...YOUR STORY ISN'T THROUGH JUST YET.

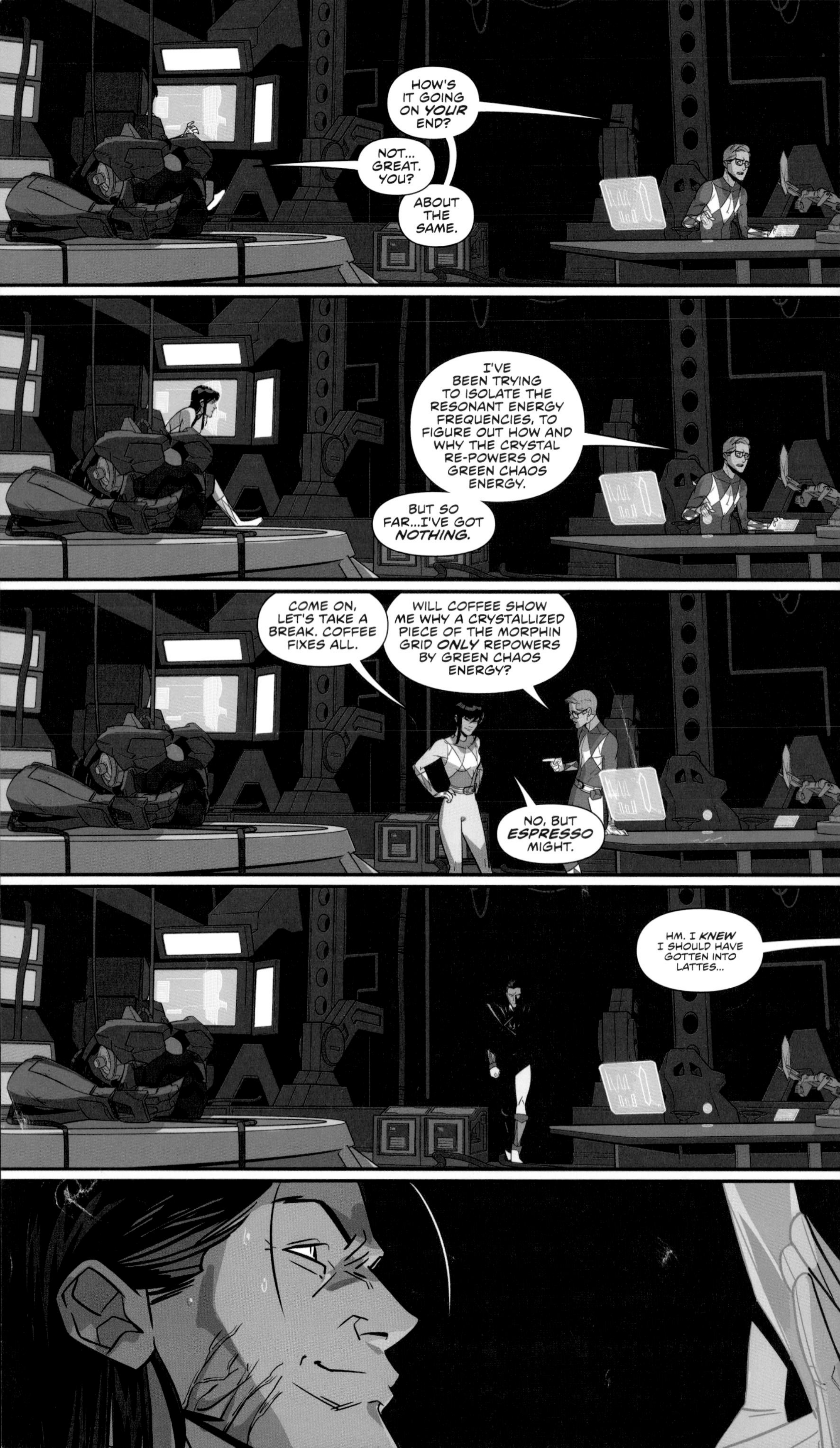
HOW'S IT GOING ON YOUR END?
NOT... GREAT. YOU?
ABOUT THE SAME.
I'VE BEEN TRYING TO ISOLATE THE RESONANT ENERGY FREQUENCIES, TO FIGURE OUT HOW AND WHY THE CRYSTAL RE-POWERS ON GREEN CHAOS ENERGY.
BUT SO FAR...I'VE GOT NOTHING.
COME ON, LET'S TAKE A BREAK. COFFEE FIXES ALL.
WILL COFFEE SHOW ME WHY A CRYSTALLIZED PIECE OF THE MORPHIN GRID ONLY REPOWERS BY GREEN CHAOS ENERGY?
NO, BUT ESPRESSO MIGHT.
HM. I KNEW I SHOULD HAVE GOTTEN INTO LATTES...

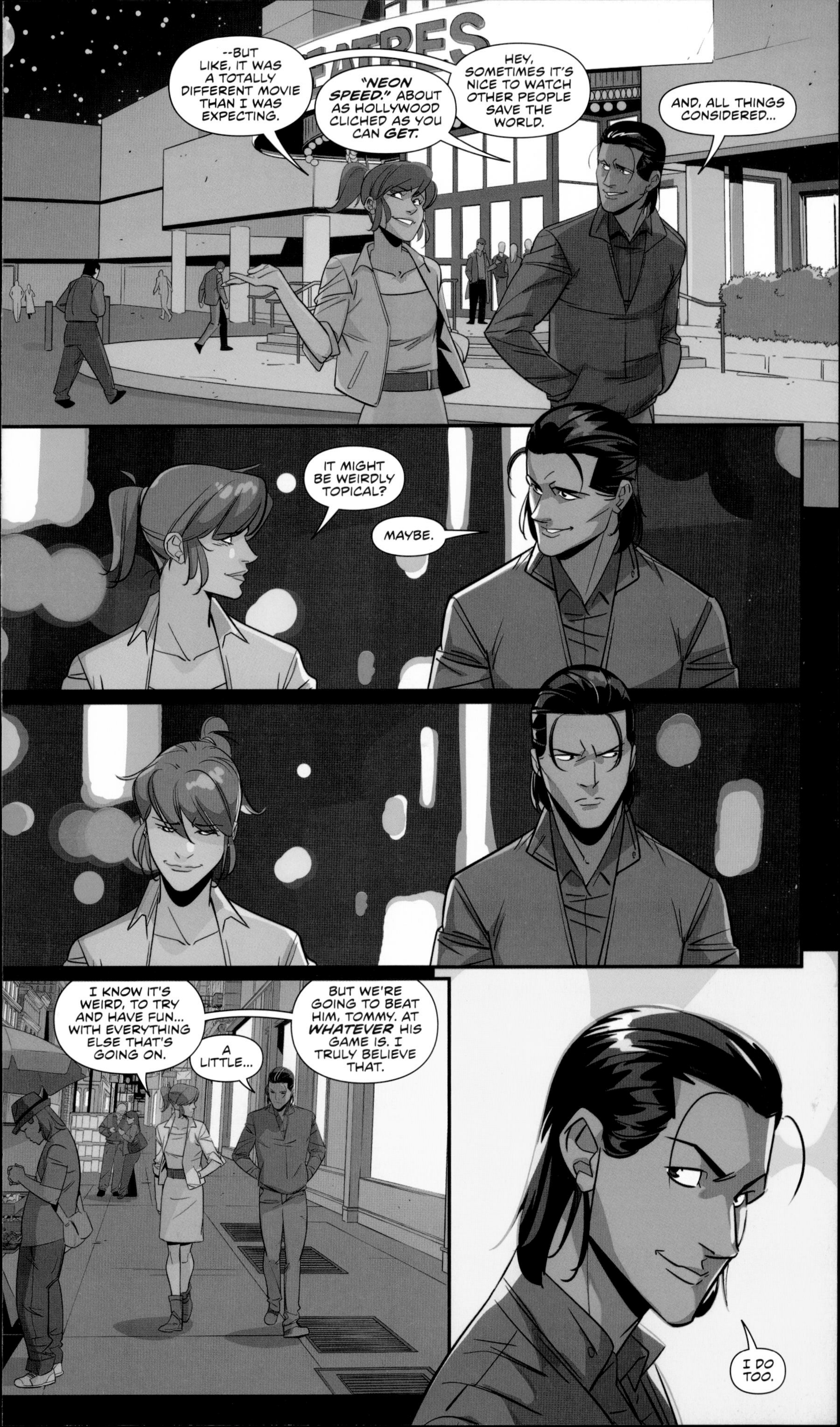

--BUT LIKE, IT WAS A TOTALLY DIFFERENT MOVIE THAN I WAS EXPECTING.
"NEON SPEED." ABOUT AS HOLLYWOOD CLICHED AS YOU CAN GET.
HEY, SOMETIMES IT'S NICE TO WATCH OTHER PEOPLE SAVE THE WORLD.
AND, ALL THINGS CONSIDERED...
IT MIGHT BE WEIRDLY TOPICAL?
MAYBE.
I KNOW IT'S WEIRD, TO TRY AND HAVE FUN... WITH EVERYTHING ELSE THAT'S GOING ON.
A LITTLE...
BUT WE'RE GOING TO BEAT HIM, TOMMY. AT WHATEVER HIS GAME IS. I TRULY BELIEVE THAT.
I DO TOO.

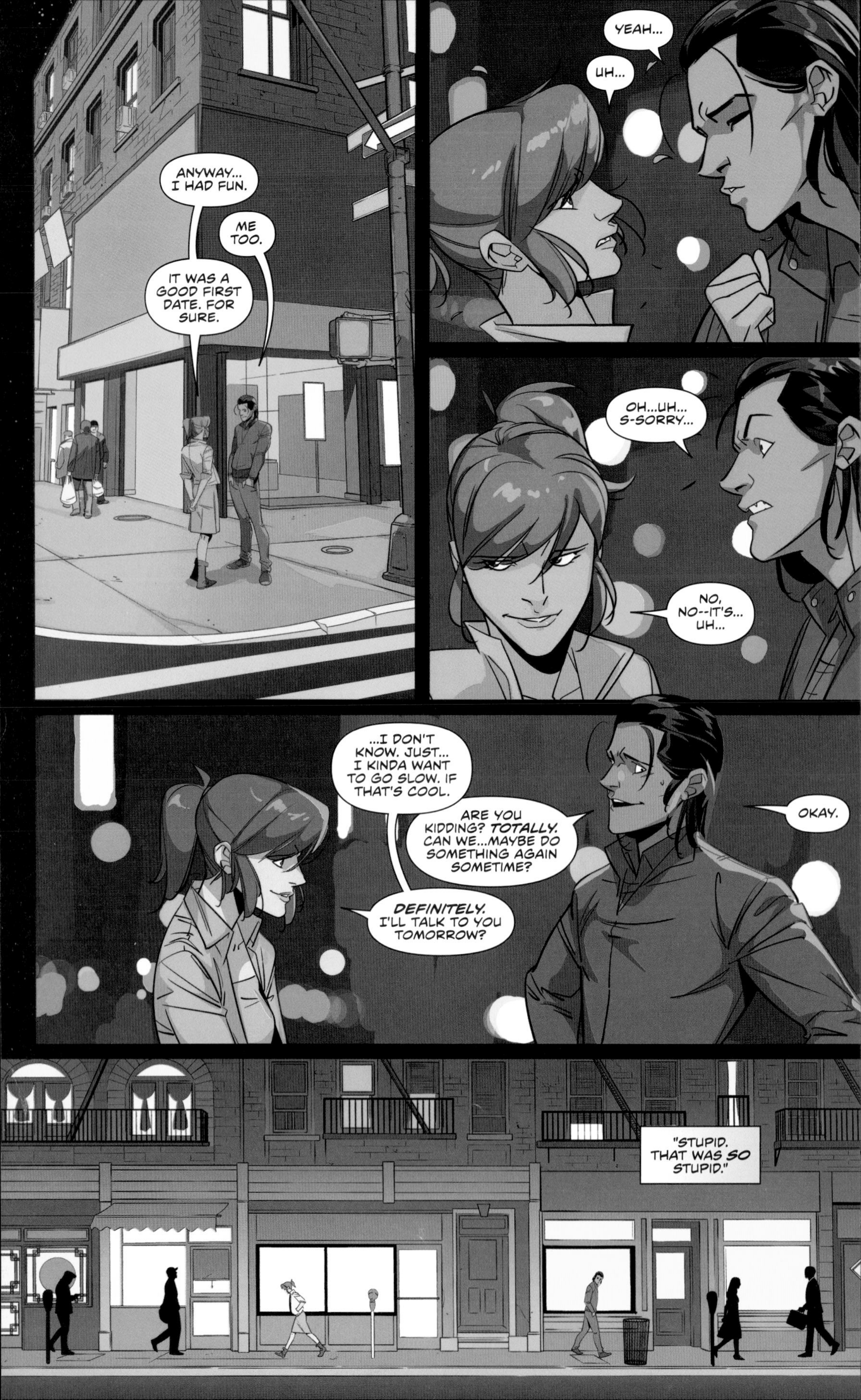
ANYWAY... I HAD FUN.
ME TOO.
IT WAS A GOOD FIRST DATE. FOR SURE.
YEAH...
UH...
OH...UH... S-SORRY...
NO, NO--IT'S... UH...
...I DON'T KNOW. JUST... I KINDA WANT TO GO SLOW. IF THAT'S COOL.
ARE YOU KIDDING? TOTALLY. CAN WE...MAYBE DO SOMETHING AGAIN SOMETIME?
DEFINITELY. I'LL TALK TO YOU TOMORROW?
OKAY.
"STUPID. THAT WAS SO STUPID."

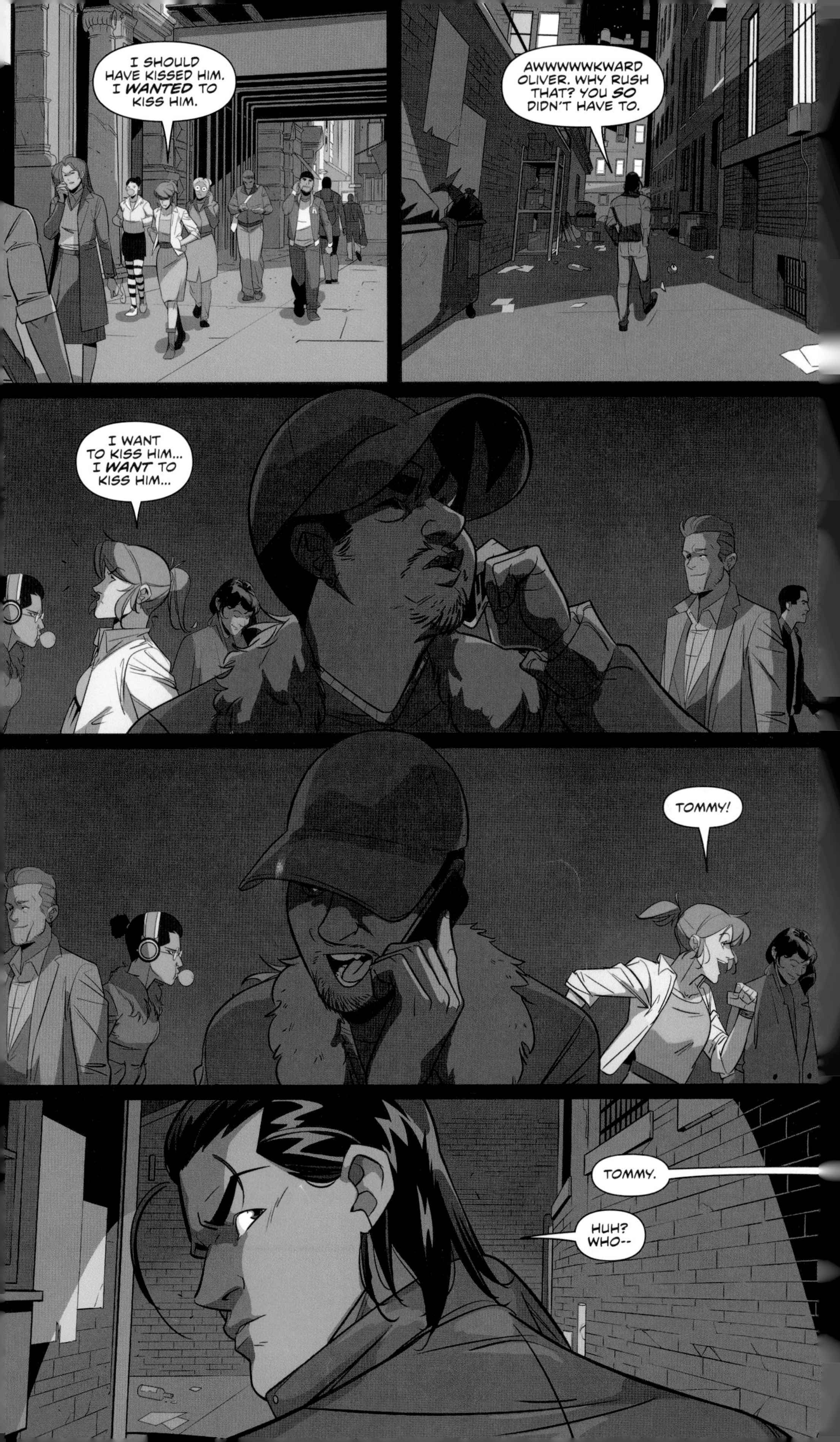
I SHOULD HAVE KISSED HIM. I WANTED TO KISS HIM.
AWWWWWKWARD OLIVER. WHY RUSH THAT? YOU SO DIDN'T HAVE TO.
I WANT TO KISS HIM... I WANT TO KISS HIM...
TOMMY!
TOMMY.
HUH? WHO--

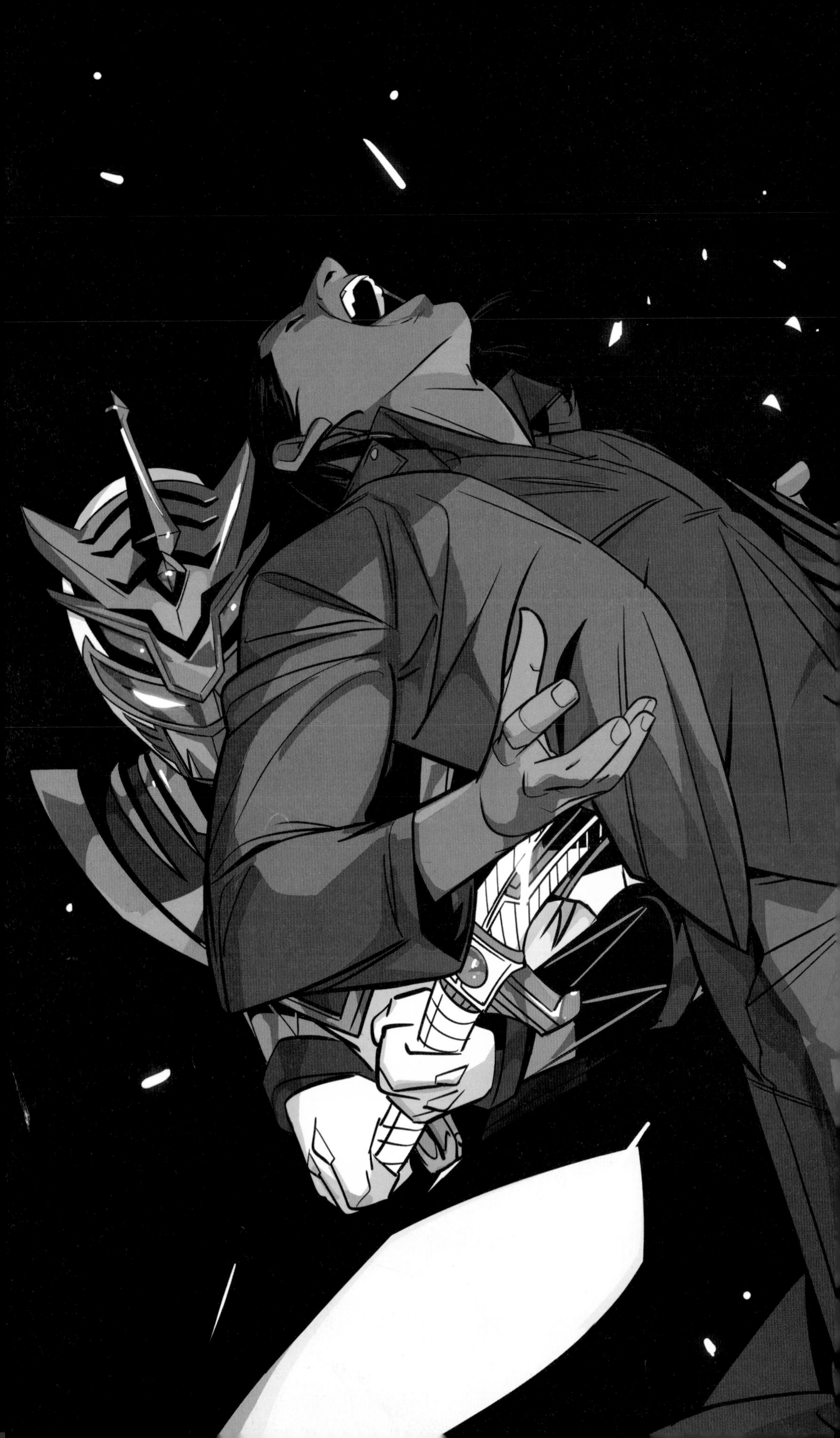

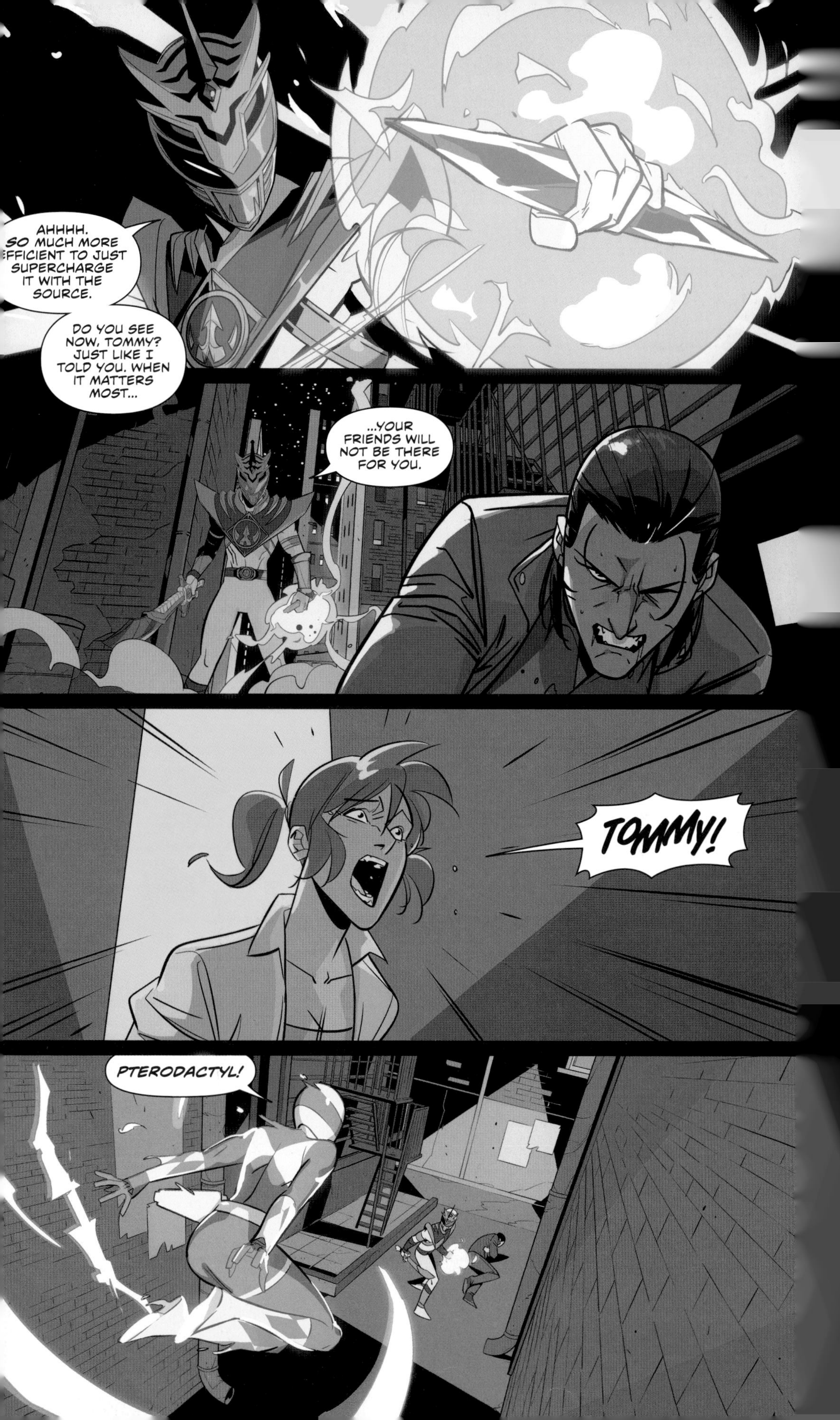
AHHHH. SO MUCH MORE EFFICIENT TO JUST SUPERCHARGE IT WITH THE SOURCE.
DO YOU SEE NOW, TOMMY? JUST LIKE I TOLD YOU. WHEN IT MATTERS MOST...
...YOUR FRIENDS WILL NOT BE THERE FOR YOU.
TOMMY!
PTERODACTYL!

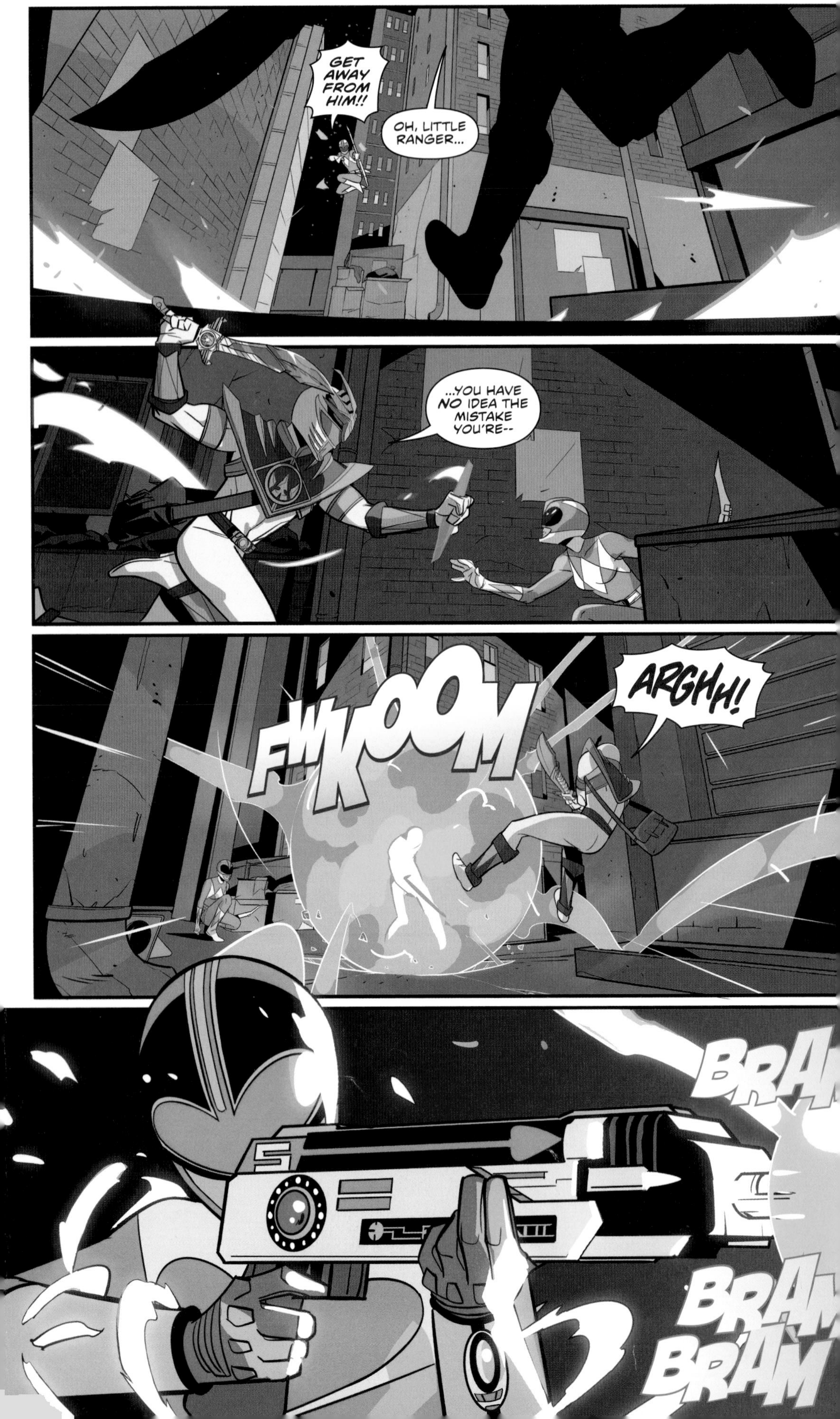
GET AWAY FROM HIM!!
OH, LITTLE RANGER...
...YOU HAVE NO IDEA THE MISTAKE YOU'RE--
FWKOOM
ARGHH!
BRAM
BRAM
BRAM

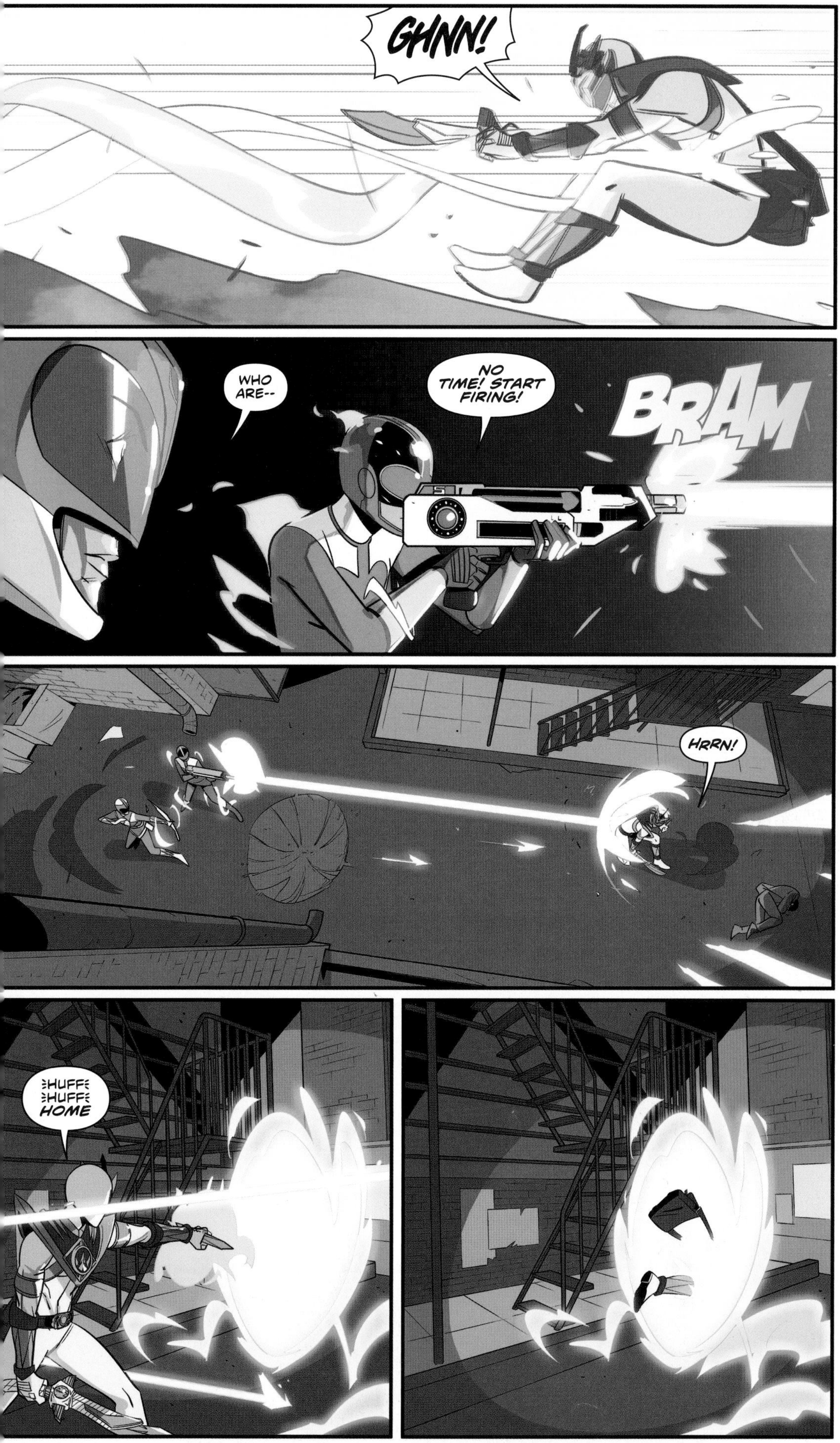
GHNN!
WHO ARE--
NO TIME! START FIRING!
BRAM
HRRN!
HUFF HUFF HOME

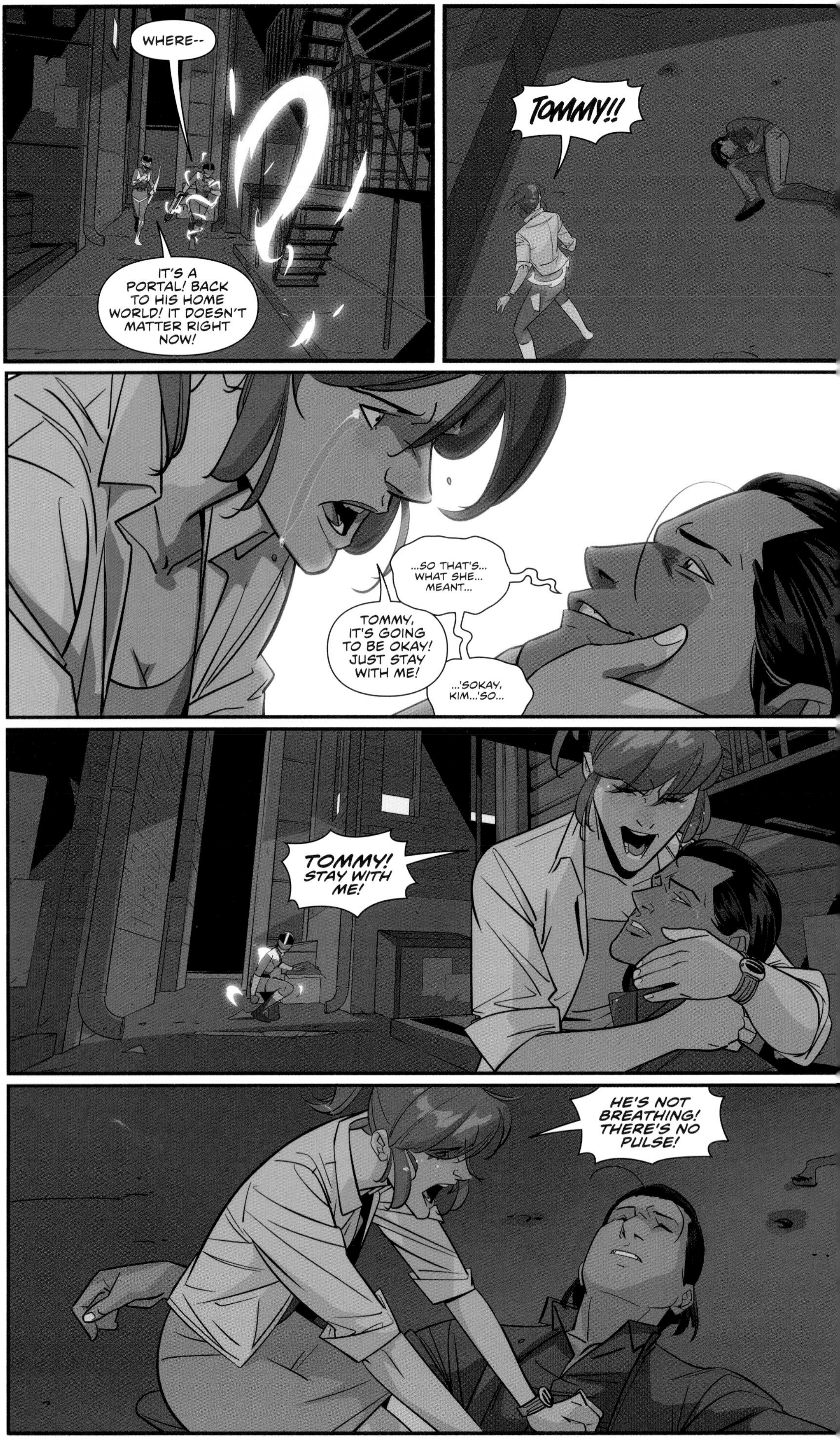
WHERE--
IT'S A PORTAL! BACK TO HIS HOME WORLD! IT DOESN'T MATTER RIGHT NOW!
TOMMY!!
TOMMY, IT'S GOING TO BE OKAY! JUST STAY WITH ME!
...SO THAT'S... WHAT SHE... MEANT...
...'SOKAY, KIM...'SO...
TOMMY! STAY WITH ME!
HE'S NOT BREATHING! THERE'S NO PULSE!

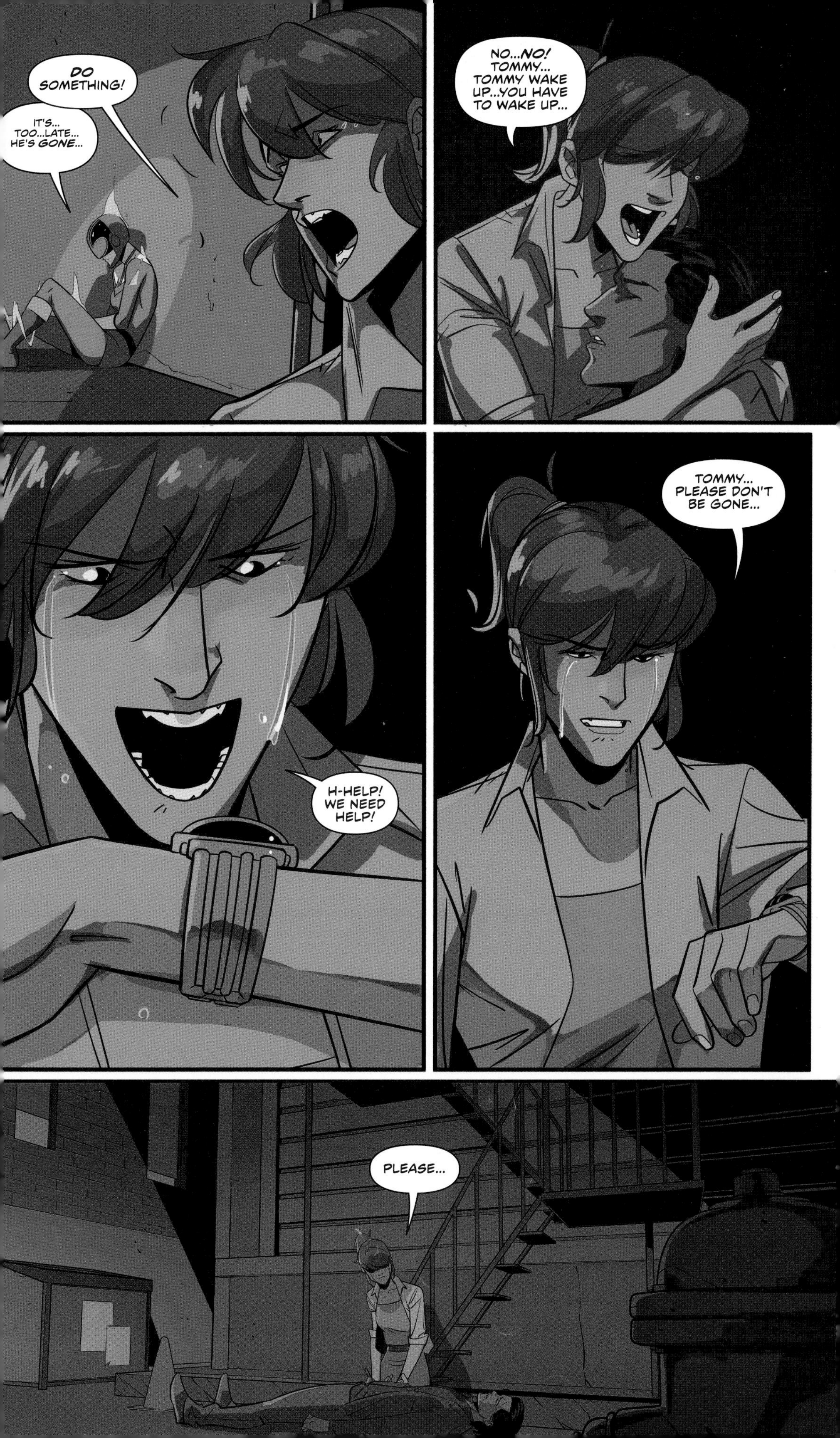
DO SOMETHING!
IT'S... TOO...LATE... HE'S GONE...
NO...NO! TOMMY... TOMMY WAKE UP...YOU HAVE TO WAKE UP...
H-HELP! WE NEED HELP!
TOMMY... PLEASE DON'T BE GONE...
PLEASE...

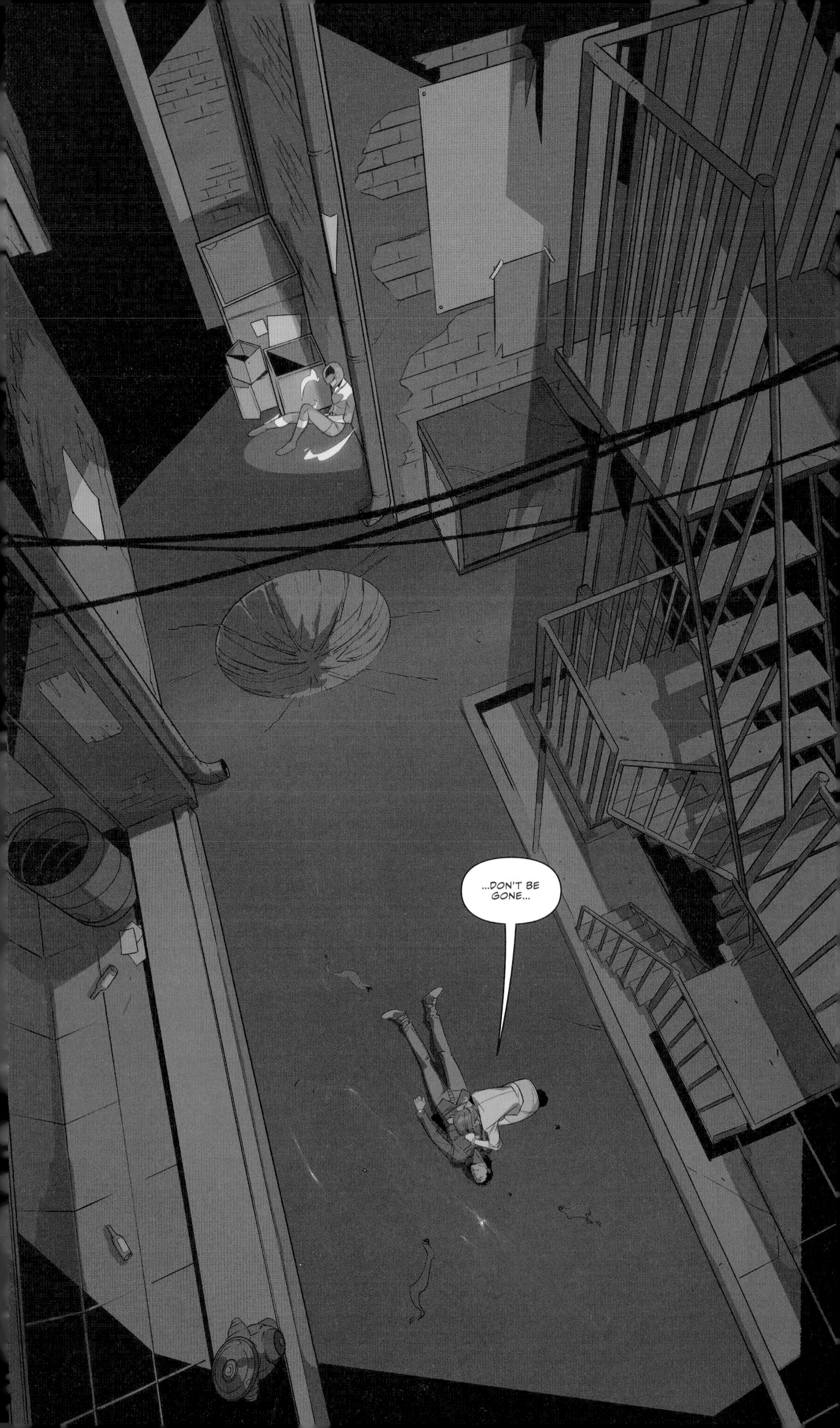
...DON'T BE GONE...

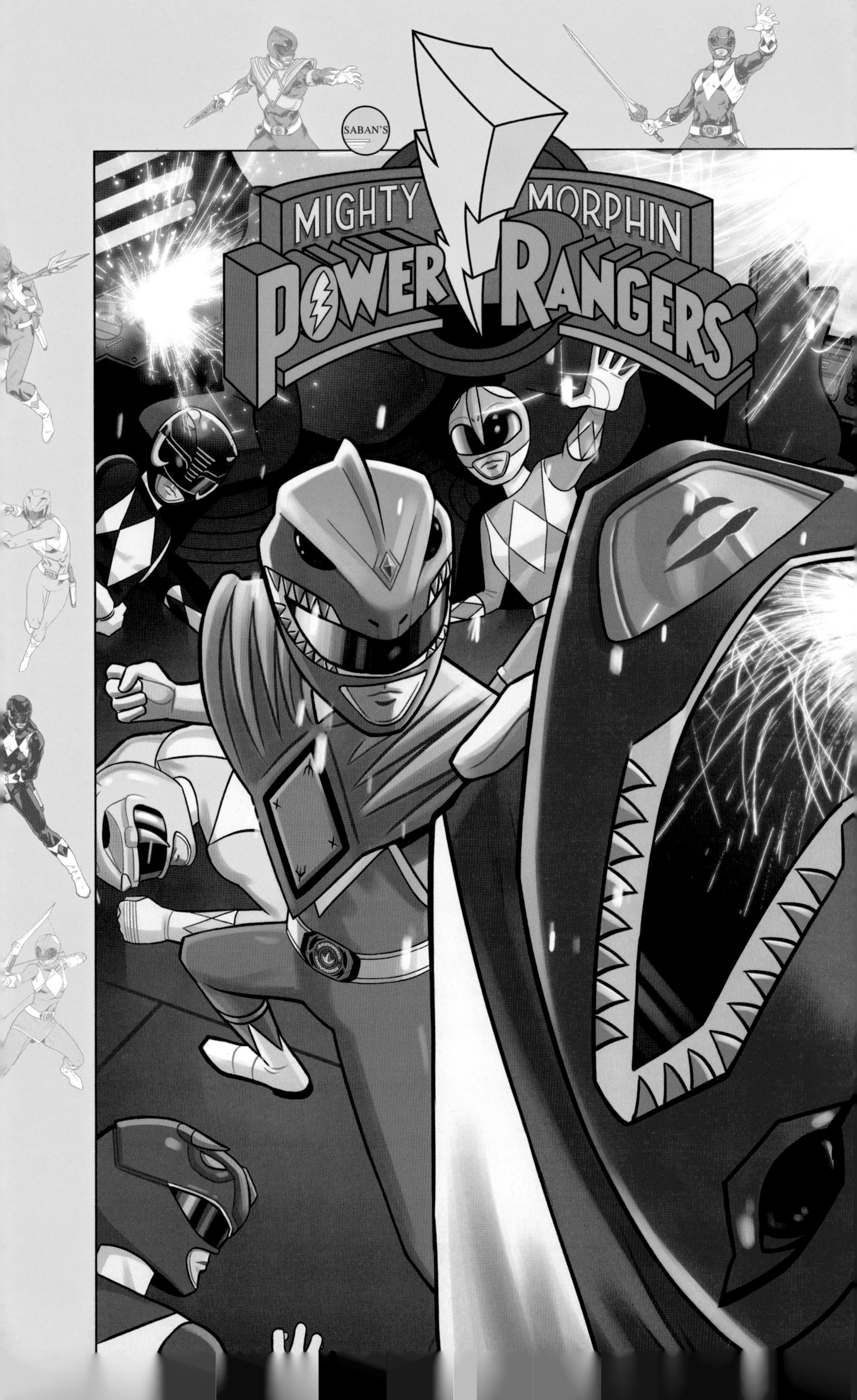
SABAN'S
MIGHTY MORPHIN
POWER RANGERS

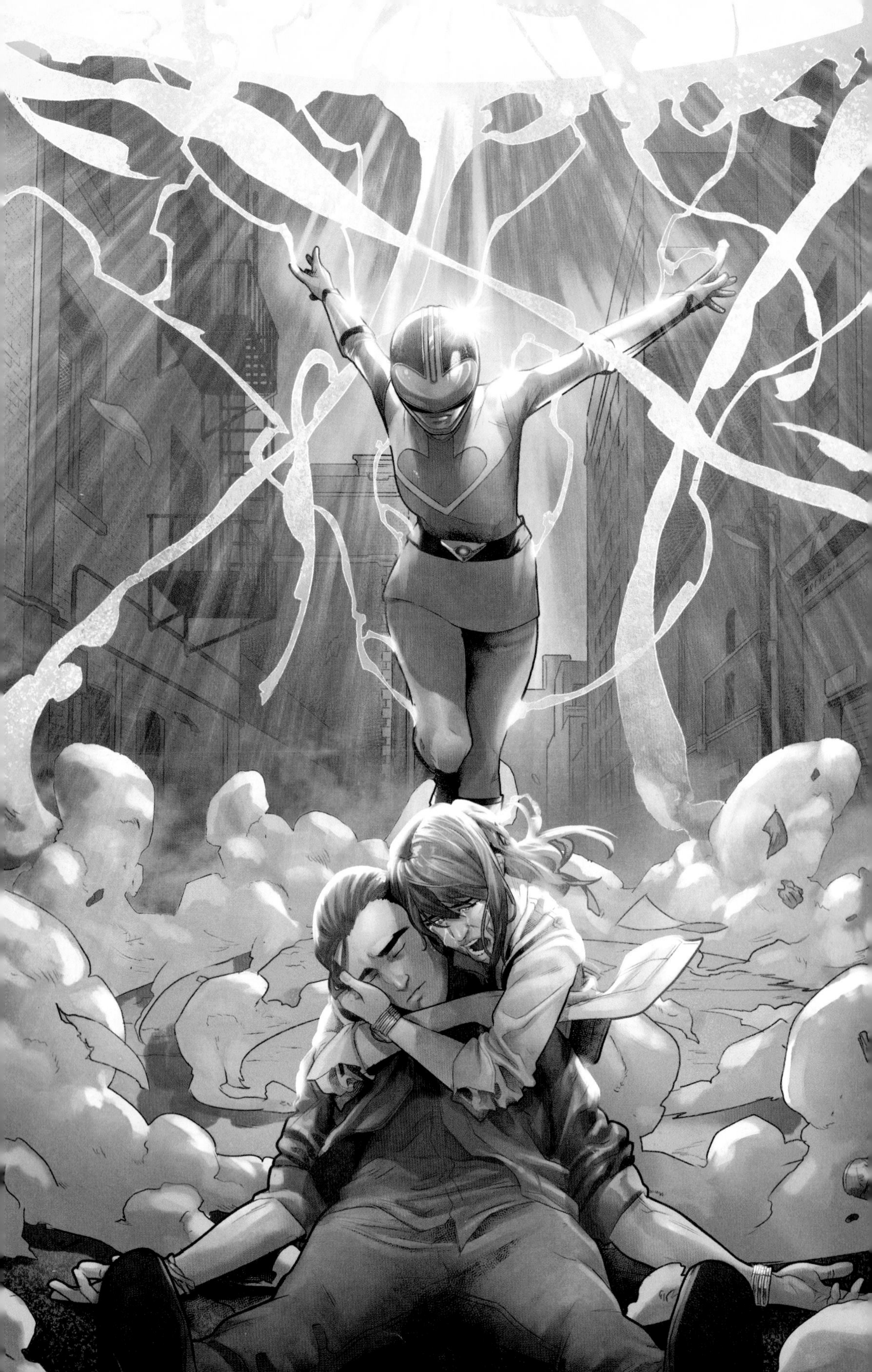

CHAPTER **TWENTY-SIX**

JAMAL CAMPBELL | ISSUE TWENTY-SIX COVER

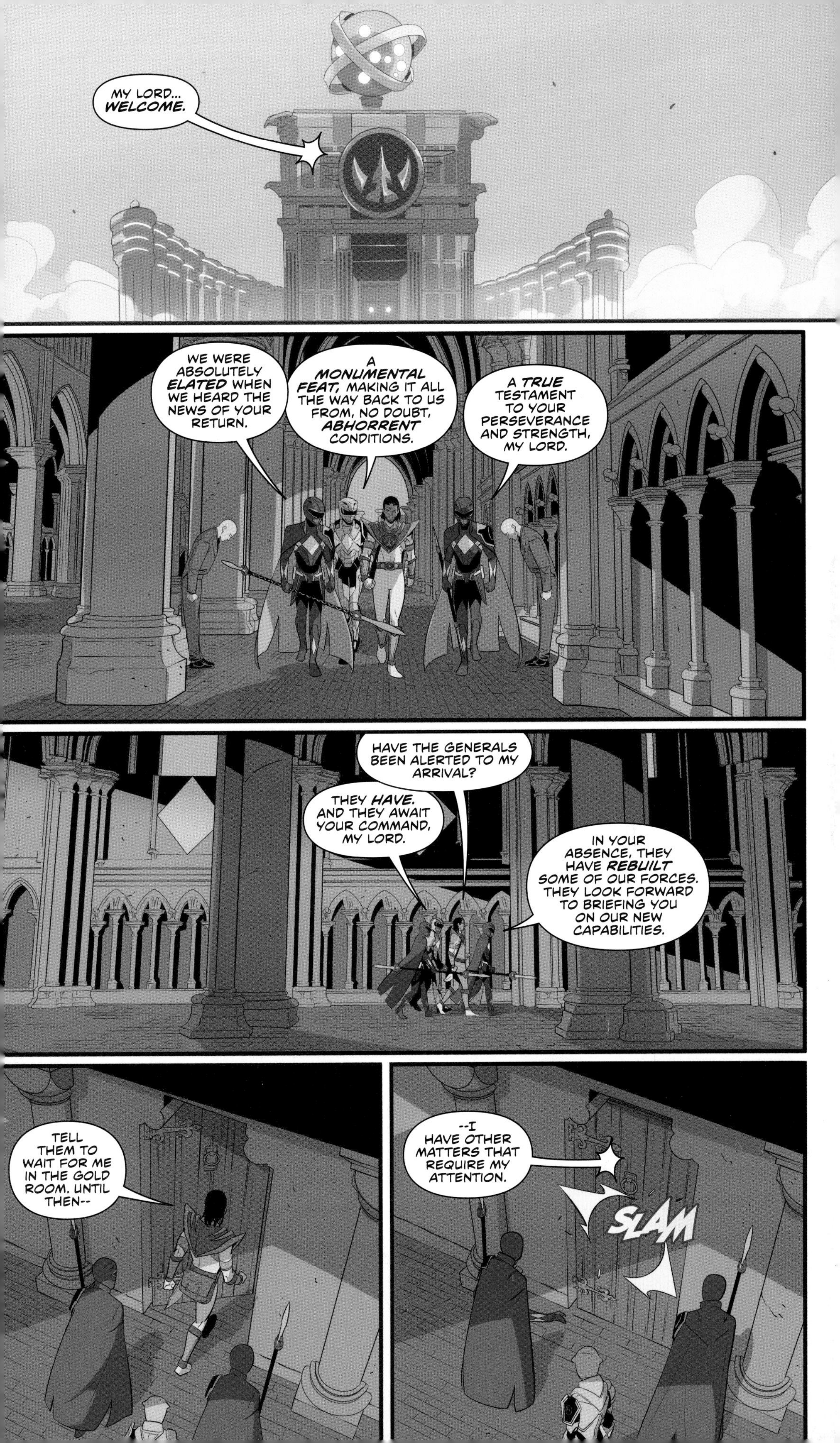
MY LORD... WELCOME.
WE WERE ABSOLUTELY ELATED WHEN WE HEARD THE NEWS OF YOUR RETURN.
A MONUMENTAL FEAT, MAKING IT ALL THE WAY BACK TO US FROM, NO DOUBT, ABHORRENT CONDITIONS.
A TRUE TESTAMENT TO YOUR PERSEVERANCE AND STRENGTH, MY LORD.
HAVE THE GENERALS BEEN ALERTED TO MY ARRIVAL?
THEY HAVE. AND THEY AWAIT YOUR COMMAND, MY LORD.
IN YOUR ABSENCE, THEY HAVE REBUILT SOME OF OUR FORCES. THEY LOOK FORWARD TO BRIEFING YOU ON OUR NEW CAPABILITIES.
TELL THEM TO WAIT FOR ME IN THE GOLD ROOM. UNTIL THEN--
--I HAVE OTHER MATTERS THAT REQUIRE MY ATTENTION.
SLAM

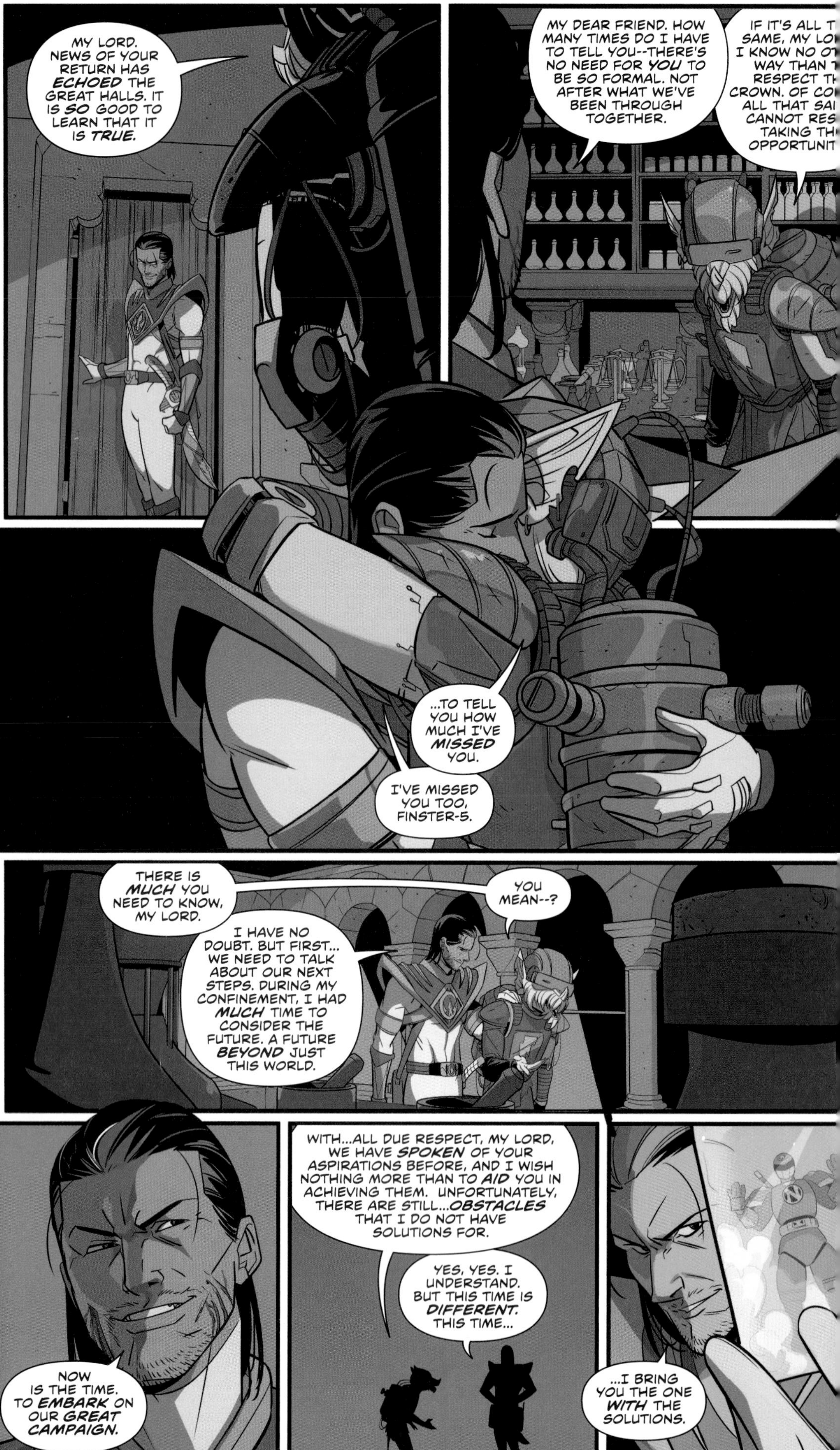
MY LORD. NEWS OF YOUR RETURN HAS ECHOED THE GREAT HALLS. IT IS SO GOOD TO LEARN THAT IT IS TRUE.
MY DEAR FRIEND. HOW MANY TIMES DO I HAVE TO TELL YOU--THERE'S NO NEED FOR YOU TO BE SO FORMAL. NOT AFTER WHAT WE'VE BEEN THROUGH TOGETHER.
IF IT'S ALL T SAME, MY LO I KNOW NO OT WAY THAN T RESPECT T CROWN. OF CO ALL THAT SA CANNOT RES TAKING TH OPPORTUNIT
...TO TELL YOU HOW MUCH I'VE MISSED YOU.
I'VE MISSED YOU TOO, FINSTER-5.
THERE IS MUCH YOU NEED TO KNOW, MY LORD.
YOU MEAN--?
I HAVE NO DOUBT. BUT FIRST... WE NEED TO TALK ABOUT OUR NEXT STEPS. DURING MY CONFINEMENT, I HAD MUCH TIME TO CONSIDER THE FUTURE. A FUTURE BEYOND JUST THIS WORLD.
NOW IS THE TIME. TO EMBARK ON OUR GREAT CAMPAIGN.
WITH...ALL DUE RESPECT, MY LORD, WE HAVE SPOKEN OF YOUR ASPIRATIONS BEFORE, AND I WISH NOTHING MORE THAN TO AID YOU IN ACHIEVING THEM. UNFORTUNATELY, THERE ARE STILL...OBSTACLES THAT I DO NOT HAVE SOLUTIONS FOR.
YES, YES. I UNDERSTAND. BUT THIS TIME IS DIFFERENT. THIS TIME...
...I BRING YOU THE ONE WITH THE SOLUTIONS.

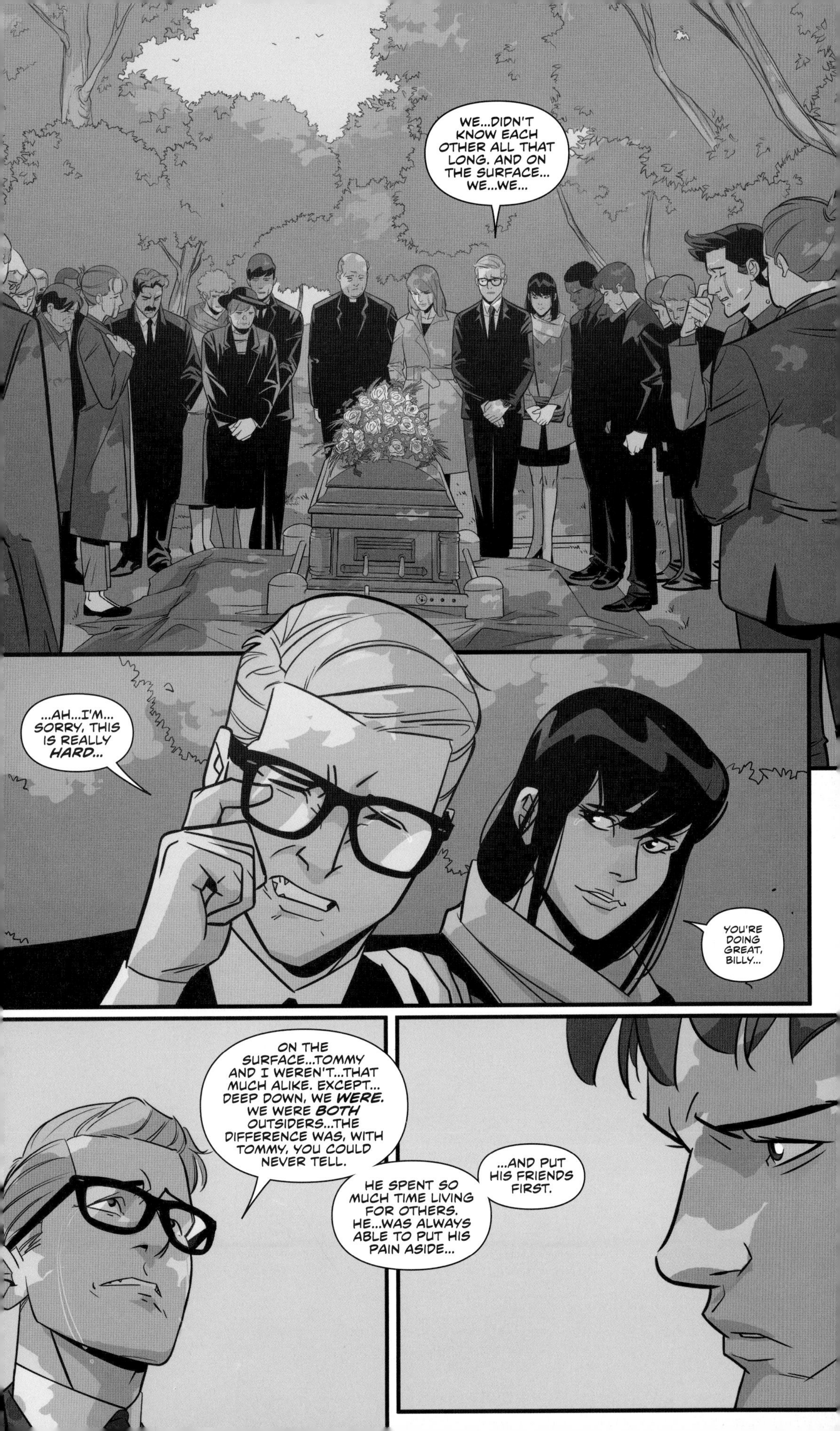
WE...DIDN'T KNOW EACH OTHER ALL THAT LONG. AND ON THE SURFACE... WE...WE...
...AH...I'M... SORRY, THIS IS REALLY *HARD*...
YOU'RE DOING GREAT, BILLY...
ON THE SURFACE...TOMMY AND I WEREN'T...THAT MUCH ALIKE. EXCEPT... DEEP DOWN, WE *WERE*. WE WERE *BOTH* OUTSIDERS...THE DIFFERENCE WAS, WITH TOMMY, YOU COULD NEVER TELL.
HE SPENT SO MUCH TIME LIVING FOR OTHERS. HE...WAS ALWAYS ABLE TO PUT HIS PAIN ASIDE...
...AND PUT HIS FRIENDS FIRST.

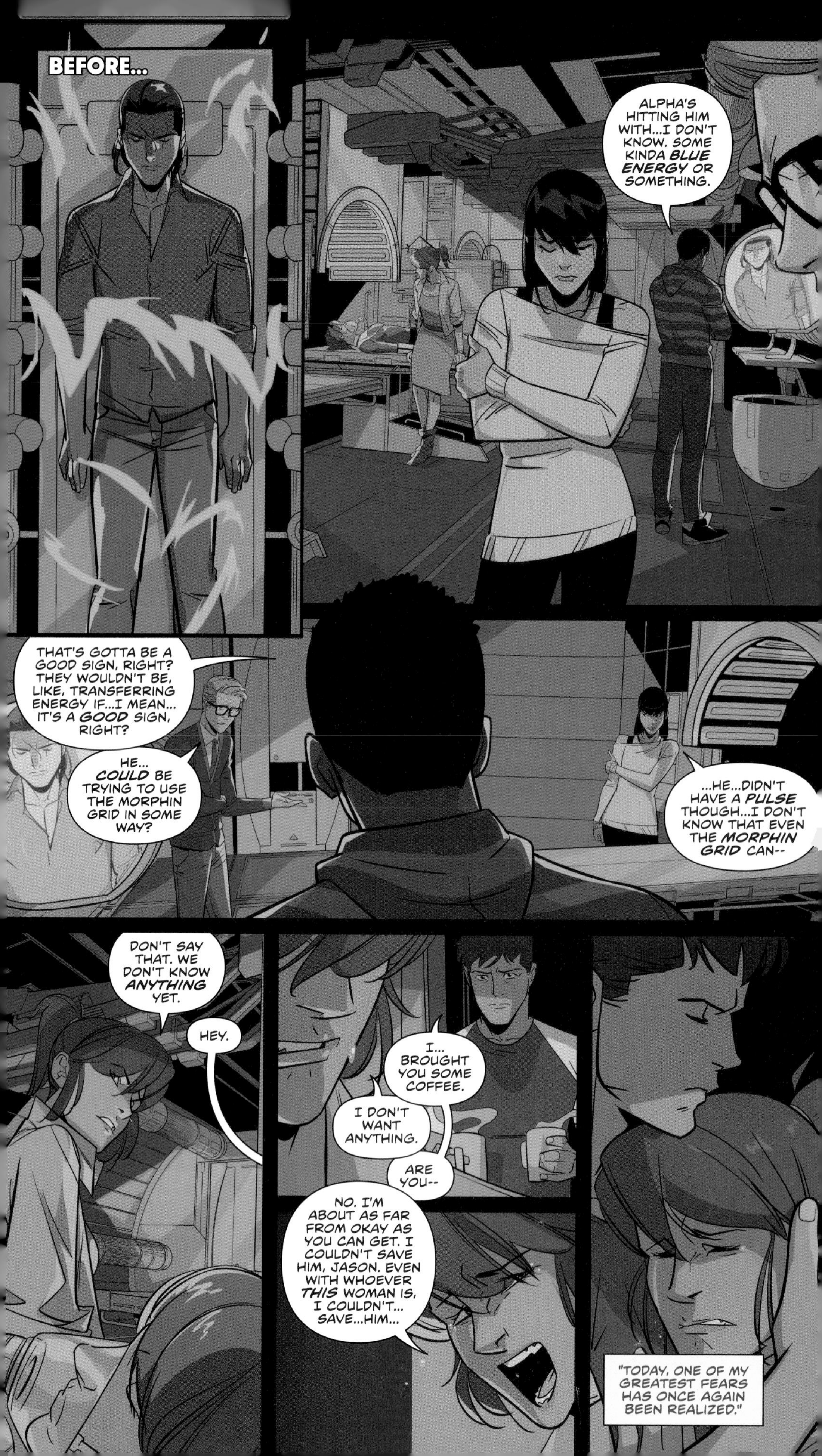
BEFORE...
ALPHA'S HITTING HIM WITH...I DON'T KNOW. SOME KINDA BLUE ENERGY OR SOMETHING.
THAT'S GOTTA BE A GOOD SIGN, RIGHT? THEY WOULDN'T BE, LIKE, TRANSFERRING ENERGY IF...I MEAN... IT'S A GOOD SIGN, RIGHT?
HE... COULD BE TRYING TO USE THE MORPHIN GRID IN SOME WAY?
...HE...DIDN'T HAVE A PULSE THOUGH...I DON'T KNOW THAT EVEN THE MORPHIN GRID CAN--
DON'T SAY THAT. WE DON'T KNOW ANYTHING YET.
HEY.
I... BROUGHT YOU SOME COFFEE.
I DON'T WANT ANYTHING.
ARE YOU--
NO. I'M ABOUT AS FAR FROM OKAY AS YOU CAN GET. I COULDN'T SAVE HIM, JASON. EVEN WITH WHOEVER THIS WOMAN IS, I COULDN'T... SAVE...HIM...
"TODAY, ONE OF MY GREATEST FEARS HAS ONCE AGAIN BEEN REALIZED."

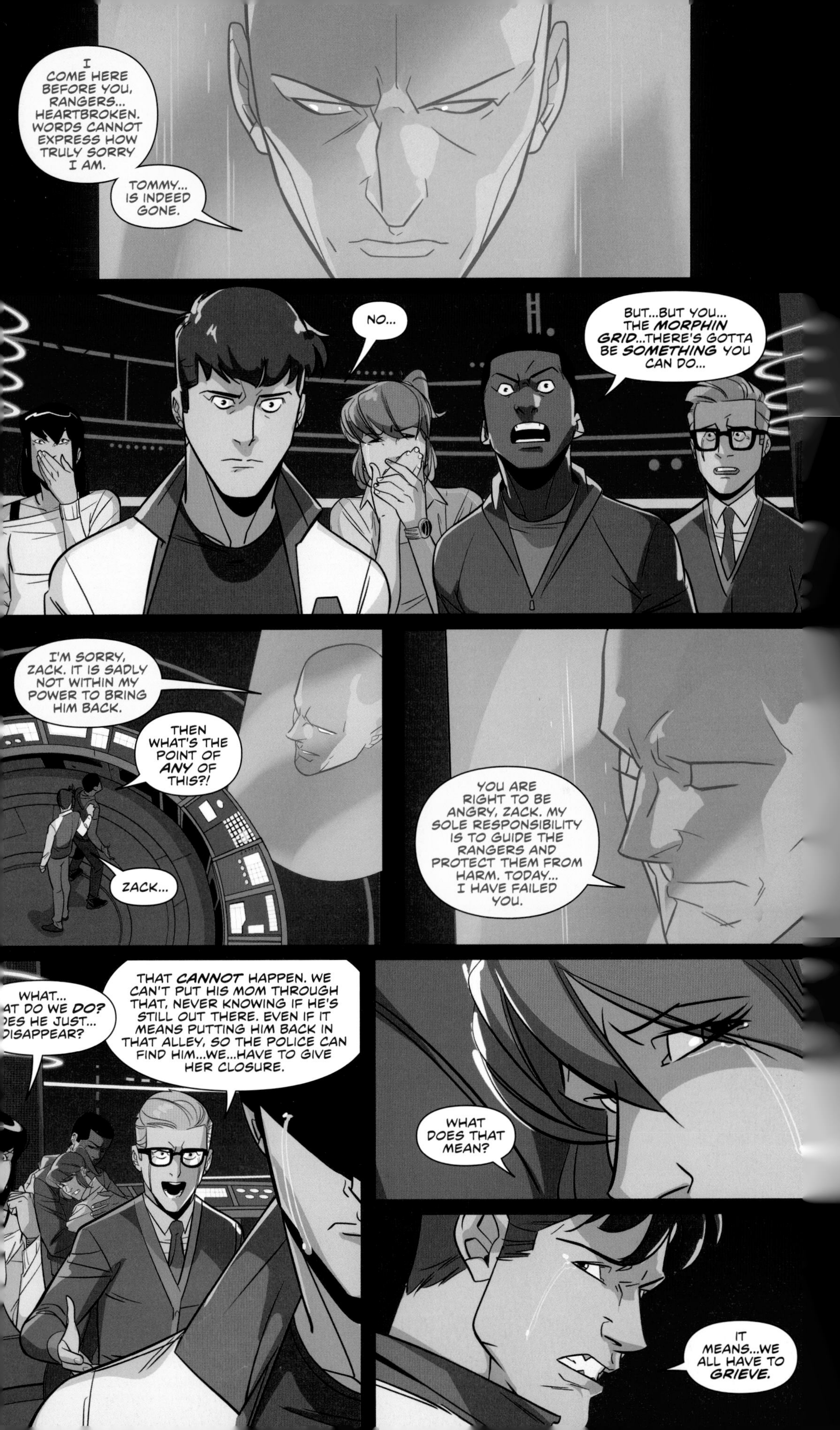
I COME HERE BEFORE YOU, RANGERS... HEARTBROKEN. WORDS CANNOT EXPRESS HOW TRULY SORRY I AM.
TOMMY... IS INDEED GONE.
NO...
BUT...BUT YOU... THE *MORPHIN GRID*...THERE'S GOTTA BE *SOMETHING* YOU CAN DO...
I'M SORRY, ZACK. IT IS SADLY NOT WITHIN MY POWER TO BRING HIM BACK.
THEN WHAT'S THE POINT OF *ANY* OF THIS?!
ZACK...
YOU ARE RIGHT TO BE ANGRY, ZACK. MY SOLE RESPONSIBILITY IS TO GUIDE THE RANGERS AND PROTECT THEM FROM HARM. TODAY... I HAVE FAILED YOU.
WHAT... AT DO WE *DO?* DES HE JUST... DISAPPEAR?
THAT *CANNOT* HAPPEN. WE CAN'T PUT HIS MOM THROUGH THAT, NEVER KNOWING IF HE'S STILL OUT THERE. EVEN IF IT MEANS PUTTING HIM BACK IN THAT ALLEY, SO THE POLICE CAN FIND HIM...WE...HAVE TO GIVE HER CLOSURE.
WHAT DOES THAT MEAN?
IT MEANS...WE ALL HAVE TO *GRIEVE.*

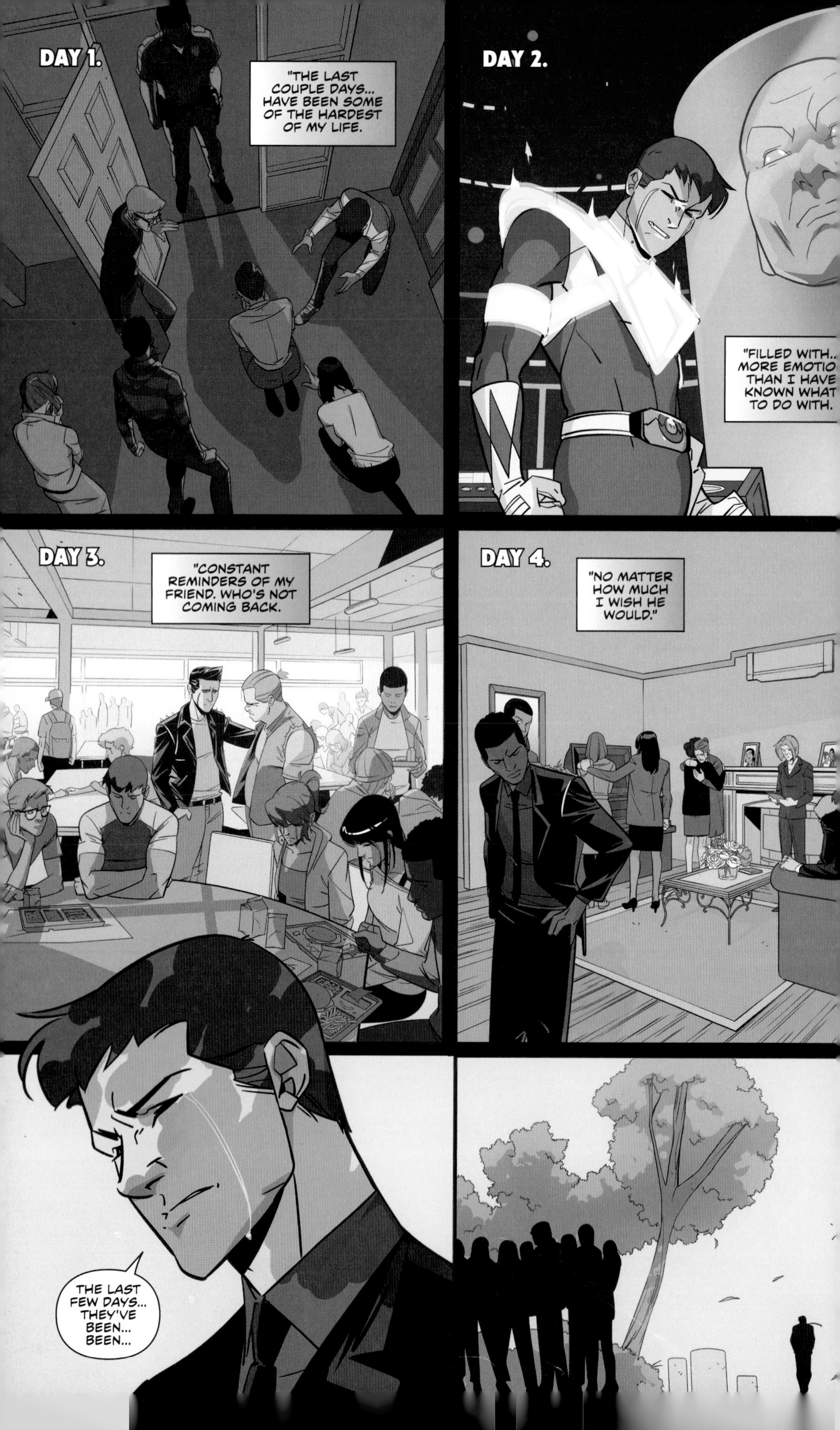
DAY 1.
"THE LAST COUPLE DAYS... HAVE BEEN SOME OF THE HARDEST OF MY LIFE.
DAY 2.
"FILLED WITH... MORE EMOTIO THAN I HAVE KNOWN WHAT TO DO WITH.
DAY 3.
"CONSTANT REMINDERS OF MY FRIEND. WHO'S NOT COMING BACK.
DAY 4.
"NO MATTER HOW MUCH I WISH HE WOULD."
THE LAST FEW DAYS... THEY'VE BEEN... BEEN...

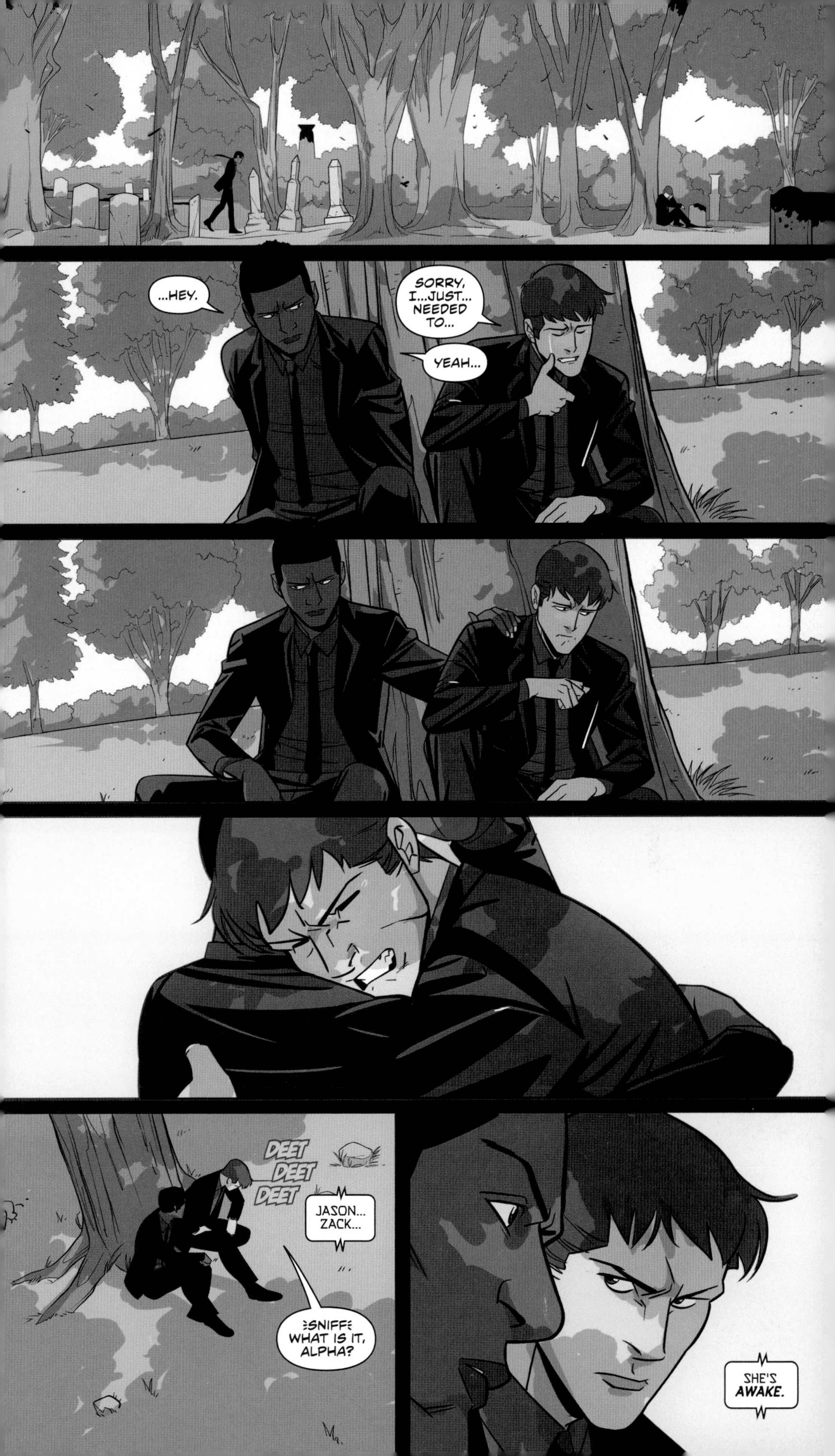
...HEY.
SORRY, I...JUST... NEEDED TO...
YEAH...
DEET DEET DEET
JASON... ZACK...
SNIFF WHAT IS IT, ALPHA?
SHE'S AWAKE.

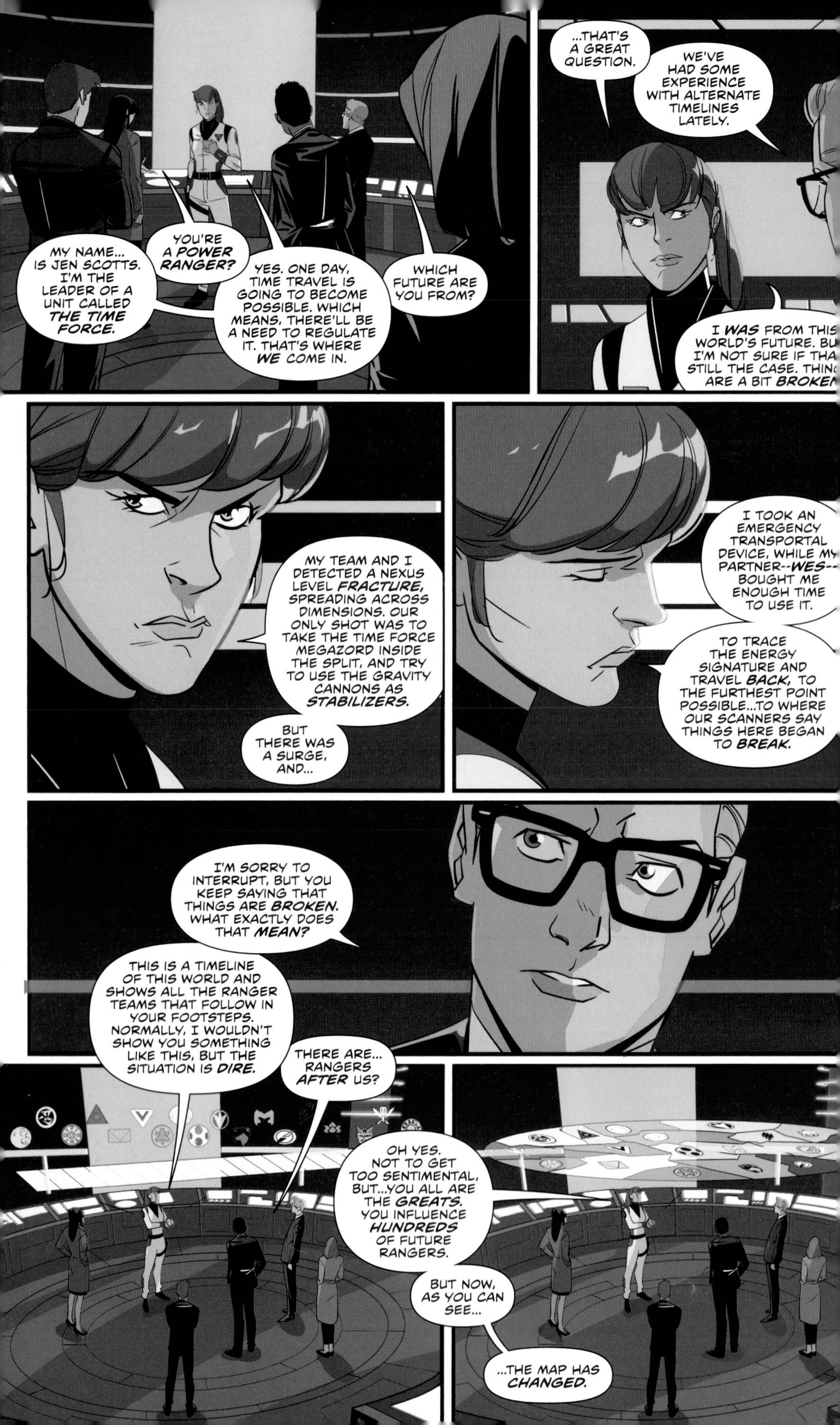

MY NAME... IS JEN SCOTTS. I'M THE LEADER OF A UNIT CALLED THE TIME FORCE.
YOU'RE A POWER RANGER?
YES. ONE DAY, TIME TRAVEL IS GOING TO BECOME POSSIBLE. WHICH MEANS, THERE'LL BE A NEED TO REGULATE IT. THAT'S WHERE WE COME IN.
WHICH FUTURE ARE YOU FROM?
...THAT'S A GREAT QUESTION.
WE'VE HAD SOME EXPERIENCE WITH ALTERNATE TIMELINES LATELY.
I WAS FROM THIS WORLD'S FUTURE. BU I'M NOT SURE IF THA STILL THE CASE. THIN ARE A BIT BROKEN
MY TEAM AND I DETECTED A NEXUS LEVEL FRACTURE, SPREADING ACROSS DIMENSIONS. OUR ONLY SHOT WAS TO TAKE THE TIME FORCE MEGAZORD INSIDE THE SPLIT, AND TRY TO USE THE GRAVITY CANNONS AS STABILIZERS.
BUT THERE WAS A SURGE, AND...
I TOOK AN EMERGENCY TRANSPORTAL DEVICE, WHILE MY PARTNER--WES-- BOUGHT ME ENOUGH TIME TO USE IT.
TO TRACE THE ENERGY SIGNATURE AND TRAVEL BACK, TO THE FURTHEST POINT POSSIBLE...TO WHERE OUR SCANNERS SAY THINGS HERE BEGAN TO BREAK.
I'M SORRY TO INTERRUPT, BUT YOU KEEP SAYING THAT THINGS ARE BROKEN. WHAT EXACTLY DOES THAT MEAN?
THIS IS A TIMELINE OF THIS WORLD AND SHOWS ALL THE RANGER TEAMS THAT FOLLOW IN YOUR FOOTSTEPS. NORMALLY, I WOULDN'T SHOW YOU SOMETHING LIKE THIS, BUT THE SITUATION IS DIRE.
THERE ARE... RANGERS AFTER US?
OH YES. NOT TO GET TOO SENTIMENTAL, BUT...YOU ALL ARE THE GREATS. YOU INFLUENCE HUNDREDS OF FUTURE RANGERS.
BUT NOW, AS YOU CAN SEE...
...THE MAP HAS CHANGED.

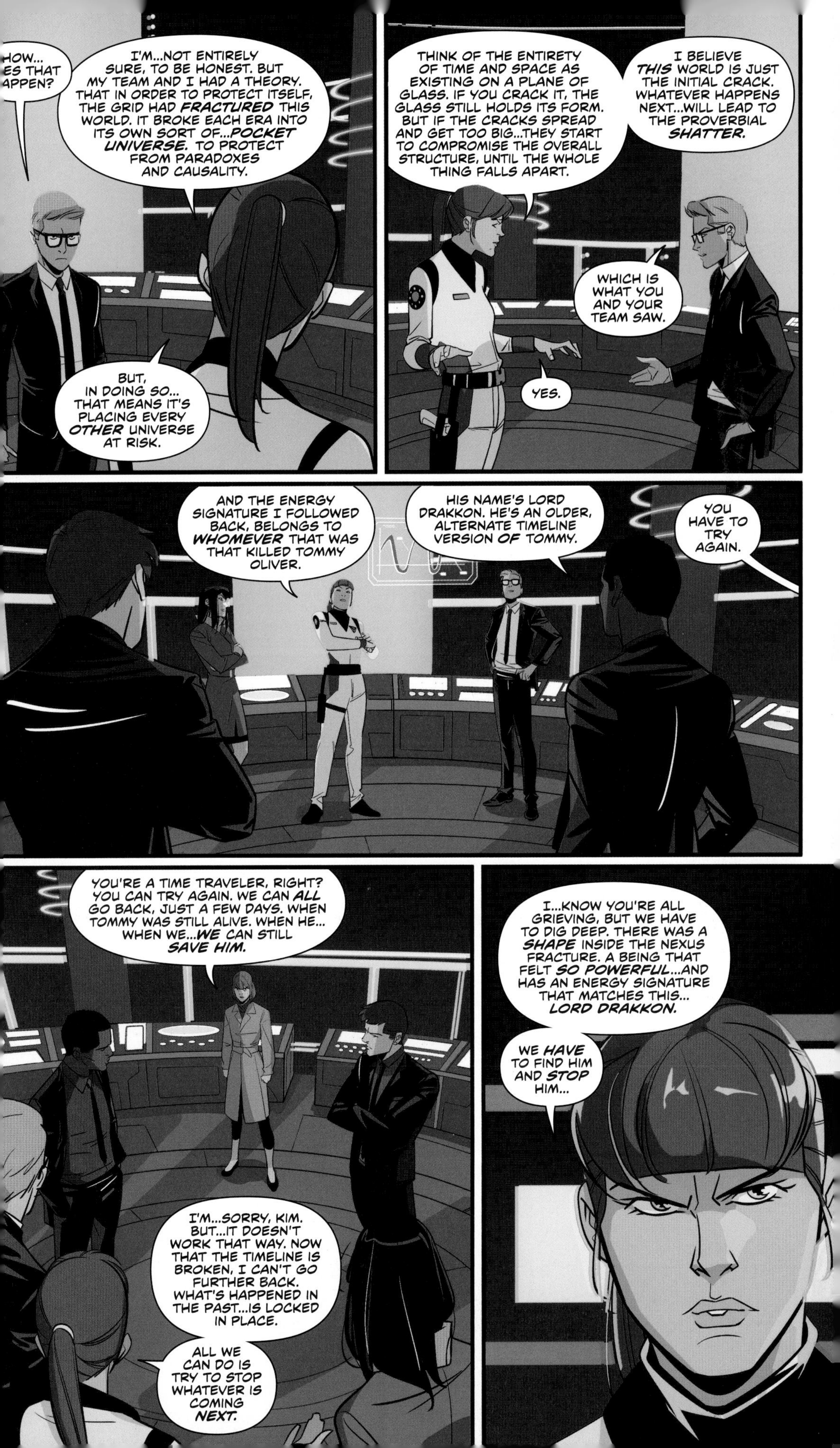
HOW... ES THAT APPEN?
I'M...NOT ENTIRELY SURE, TO BE HONEST. BUT MY TEAM AND I HAD A THEORY. THAT IN ORDER TO PROTECT ITSELF, THE GRID HAD FRACTURED THIS WORLD. IT BROKE EACH ERA INTO ITS OWN SORT OF...POCKET UNIVERSE. TO PROTECT FROM PARADOXES AND CAUSALITY.
BUT, IN DOING SO... THAT MEANS IT'S PLACING EVERY OTHER UNIVERSE AT RISK.
THINK OF THE ENTIRETY OF TIME AND SPACE AS EXISTING ON A PLANE OF GLASS. IF YOU CRACK IT, THE GLASS STILL HOLDS ITS FORM. BUT IF THE CRACKS SPREAD AND GET TOO BIG...THEY START TO COMPROMISE THE OVERALL STRUCTURE, UNTIL THE WHOLE THING FALLS APART.
I BELIEVE THIS WORLD IS JUST THE INITIAL CRACK. WHATEVER HAPPENS NEXT...WILL LEAD TO THE PROVERBIAL SHATTER.
WHICH IS WHAT YOU AND YOUR TEAM SAW.
YES.
AND THE ENERGY SIGNATURE I FOLLOWED BACK, BELONGS TO WHOMEVER THAT WAS THAT KILLED TOMMY OLIVER.
HIS NAME'S LORD DRAKKON. HE'S AN OLDER, ALTERNATE TIMELINE VERSION OF TOMMY.
YOU HAVE TO TRY AGAIN.
YOU'RE A TIME TRAVELER, RIGHT? YOU CAN TRY AGAIN. WE CAN ALL GO BACK, JUST A FEW DAYS. WHEN TOMMY WAS STILL ALIVE. WHEN HE... WHEN WE...WE CAN STILL SAVE HIM.
I'M...SORRY, KIM. BUT...IT DOESN'T WORK THAT WAY. NOW THAT THE TIMELINE IS BROKEN, I CAN'T GO FURTHER BACK. WHAT'S HAPPENED IN THE PAST...IS LOCKED IN PLACE.
ALL WE CAN DO IS TRY TO STOP WHATEVER IS COMING NEXT.
I...KNOW YOU'RE ALL GRIEVING, BUT WE HAVE TO DIG DEEP. THERE WAS A SHAPE INSIDE THE NEXUS FRACTURE. A BEING THAT FELT SO POWERFUL...AND HAS AN ENERGY SIGNATURE THAT MATCHES THIS... LORD DRAKKON.
WE HAVE TO FIND HIM AND STOP HIM...

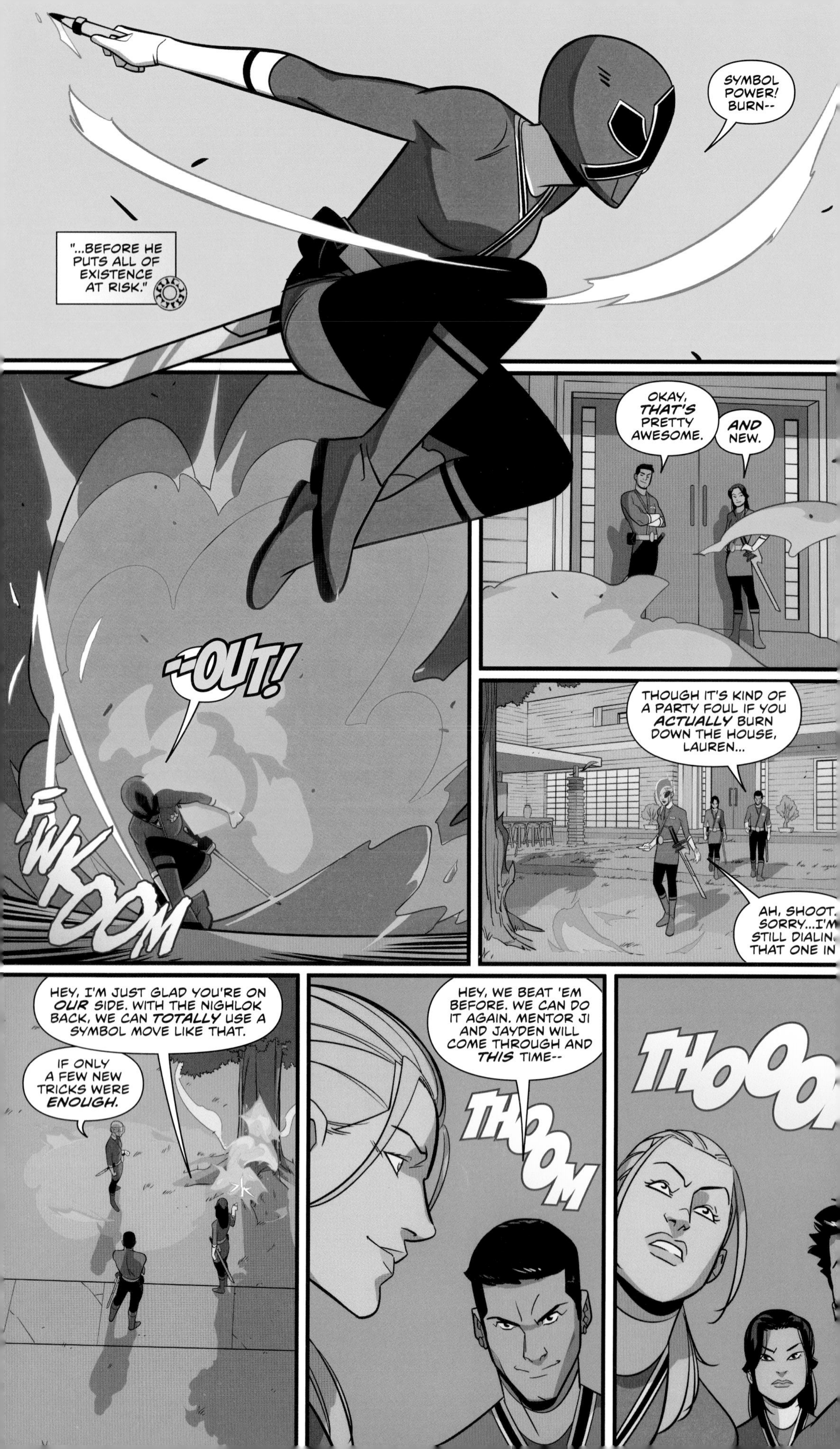

SYMBOL POWER! BURN--
"...BEFORE HE PUTS ALL OF EXISTENCE AT RISK."
--OUT!
FWKOOM
OKAY, THAT'S PRETTY AWESOME.
AND NEW.
THOUGH IT'S KIND OF A PARTY FOUL IF YOU ACTUALLY BURN DOWN THE HOUSE, LAUREN...
AH, SHOOT. SORRY...I'M STILL DIALIN THAT ONE IN
HEY, I'M JUST GLAD YOU'RE ON OUR SIDE. WITH THE NIGHLOK BACK, WE CAN TOTALLY USE A SYMBOL MOVE LIKE THAT.
IF ONLY A FEW NEW TRICKS WERE ENOUGH.
HEY, WE BEAT 'EM BEFORE. WE CAN DO IT AGAIN. MENTOR JI AND JAYDEN WILL COME THROUGH AND THIS TIME--
THOOOM
THOOO

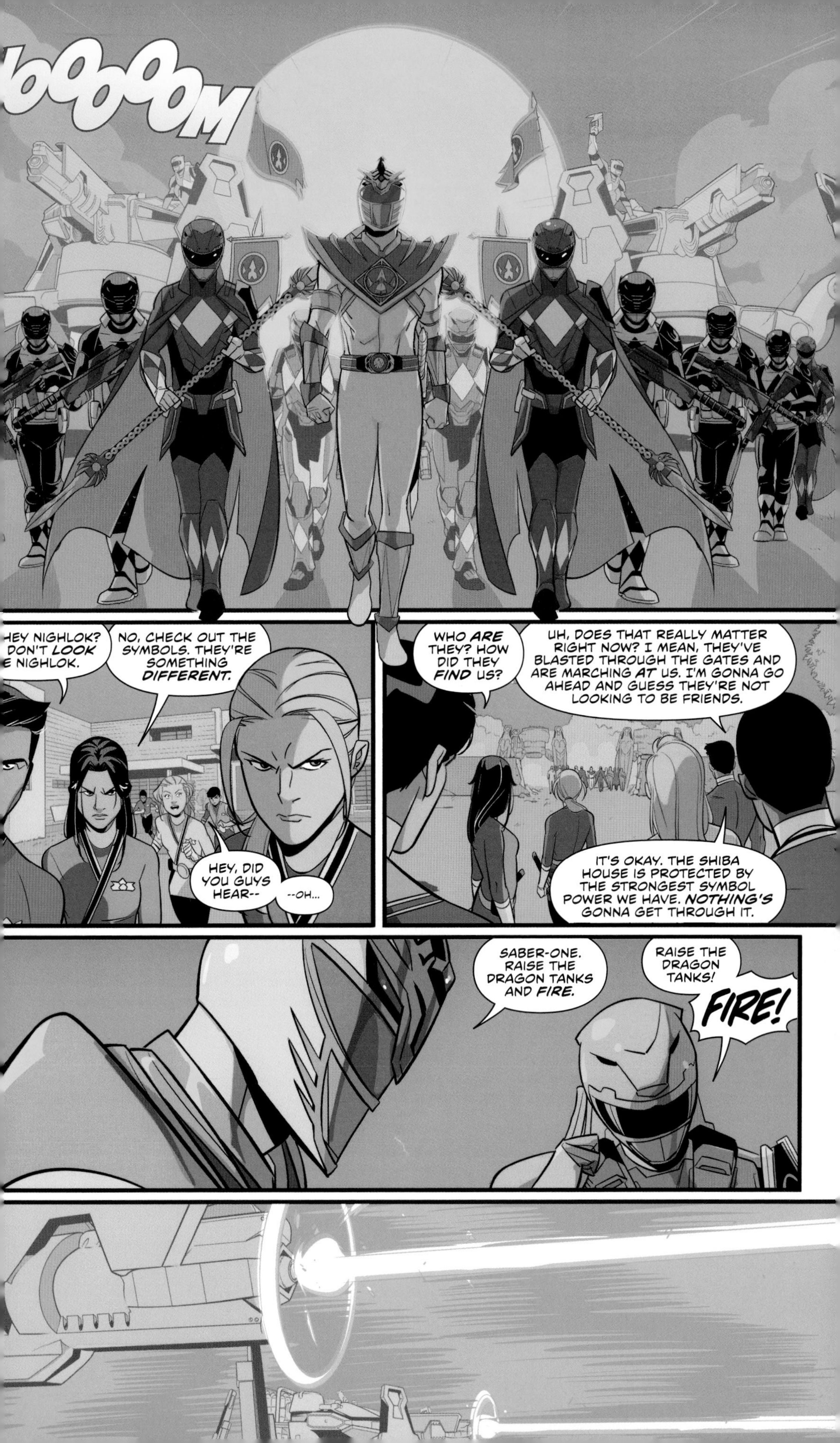
OOOOOM
HEY NIGHLOK? DON'T LOOK E NIGHLOK.
NO, CHECK OUT THE SYMBOLS. THEY'RE SOMETHING DIFFERENT.
HEY, DID YOU GUYS HEAR--
--OH...
WHO ARE THEY? HOW DID THEY FIND US?
UH, DOES THAT REALLY MATTER RIGHT NOW? I MEAN, THEY'VE BLASTED THROUGH THE GATES AND ARE MARCHING AT US. I'M GONNA GO AHEAD AND GUESS THEY'RE NOT LOOKING TO BE FRIENDS.
IT'S OKAY. THE SHIBA HOUSE IS PROTECTED BY THE STRONGEST SYMBOL POWER WE HAVE. NOTHING'S GONNA GET THROUGH IT.
SABER-ONE. RAISE THE DRAGON TANKS AND FIRE.
RAISE THE DRAGON TANKS!
FIRE!

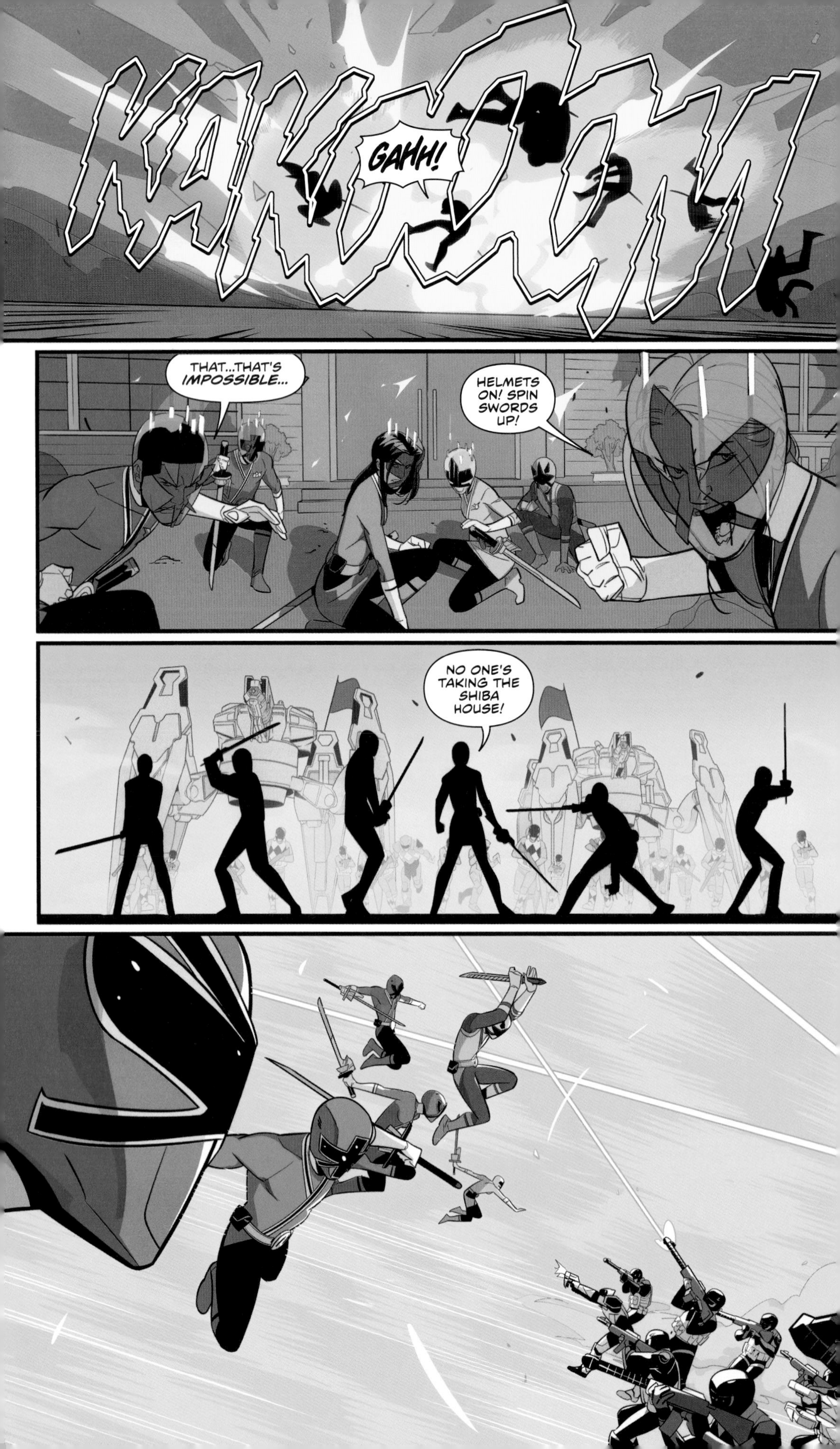
KAKOOM
GAHH!
THAT...THAT'S *IMPOSSIBLE*...
HELMETS ON! SPIN SWORDS UP!
NO ONE'S TAKING THE SHIBA HOUSE!

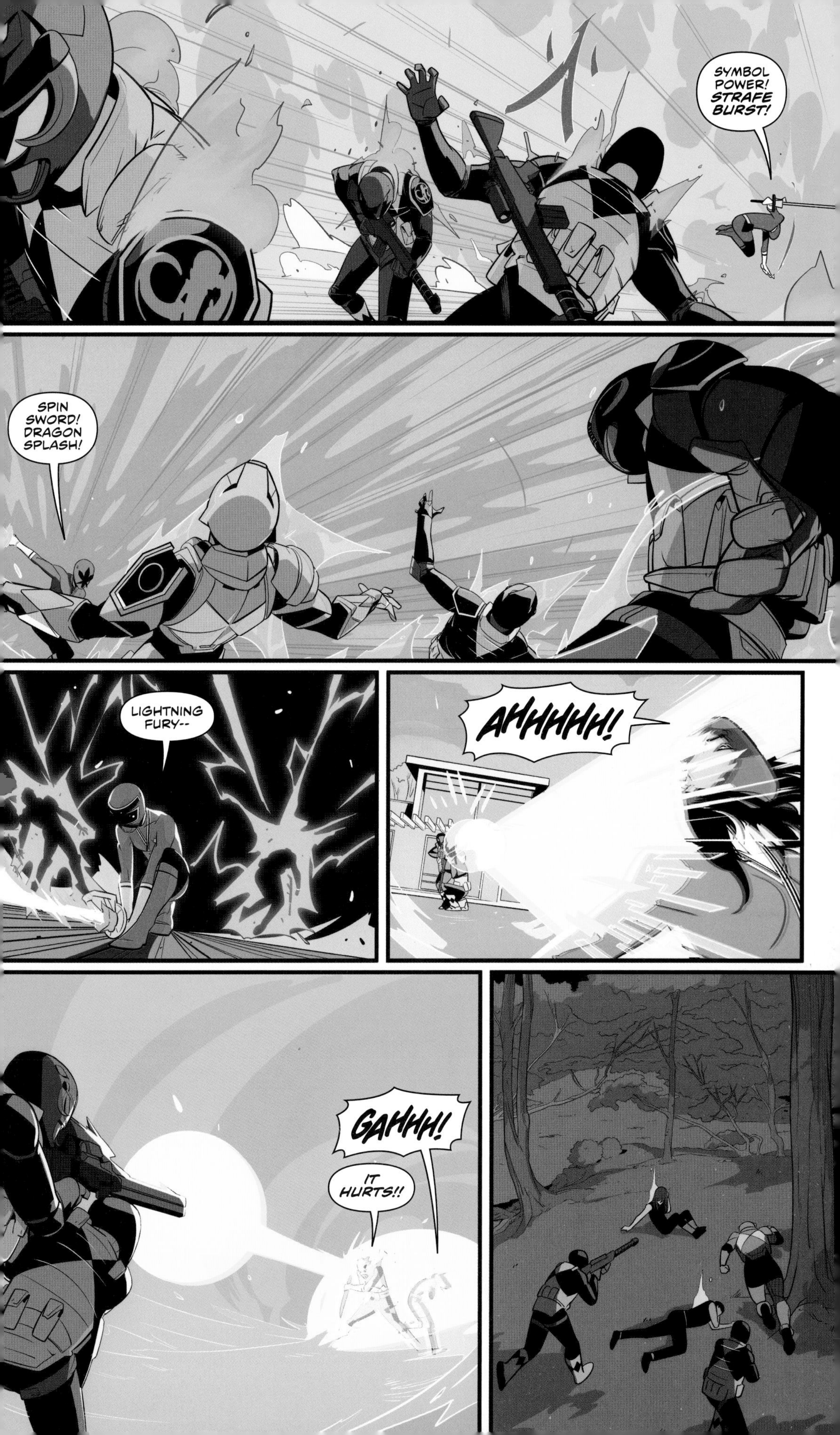
SYMBOL POWER! STRAFE BURST!
SPIN SWORD! DRAGON SPLASH!
LIGHTNING FURY--
AHHHHH!
GAHHH!
IT HURTS!!

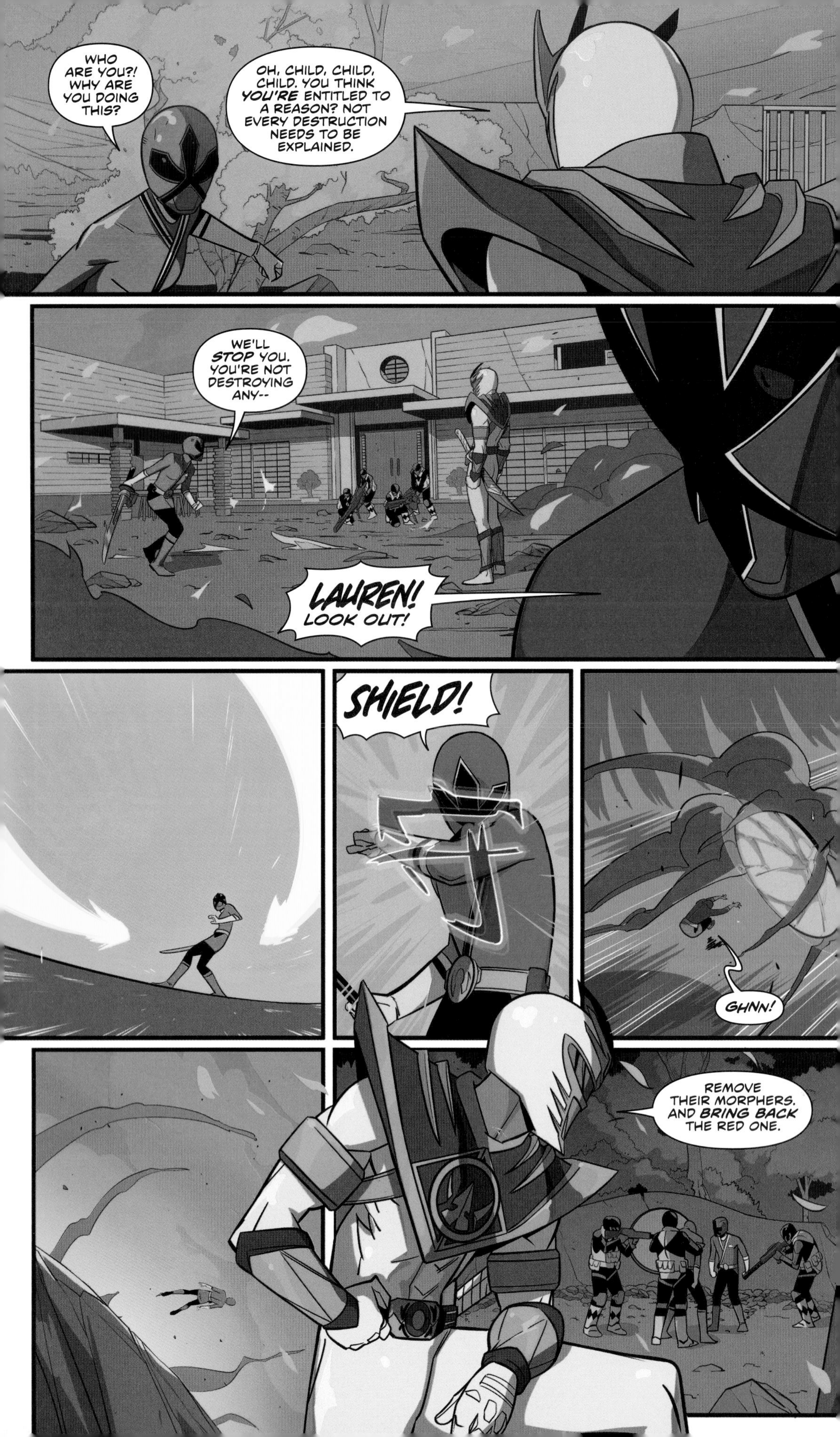
WHO ARE YOU?! WHY ARE YOU DOING THIS?
OH, CHILD, CHILD, CHILD. YOU THINK *YOU'RE* ENTITLED TO A REASON? NOT EVERY DESTRUCTION NEEDS TO BE EXPLAINED.
WE'LL *STOP* YOU. YOU'RE NOT DESTROYING ANY--
LAUREN! LOOK OUT!
SHIELD!
GHNN!
REMOVE THEIR MORPHERS. AND *BRING BACK* THE RED ONE.

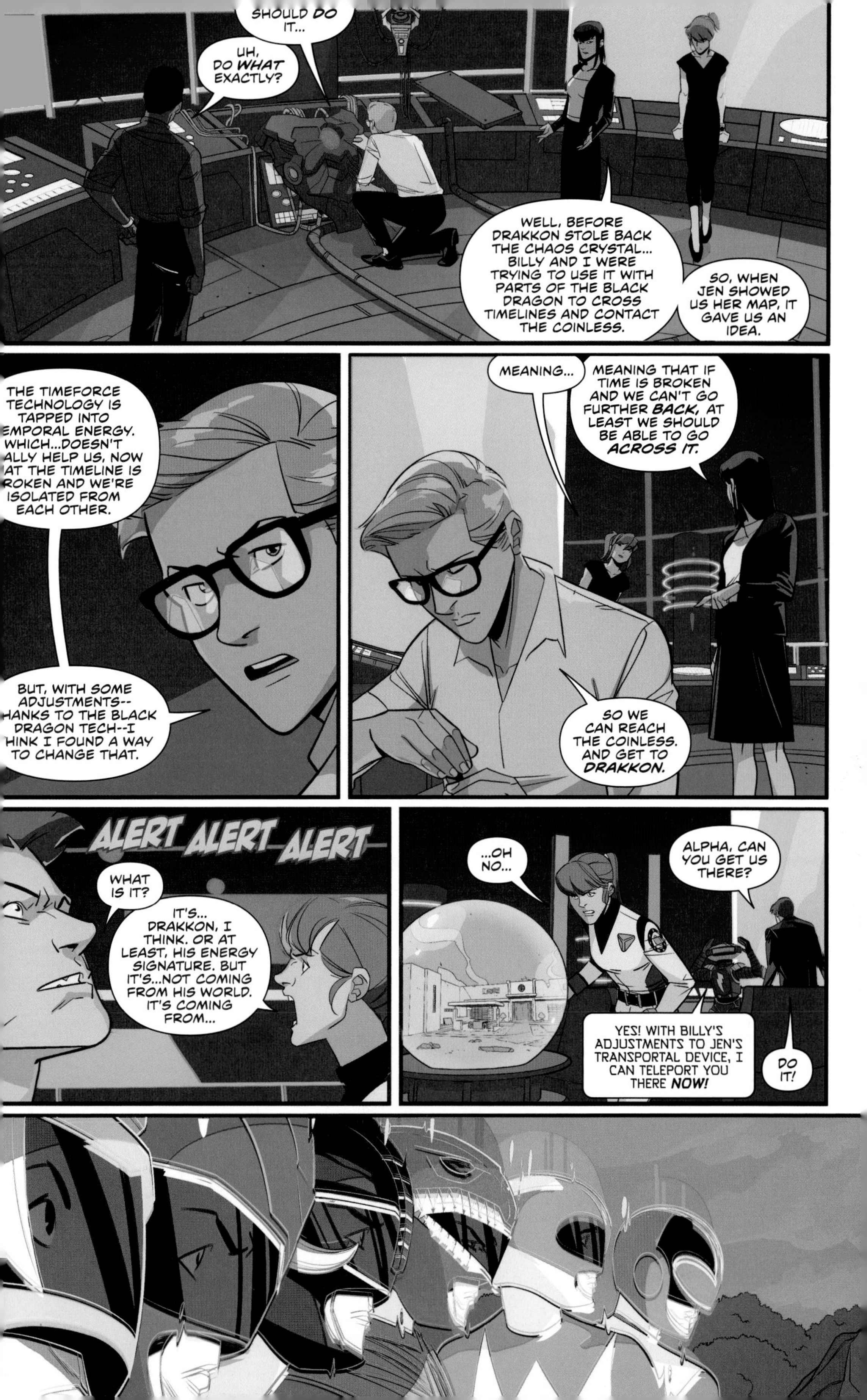
SHOULD DO IT...
UH, DO WHAT EXACTLY?
WELL, BEFORE DRAKKON STOLE BACK THE CHAOS CRYSTAL... BILLY AND I WERE TRYING TO USE IT WITH PARTS OF THE BLACK DRAGON TO CROSS TIMELINES AND CONTACT THE COINLESS.
SO, WHEN JEN SHOWED US HER MAP, IT GAVE US AN IDEA.
THE TIMEFORCE TECHNOLOGY IS TAPPED INTO EMPORAL ENERGY. WHICH...DOESN'T ALLY HELP US, NOW AT THE TIMELINE IS ROKEN AND WE'RE ISOLATED FROM EACH OTHER.
BUT, WITH SOME ADJUSTMENTS-- HANKS TO THE BLACK DRAGON TECH--I HINK I FOUND A WAY TO CHANGE THAT.
MEANING...
MEANING THAT IF TIME IS BROKEN AND WE CAN'T GO FURTHER BACK, AT LEAST WE SHOULD BE ABLE TO GO ACROSS IT.
SO WE CAN REACH THE COINLESS. AND GET TO DRAKKON.
ALERT ALERT ALERT
WHAT IS IT?
IT'S... DRAKKON, I THINK. OR AT LEAST, HIS ENERGY SIGNATURE. BUT IT'S...NOT COMING FROM HIS WORLD. IT'S COMING FROM...
...OH NO...
ALPHA, CAN YOU GET US THERE?
YES! WITH BILLY'S ADJUSTMENTS TO JEN'S TRANSPORTAL DEVICE, I CAN TELEPORT YOU THERE NOW!
DO IT!

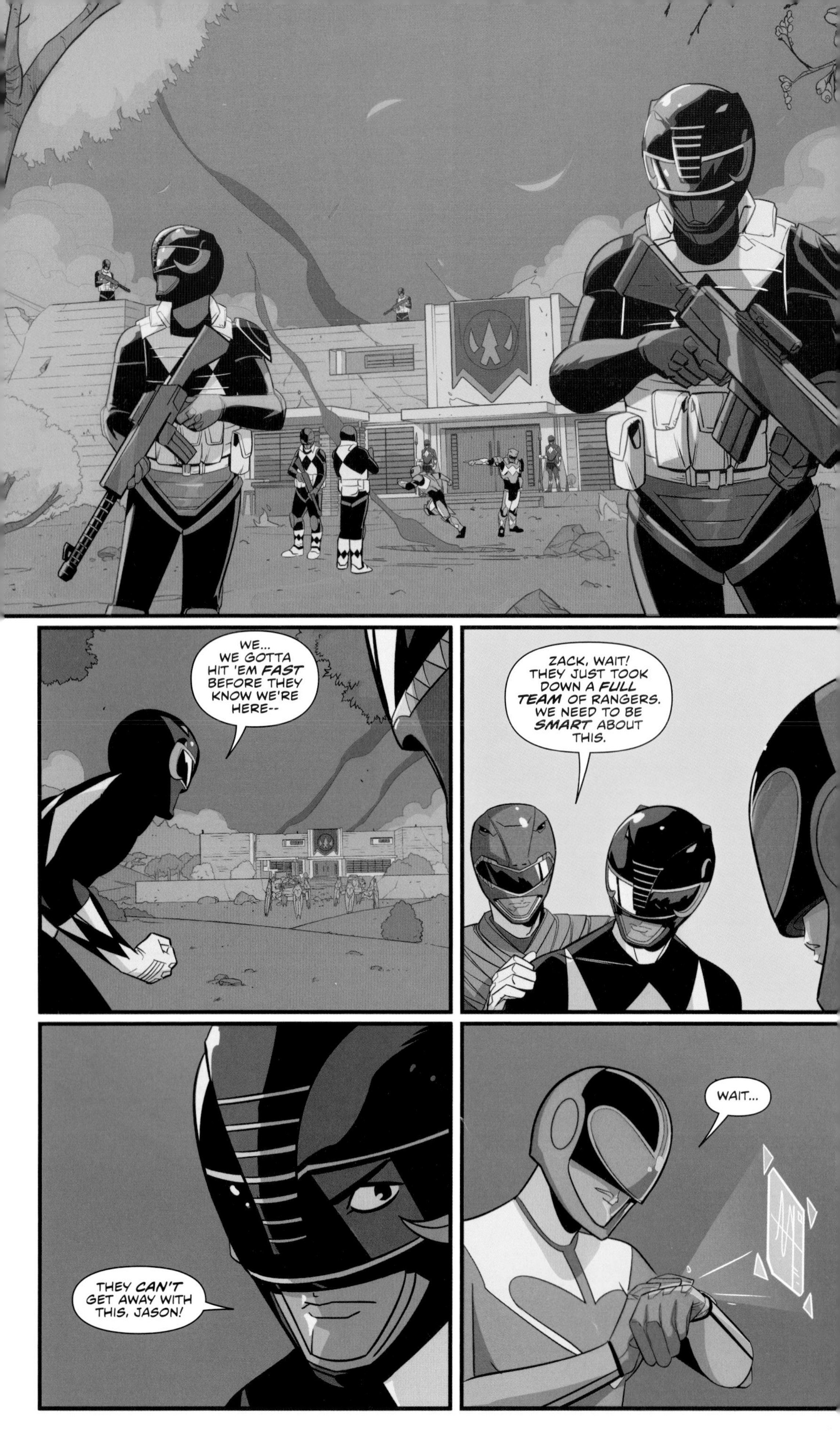
WE... WE GOTTA HIT 'EM *FAST* BEFORE THEY KNOW WE'RE HERE--
ZACK, WAIT! THEY JUST TOOK DOWN A *FULL TEAM* OF RANGERS. WE NEED TO BE *SMART* ABOUT THIS.
THEY *CAN'T* GET AWAY WITH THIS, JASON!
WAIT...

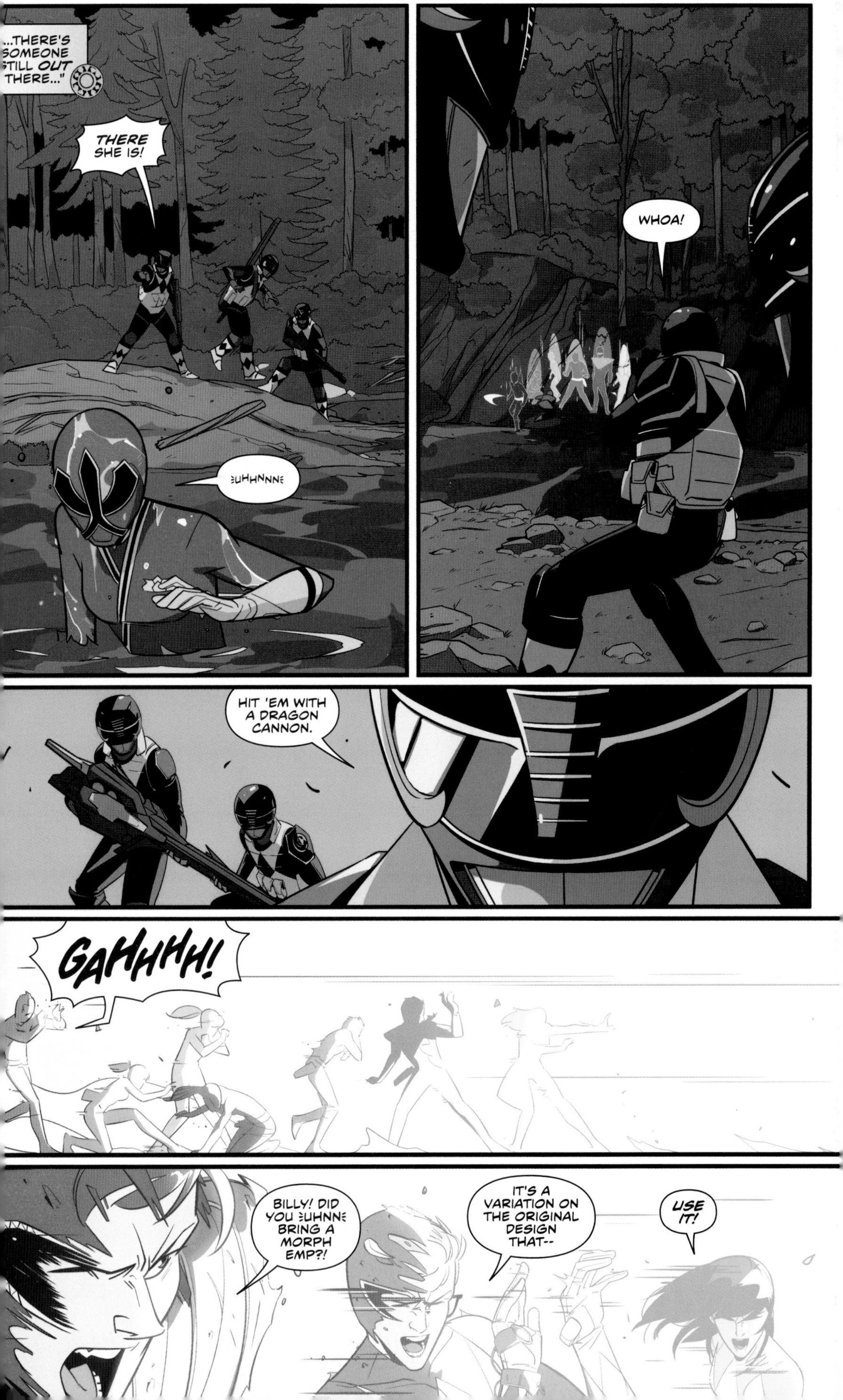

...THERE'S SOMEONE STILL OUT THERE..."
THERE SHE IS!
UHHNNN
WHOA!
HIT 'EM WITH A DRAGON CANNON.
GAHHHH!
BILLY! DID YOU UHNN BRING A MORPH EMP?!
IT'S A VARIATION ON THE ORIGINAL DESIGN THAT--
USE IT!

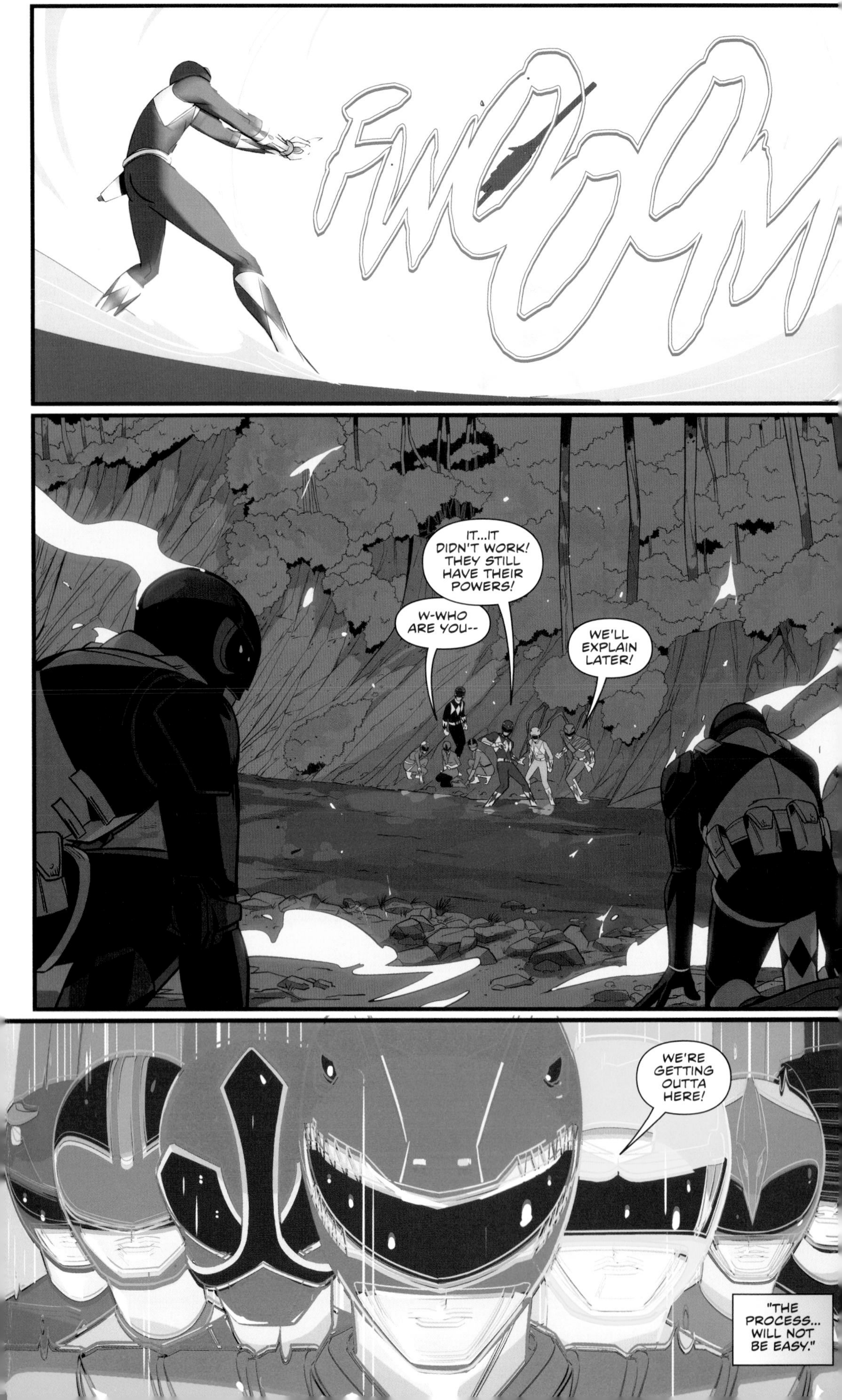
FWOOM
IT...IT DIDN'T WORK! THEY STILL HAVE THEIR POWERS!
W-WHO ARE YOU--
WE'LL EXPLAIN LATER!
WE'RE GETTING OUTTA HERE!
"THE PROCESS... WILL NOT BE EASY."

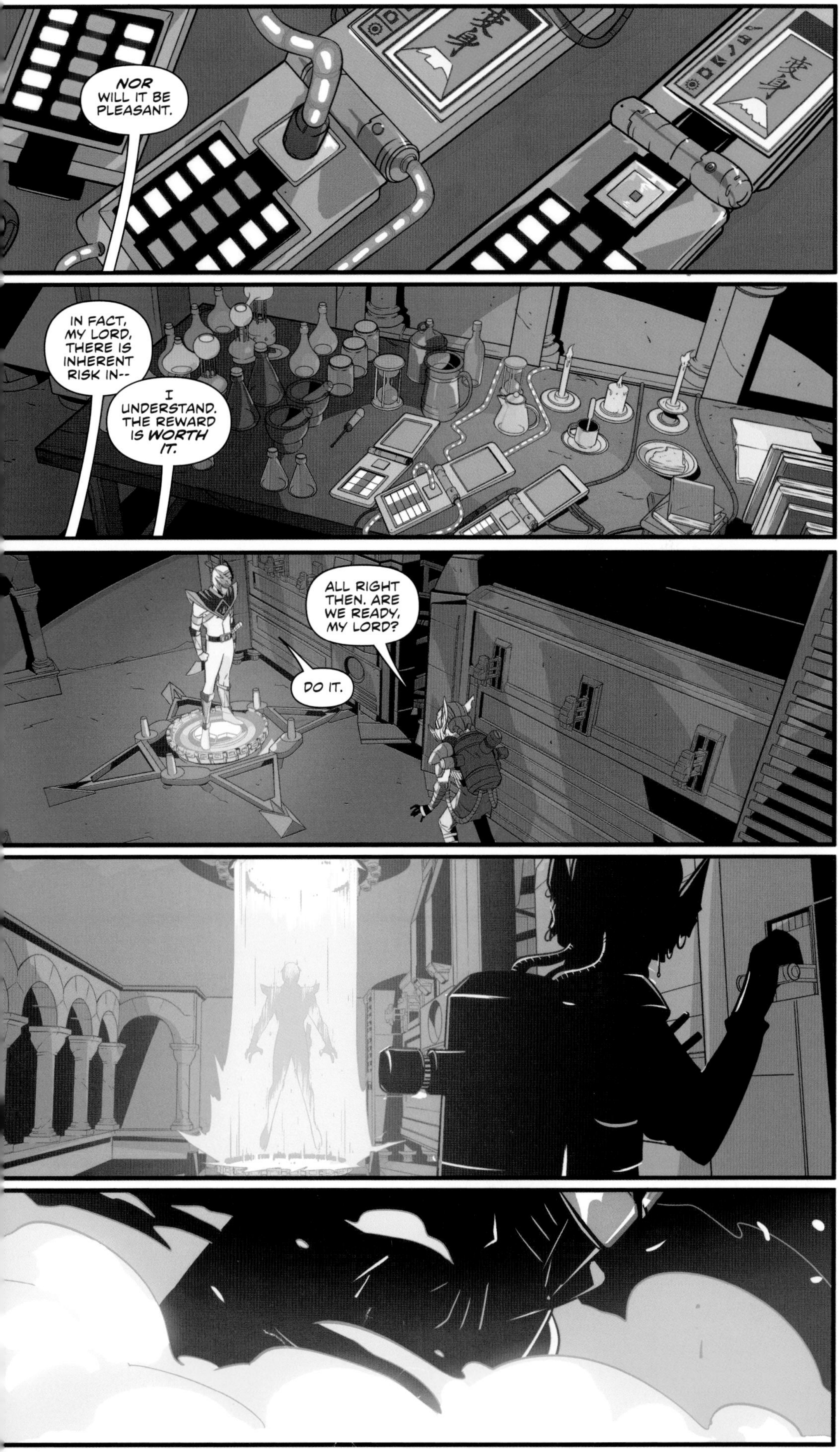
NOR WILL IT BE PLEASANT.
変身
変身
IN FACT, MY LORD, THERE IS INHERENT RISK IN--
I UNDERSTAND. THE REWARD IS WORTH IT.
ALL RIGHT THEN. ARE WE READY, MY LORD?
DO IT.

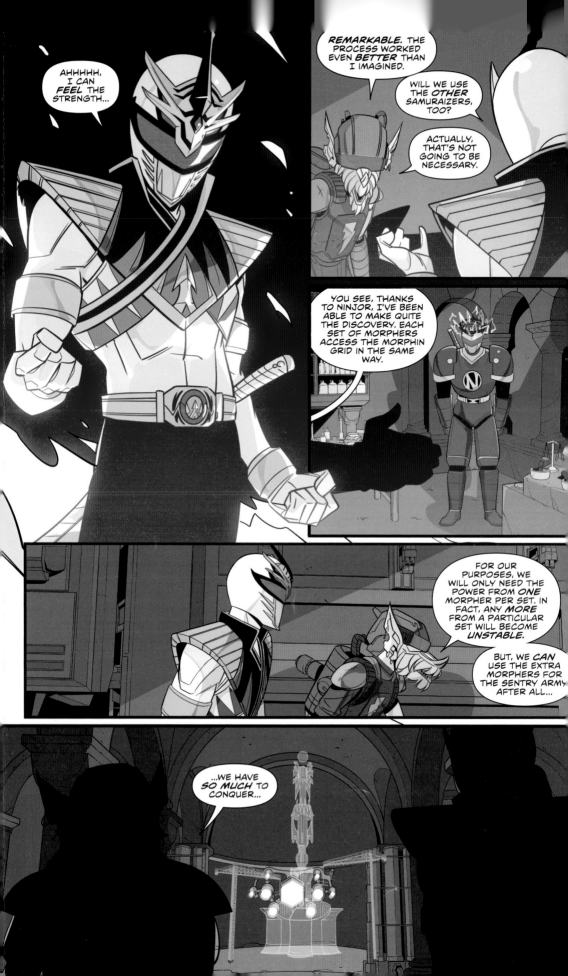

AHHHHH, I CAN *FEEL* THE STRENGTH...

REMARKABLE. THE PROCESS WORKED EVEN *BETTER* THAN I IMAGINED.

WILL WE USE THE *OTHER* SAMURAIZERS, TOO?

ACTUALLY, THAT'S NOT GOING TO BE NECESSARY.

YOU SEE, THANKS TO NINJOR, I'VE BEEN ABLE TO MAKE QUITE THE DISCOVERY. EACH SET OF MORPHERS ACCESS THE MORPHIN GRID IN THE SAME WAY.

FOR OUR PURPOSES, WE WILL ONLY NEED THE POWER FROM *ONE* MORPHER PER SET. IN FACT, ANY *MORE* FROM A PARTICULAR SET WILL BECOME *UNSTABLE.*

BUT, WE *CAN* USE THE EXTRA MORPHERS FOR THE SENTRY ARMY AFTER ALL...

...WE HAVE *SO MUCH* TO CONQUER...

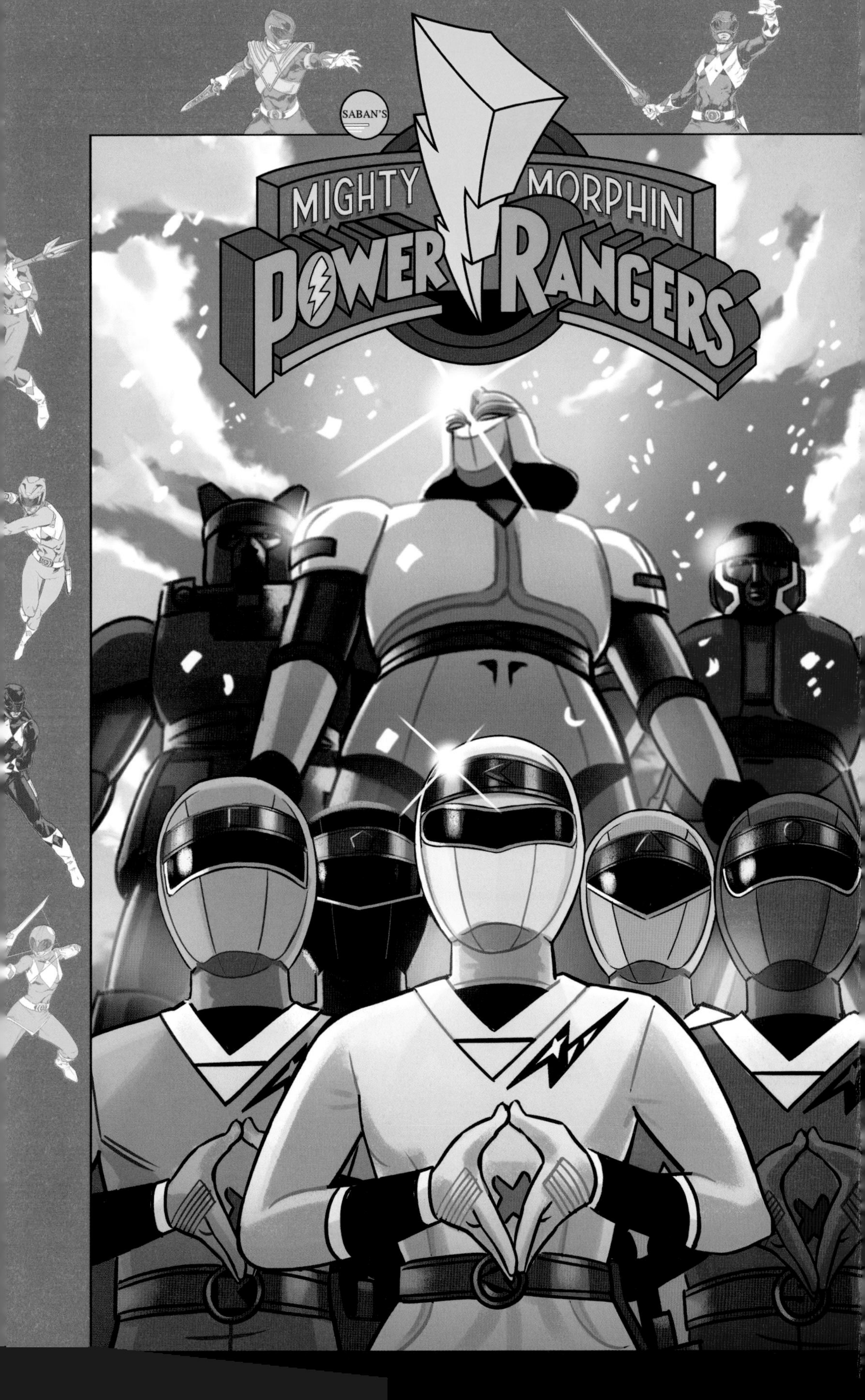
SABAN'S
MIGHTY MORPHIN
POWER RANGERS

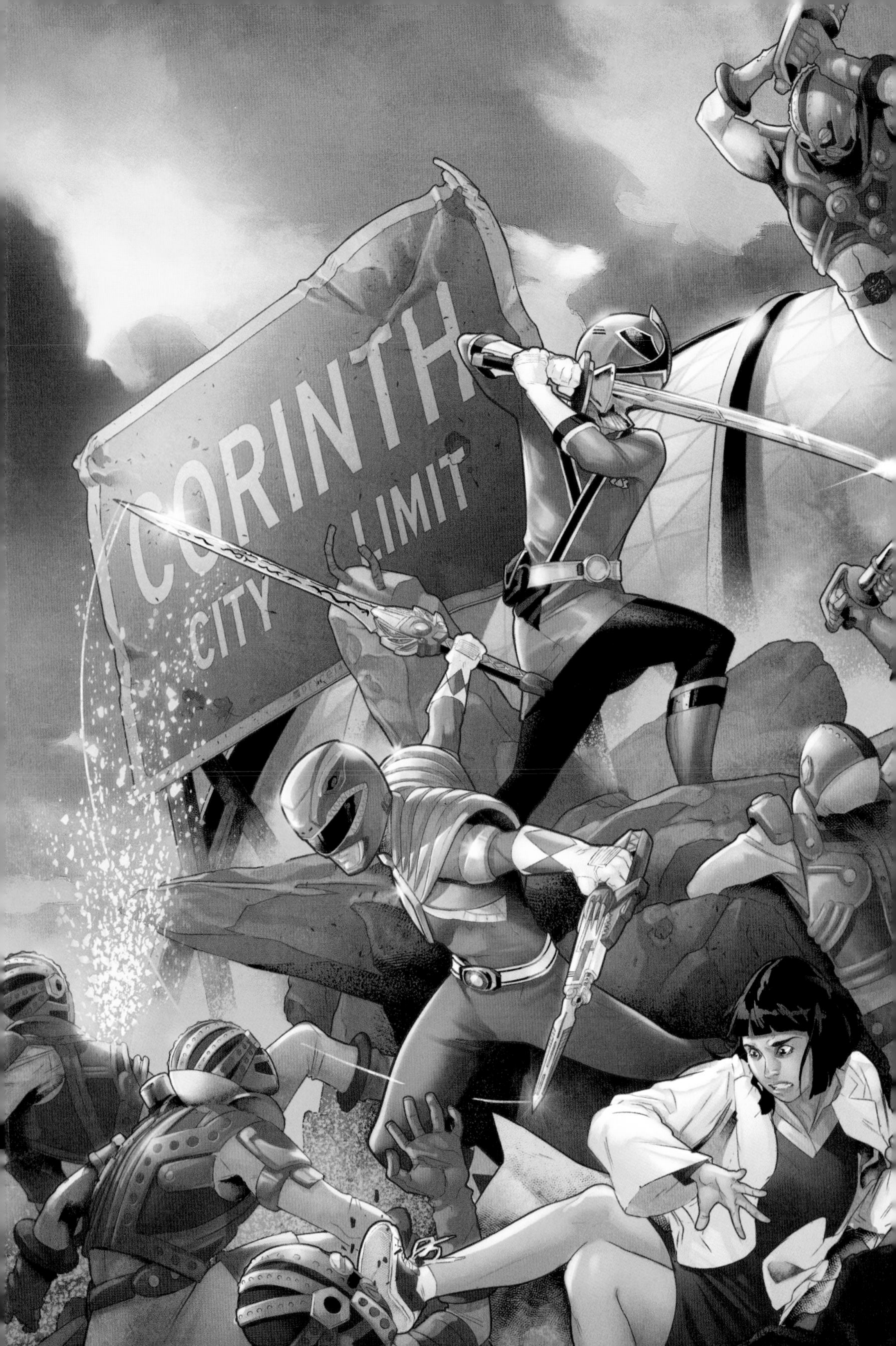
CORINTH
CITY LIMIT

CHAPTER **TWENTY-SEVEN**

JAMAL CAMPBELL ISSUE TWENTY-SEVEN COVER

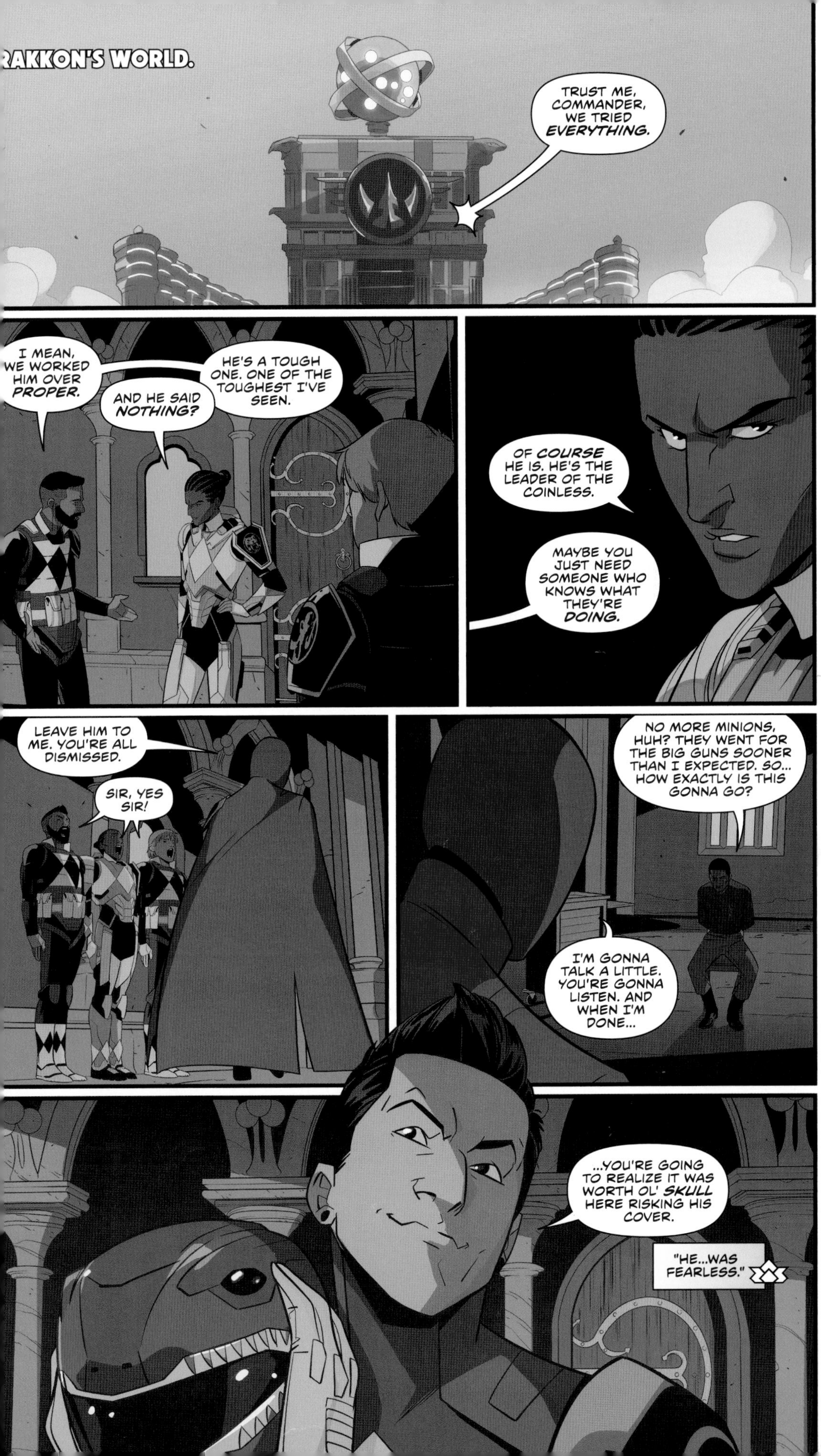
RAKKON'S WORLD.
TRUST ME, COMMANDER, WE TRIED EVERYTHING.
I MEAN, WE WORKED HIM OVER PROPER.
AND HE SAID NOTHING?
HE'S A TOUGH ONE. ONE OF THE TOUGHEST I'VE SEEN.
OF COURSE HE IS. HE'S THE LEADER OF THE COINLESS.
MAYBE YOU JUST NEED SOMEONE WHO KNOWS WHAT THEY'RE DOING.
LEAVE HIM TO ME. YOU'RE ALL DISMISSED.
SIR, YES SIR!
NO MORE MINIONS, HUH? THEY WENT FOR THE BIG GUNS SOONER THAN I EXPECTED. SO... HOW EXACTLY IS THIS GONNA GO?
I'M GONNA TALK A LITTLE. YOU'RE GONNA LISTEN. AND WHEN I'M DONE...
...YOU'RE GOING TO REALIZE IT WAS WORTH OL' SKULL HERE RISKING HIS COVER.
"HE...WAS FEARLESS."

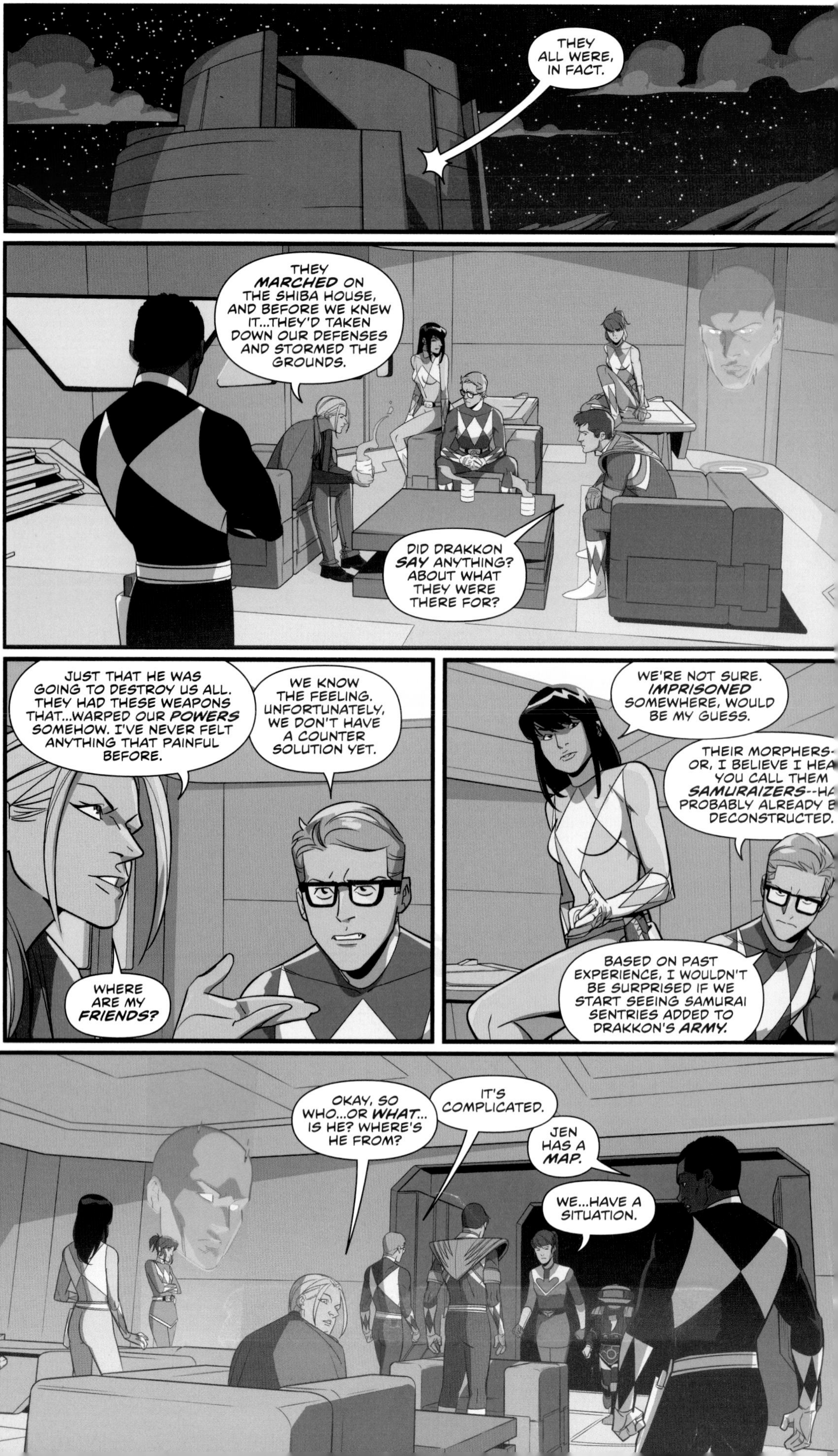
THEY ALL WERE, IN FACT.
THEY MARCHED ON THE SHIBA HOUSE, AND BEFORE WE KNEW IT...THEY'D TAKEN DOWN OUR DEFENSES AND STORMED THE GROUNDS.
DID DRAKKON SAY ANYTHING? ABOUT WHAT THEY WERE THERE FOR?
JUST THAT HE WAS GOING TO DESTROY US ALL. THEY HAD THESE WEAPONS THAT...WARPED OUR POWERS SOMEHOW. I'VE NEVER FELT ANYTHING THAT PAINFUL BEFORE.
WE KNOW THE FEELING. UNFORTUNATELY, WE DON'T HAVE A COUNTER SOLUTION YET.
WHERE ARE MY FRIENDS?
WE'RE NOT SURE. IMPRISONED SOMEWHERE, WOULD BE MY GUESS.
THEIR MORPHERS--OR, I BELIEVE I HEA YOU CALL THEM SAMURAIZERS--HA PROBABLY ALREADY B DECONSTRUCTED.
BASED ON PAST EXPERIENCE, I WOULDN'T BE SURPRISED IF WE START SEEING SAMURAI SENTRIES ADDED TO DRAKKON'S ARMY.
OKAY, SO WHO...OR WHAT... IS HE? WHERE'S HE FROM?
IT'S COMPLICATED.
JEN HAS A MAP.
WE...HAVE A SITUATION.

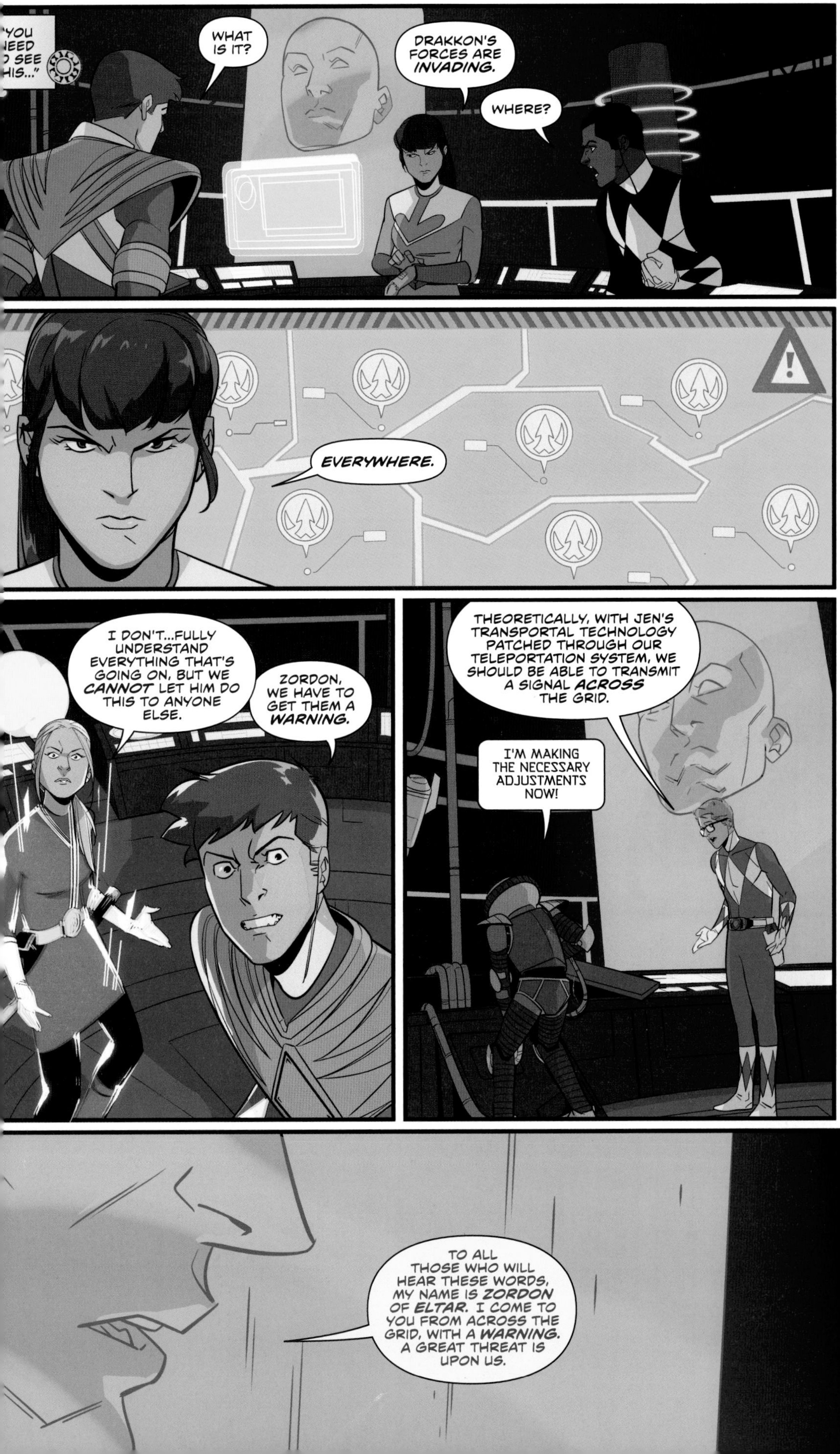

"YOU NEED TO SEE THIS..."
WHAT IS IT?
DRAKKON'S FORCES ARE INVADING.
WHERE?
EVERYWHERE.
I DON'T...FULLY UNDERSTAND EVERYTHING THAT'S GOING ON, BUT WE CANNOT LET HIM DO THIS TO ANYONE ELSE.
ZORDON, WE HAVE TO GET THEM A WARNING.
THEORETICALLY, WITH JEN'S TRANSPORTAL TECHNOLOGY PATCHED THROUGH OUR TELEPORTATION SYSTEM, WE SHOULD BE ABLE TO TRANSMIT A SIGNAL ACROSS THE GRID.
I'M MAKING THE NECESSARY ADJUSTMENTS NOW!
TO ALL THOSE WHO WILL HEAR THESE WORDS, MY NAME IS ZORDON OF ELTAR. I COME TO YOU FROM ACROSS THE GRID, WITH A WARNING. A GREAT THREAT IS UPON US.

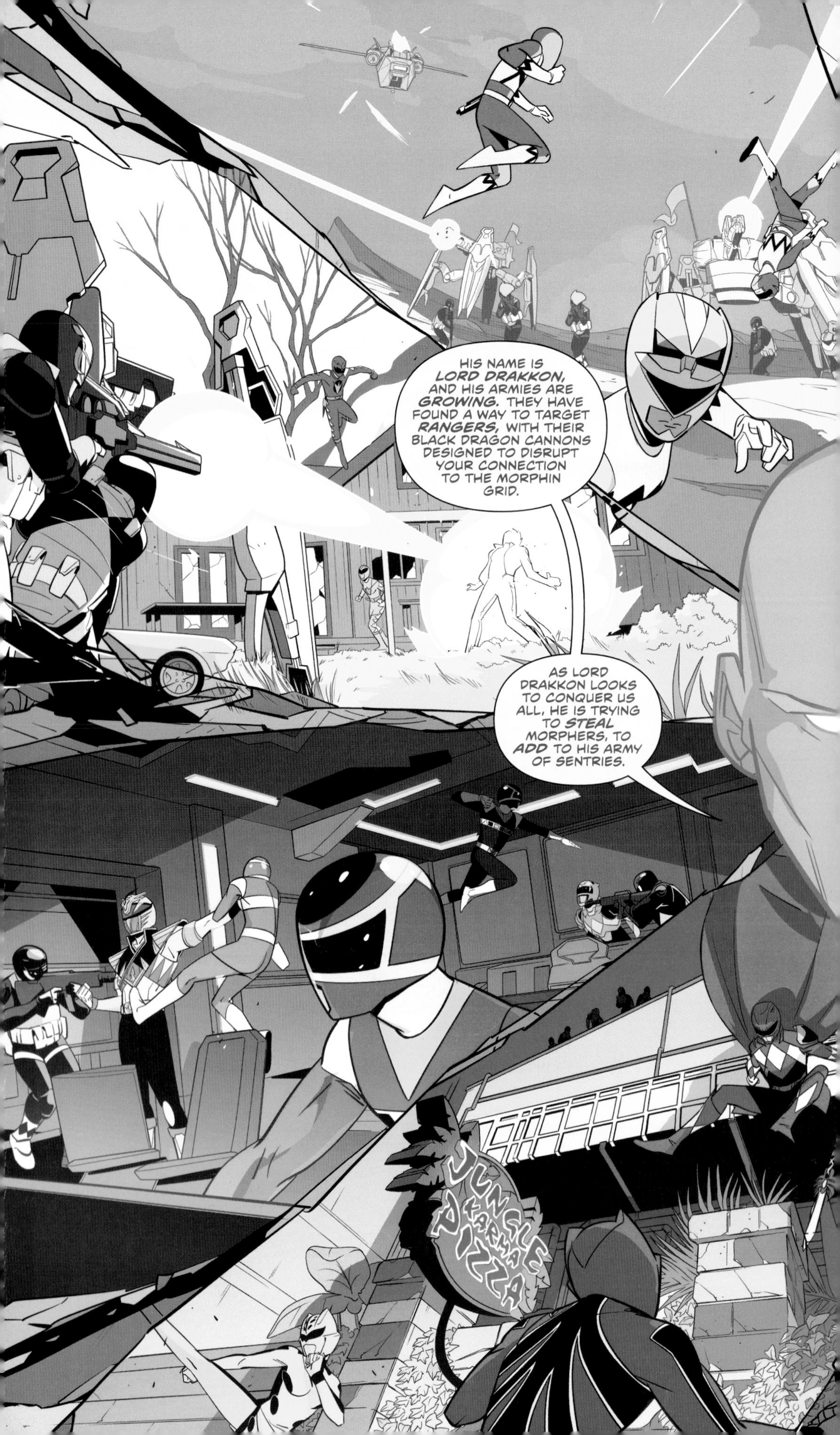
HIS NAME IS LORD DRAKKON, AND HIS ARMIES ARE GROWING. THEY HAVE FOUND A WAY TO TARGET RANGERS, WITH THEIR BLACK DRAGON CANNONS DESIGNED TO DISRUPT YOUR CONNECTION TO THE MORPHIN GRID.
AS LORD DRAKKON LOOKS TO CONQUER US ALL, HE IS TRYING TO STEAL MORPHERS, TO ADD TO HIS ARMY OF SENTRIES.
JUNGLE KARMA PIZZA

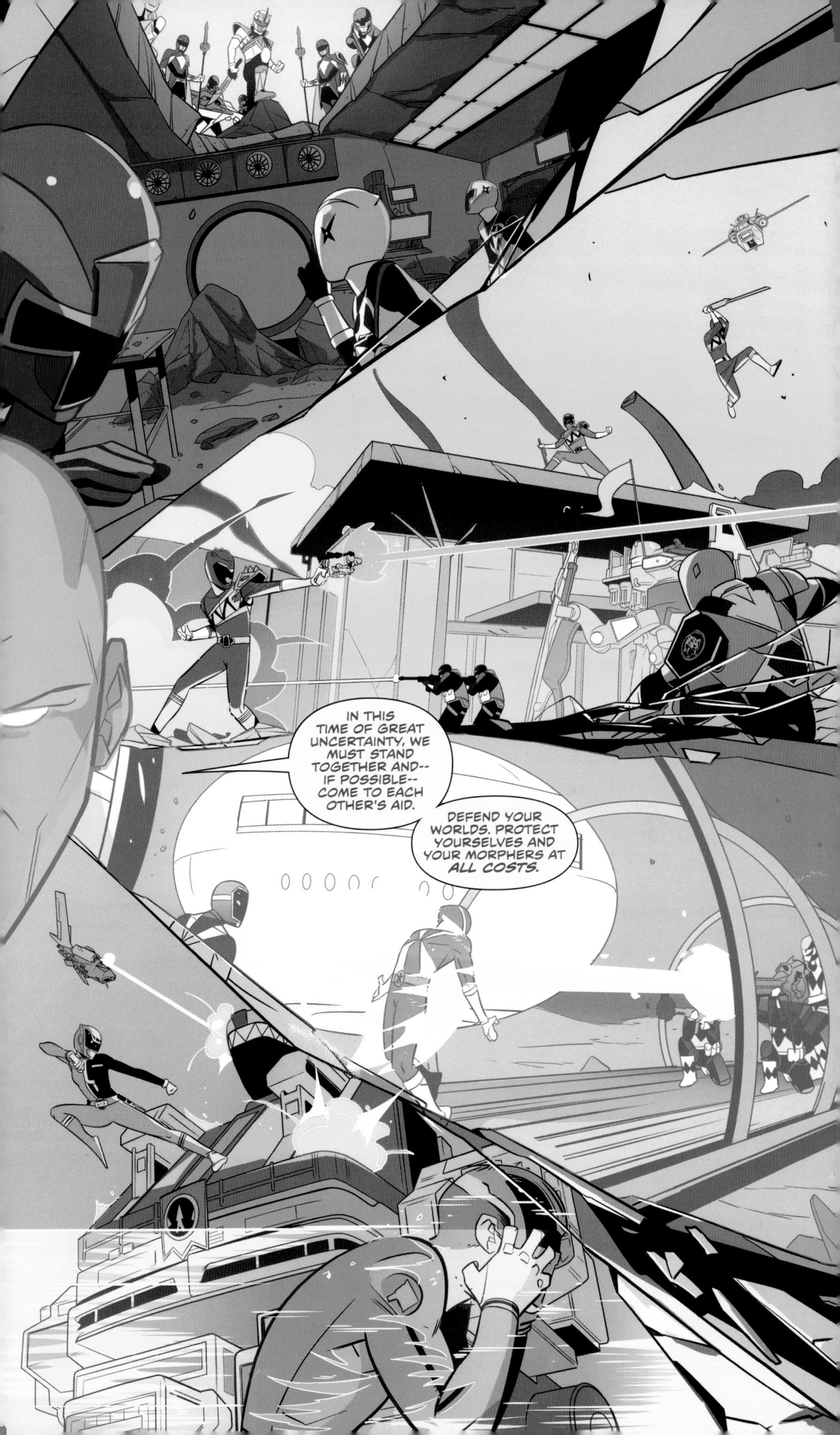
IN THIS TIME OF GREAT UNCERTAINTY, WE MUST STAND TOGETHER AND-- IF POSSIBLE-- COME TO EACH OTHER'S AID.
DEFEND YOUR WORLDS. PROTECT YOURSELVES AND YOUR MORPHERS AT ALL COSTS.

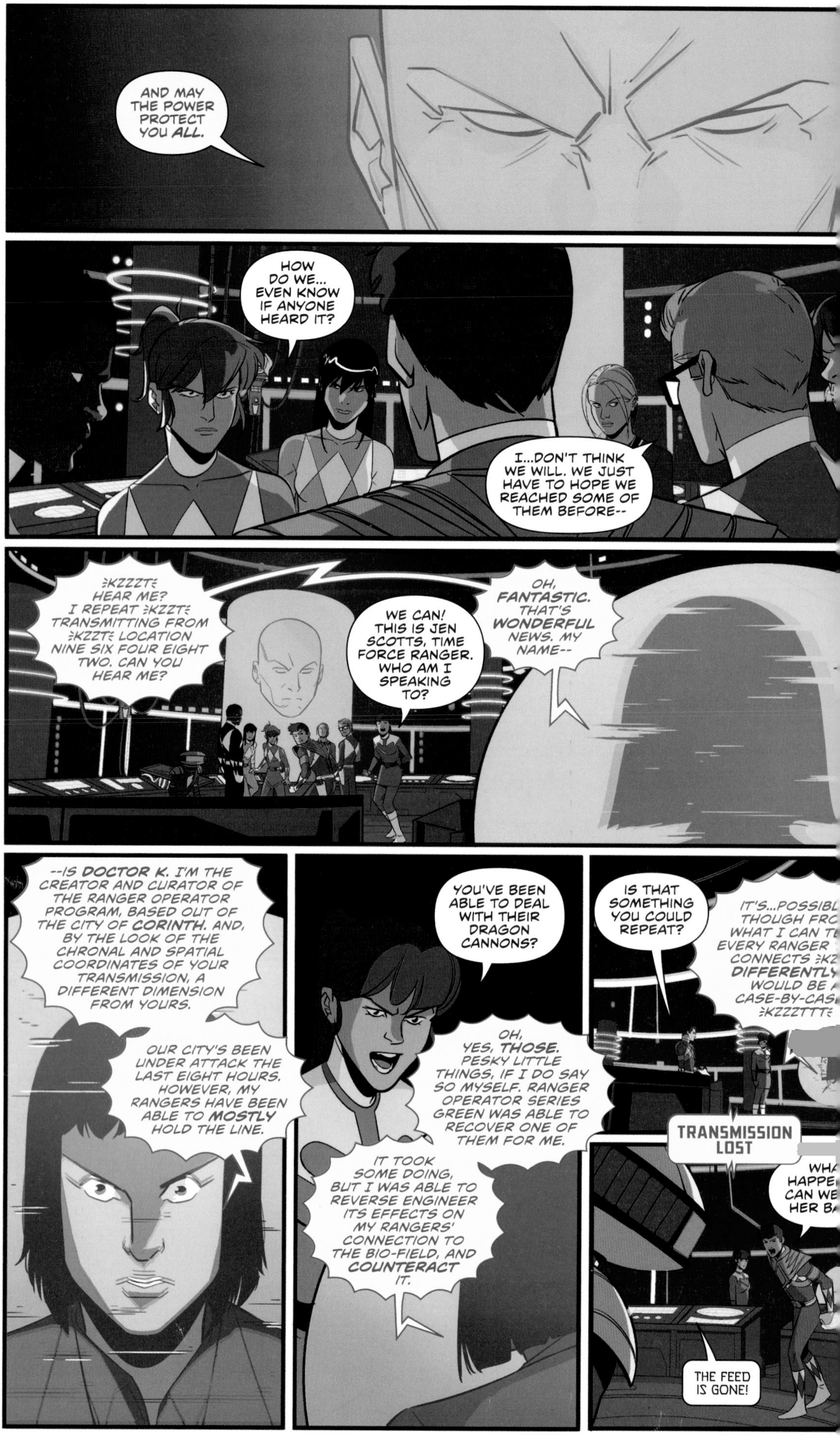
AND MAY THE POWER PROTECT YOU ALL.
HOW DO WE... EVEN KNOW IF ANYONE HEARD IT?
I...DON'T THINK WE WILL. WE JUST HAVE TO HOPE WE REACHED SOME OF THEM BEFORE--
KZZZT HEAR ME? I REPEAT KZZZT TRANSMITTING FROM KZZT LOCATION NINE SIX FOUR EIGHT TWO. CAN YOU HEAR ME?
WE CAN! THIS IS JEN SCOTTS, TIME FORCE RANGER. WHO AM I SPEAKING TO?
OH, FANTASTIC. THAT'S WONDERFUL NEWS. MY NAME--
--IS DOCTOR K. I'M THE CREATOR AND CURATOR OF THE RANGER OPERATOR PROGRAM, BASED OUT OF THE CITY OF CORINTH. AND, BY THE LOOK OF THE CHRONAL AND SPATIAL COORDINATES OF YOUR TRANSMISSION, A DIFFERENT DIMENSION FROM YOURS.
OUR CITY'S BEEN UNDER ATTACK THE LAST EIGHT HOURS. HOWEVER, MY RANGERS HAVE BEEN ABLE TO MOSTLY HOLD THE LINE.
YOU'VE BEEN ABLE TO DEAL WITH THEIR DRAGON CANNONS?
OH, YES, THOSE. PESKY LITTLE THINGS, IF I DO SAY SO MYSELF. RANGER OPERATOR SERIES GREEN WAS ABLE TO RECOVER ONE OF THEM FOR ME.
IT TOOK SOME DOING, BUT I WAS ABLE TO REVERSE ENGINEER ITS EFFECTS ON MY RANGERS' CONNECTION TO THE BIO-FIELD, AND COUNTERACT IT.
IS THAT SOMETHING YOU COULD REPEAT?
IT'S...POSSIBL THOUGH FRO WHAT I CAN T EVERY RANGER CONNECTS KZ DIFFERENTLY WOULD BE A CASE-BY-CAS KZZZTTT
TRANSMISSION LOST
WHA HAPPE CAN WE HER BA
THE FEED IS GONE!

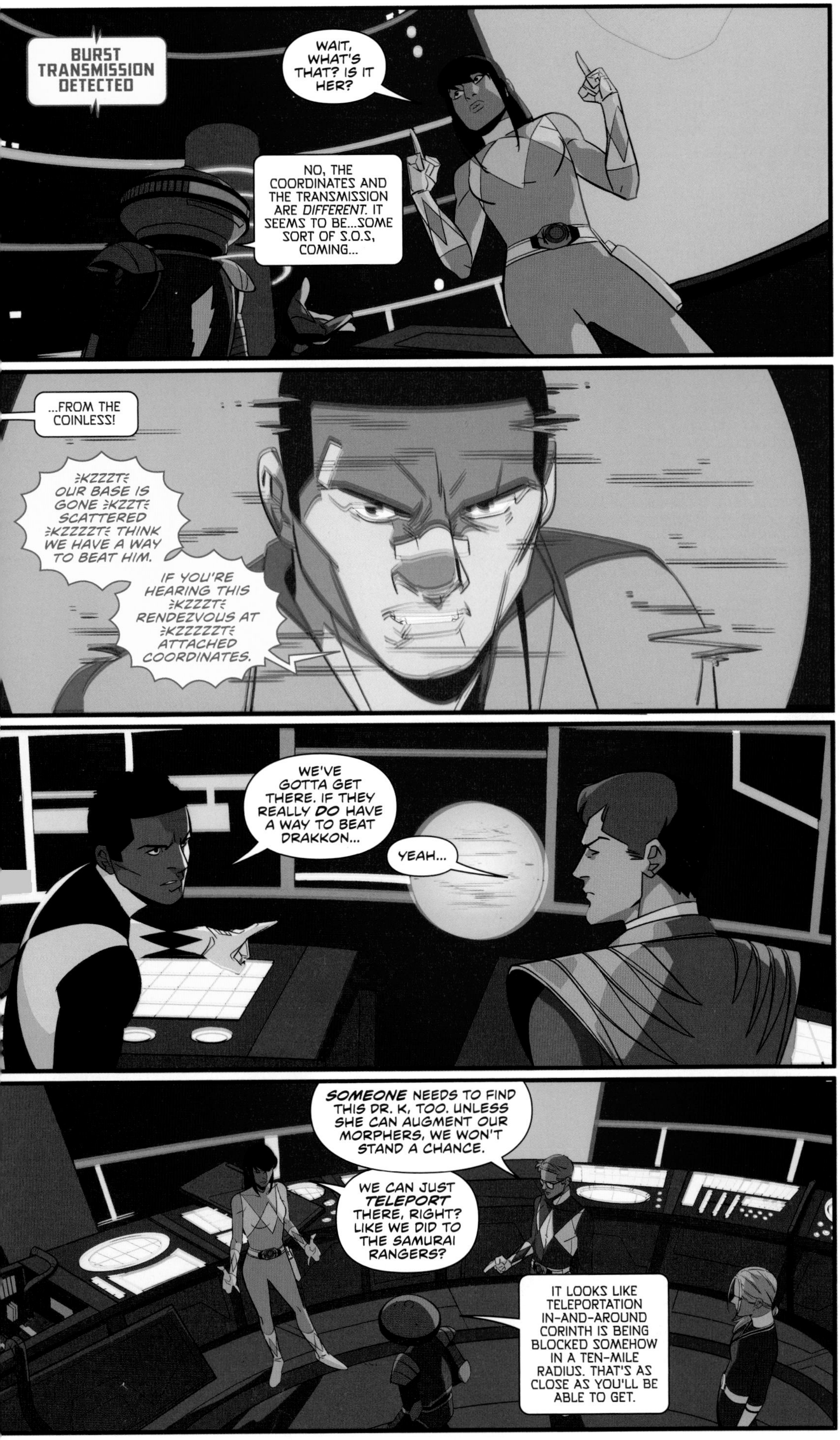
BURST TRANSMISSION DETECTED
WAIT, WHAT'S THAT? IS IT HER?
NO, THE COORDINATES AND THE TRANSMISSION ARE *DIFFERENT*. IT SEEMS TO BE...SOME SORT OF S.O.S, COMING...
...FROM THE COINLESS!
KZZZT OUR BASE IS GONE KZZT SCATTERED KZZZZT THINK WE HAVE A WAY TO BEAT HIM.
IF YOU'RE HEARING THIS KZZZT RENDEZVOUS AT KZZZZZT ATTACHED COORDINATES.
WE'VE GOTTA GET THERE. IF THEY REALLY **DO** HAVE A WAY TO BEAT DRAKKON...
YEAH...
SOMEONE NEEDS TO FIND THIS DR. K, TOO. UNLESS SHE CAN AUGMENT OUR MORPHERS, WE WON'T STAND A CHANCE.
WE CAN JUST ***TELEPORT*** THERE, RIGHT? LIKE WE DID TO THE SAMURAI RANGERS?
IT LOOKS LIKE TELEPORTATION IN-AND-AROUND CORINTH IS BEING BLOCKED SOMEHOW IN A TEN-MILE RADIUS. THAT'S AS CLOSE AS YOU'LL BE ABLE TO GET.

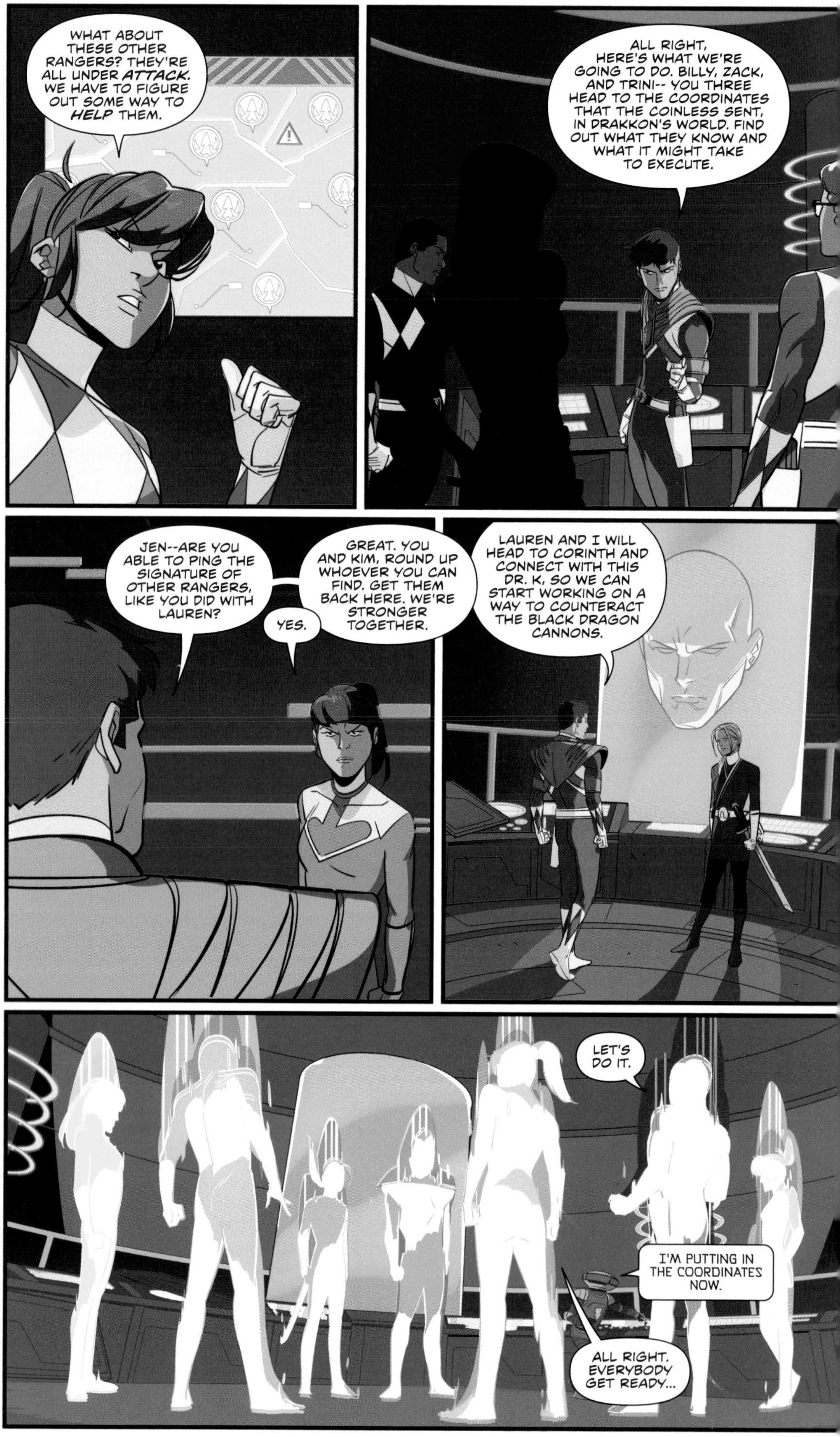
WHAT ABOUT THESE OTHER RANGERS? THEY'RE ALL UNDER ATTACK. WE HAVE TO FIGURE OUT SOME WAY TO HELP THEM.
ALL RIGHT, HERE'S WHAT WE'RE GOING TO DO. BILLY, ZACK, AND TRINI-- YOU THREE HEAD TO THE COORDINATES THAT THE COINLESS SENT, IN DRAKKON'S WORLD. FIND OUT WHAT THEY KNOW AND WHAT IT MIGHT TAKE TO EXECUTE.
JEN--ARE YOU ABLE TO PING THE SIGNATURE OF OTHER RANGERS, LIKE YOU DID WITH LAUREN?
YES.
GREAT. YOU AND KIM, ROUND UP WHOEVER YOU CAN FIND. GET THEM BACK HERE. WE'RE STRONGER TOGETHER.
LAUREN AND I WILL HEAD TO CORINTH AND CONNECT WITH THIS DR. K, SO WE CAN START WORKING ON A WAY TO COUNTERACT THE BLACK DRAGON CANNONS.
LET'S DO IT.
I'M PUTTING IN THE COORDINATES NOW.
ALL RIGHT. EVERYBODY GET READY...

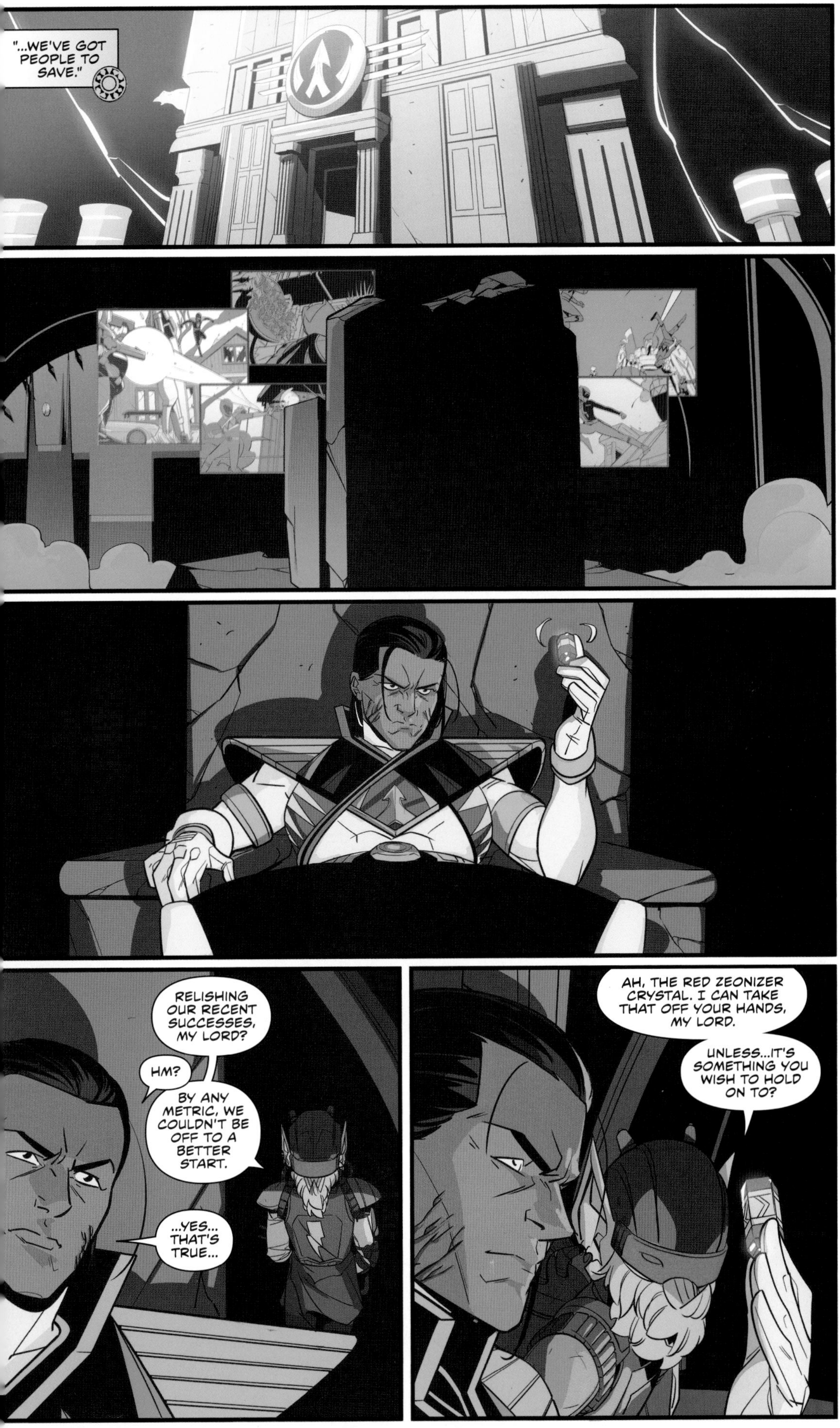
"...WE'VE GOT PEOPLE TO SAVE."
RELISHING OUR RECENT SUCCESSES, MY LORD?
HM?
BY ANY METRIC, WE COULDN'T BE OFF TO A BETTER START.
...YES... THAT'S TRUE...
AH, THE RED ZEONIZER CRYSTAL. I CAN TAKE THAT OFF YOUR HANDS, MY LORD.
UNLESS...IT'S SOMETHING YOU WISH TO HOLD ON TO?

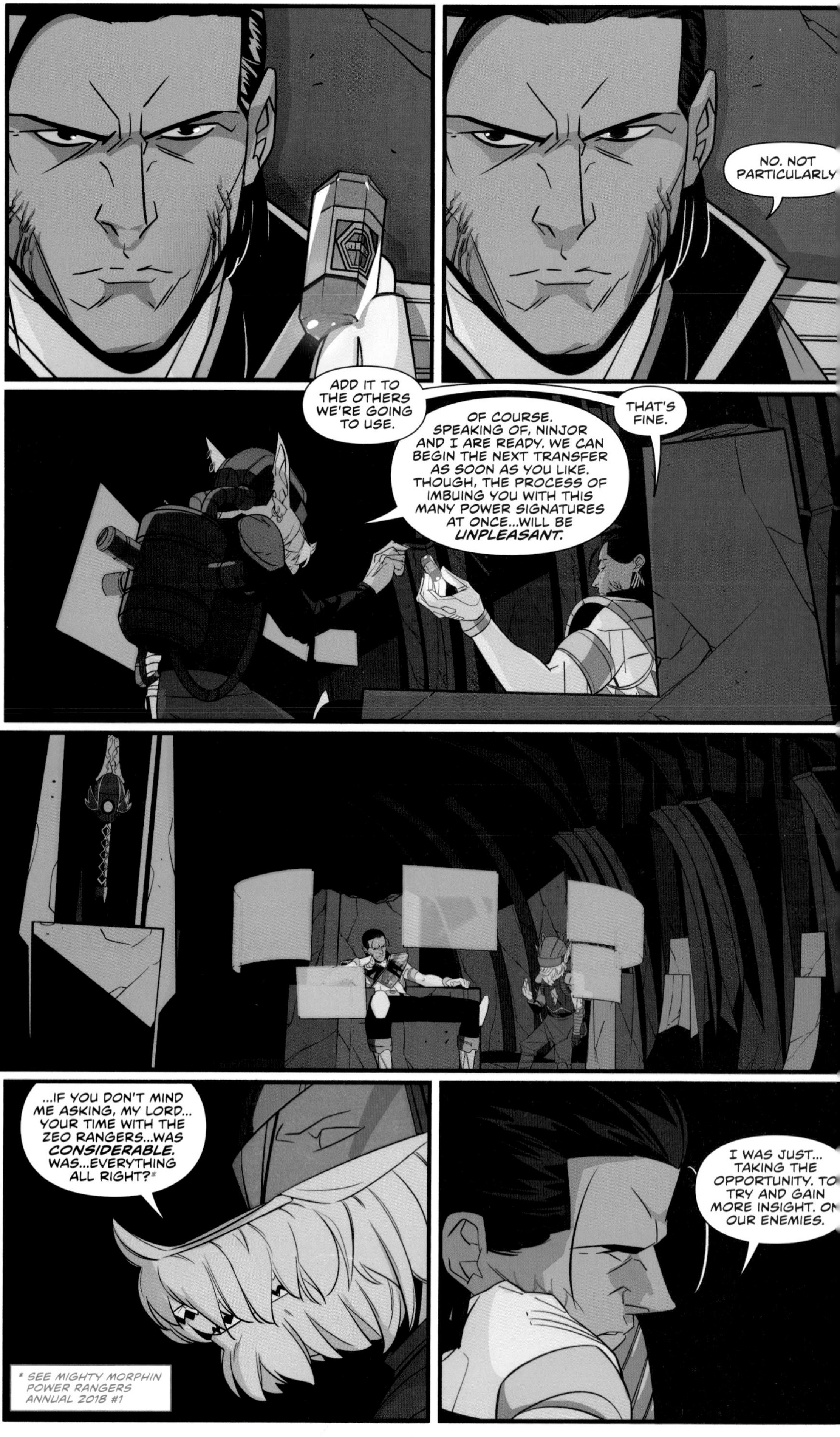
NO. NOT PARTICULARLY
ADD IT TO THE OTHERS WE'RE GOING TO USE.
THAT'S FINE.
OF COURSE. SPEAKING OF, NINJOR AND I ARE READY. WE CAN BEGIN THE NEXT TRANSFER AS SOON AS YOU LIKE. THOUGH, THE PROCESS OF IMBUING YOU WITH THIS MANY POWER SIGNATURES AT ONCE...WILL BE ***UNPLEASANT.***
...IF YOU DON'T MIND ME ASKING, MY LORD... YOUR TIME WITH THE ZEO RANGERS...WAS ***CONSIDERABLE.*** WAS...EVERYTHING ALL RIGHT?*
I WAS JUST... TAKING THE OPPORTUNITY. TO TRY AND GAIN MORE INSIGHT. ON OUR ENEMIES.
* SEE MIGHTY MORPHIN POWER RANGERS ANNUAL 2018 #1

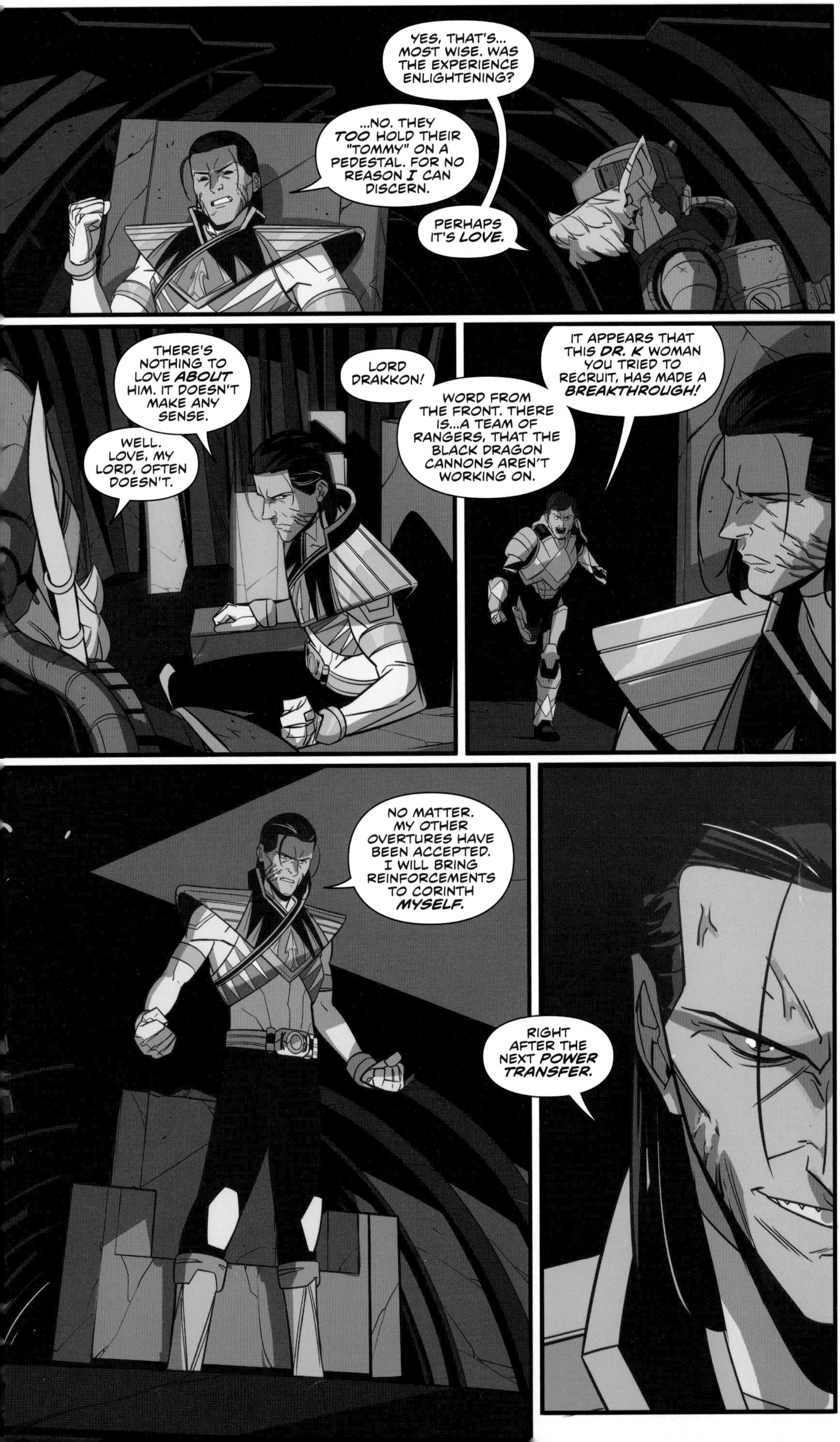
YES, THAT'S... MOST WISE. WAS THE EXPERIENCE ENLIGHTENING?
...NO. THEY TOO HOLD THEIR "TOMMY" ON A PEDESTAL. FOR NO REASON I CAN DISCERN.
PERHAPS IT'S LOVE.
THERE'S NOTHING TO LOVE ABOUT HIM. IT DOESN'T MAKE ANY SENSE.
WELL. LOVE, MY LORD, OFTEN DOESN'T.
LORD DRAKKON!
WORD FROM THE FRONT. THERE IS...A TEAM OF RANGERS, THAT THE BLACK DRAGON CANNONS AREN'T WORKING ON.
IT APPEARS THAT THIS DR. K WOMAN YOU TRIED TO RECRUIT, HAS MADE A BREAKTHROUGH!
NO MATTER. MY OTHER OVERTURES HAVE BEEN ACCEPTED. I WILL BRING REINFORCEMENTS TO CORINTH MYSELF.
RIGHT AFTER THE NEXT POWER TRANSFER.

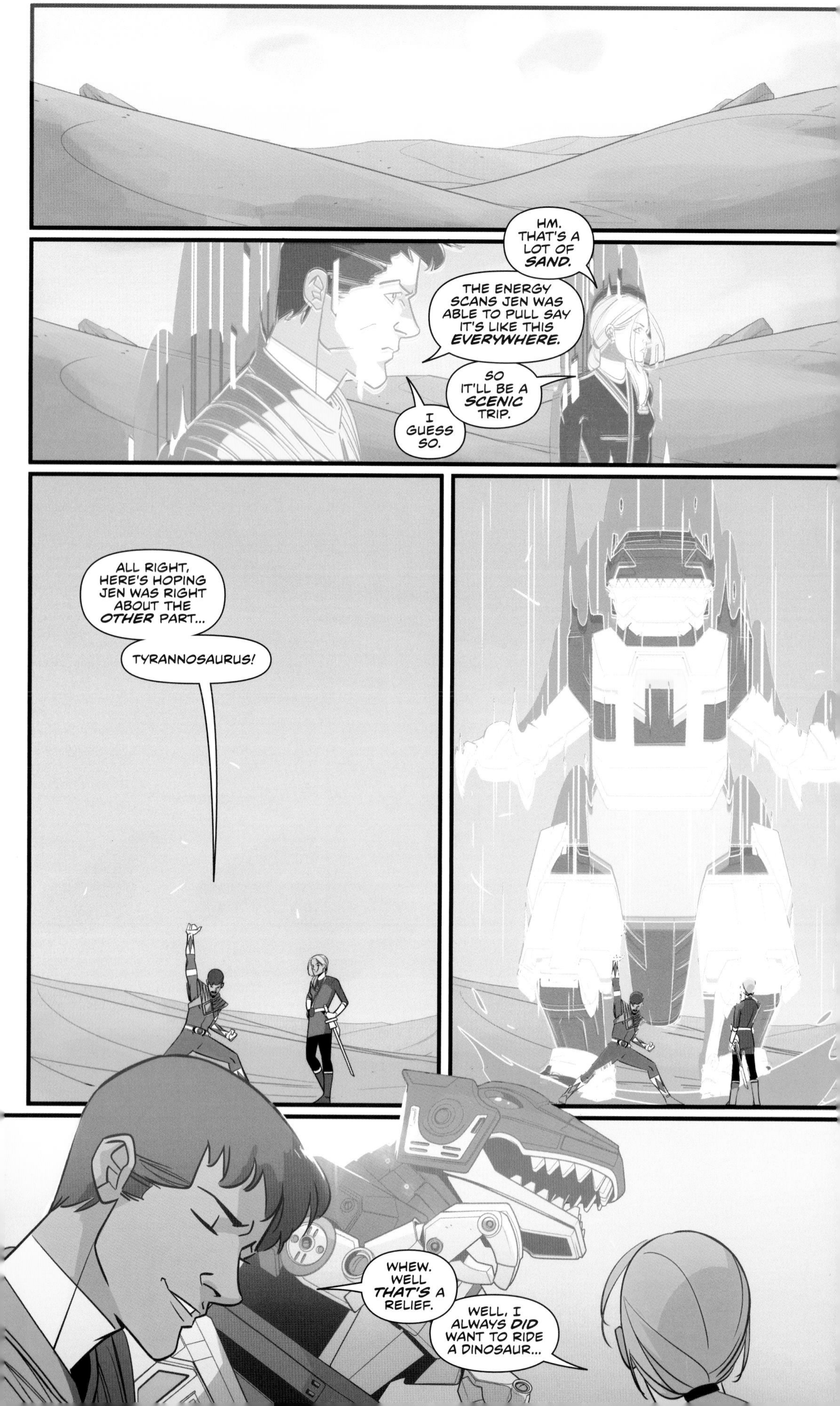
HM. THAT'S A LOT OF SAND.
THE ENERGY SCANS JEN WAS ABLE TO PULL SAY IT'S LIKE THIS EVERYWHERE.
SO IT'LL BE A SCENIC TRIP.
I GUESS SO.
ALL RIGHT, HERE'S HOPING JEN WAS RIGHT ABOUT THE OTHER PART...
TYRANNOSAURUS!
WHEW. WELL THAT'S A RELIEF.
WELL, I ALWAYS DID WANT TO RIDE A DINOSAUR...

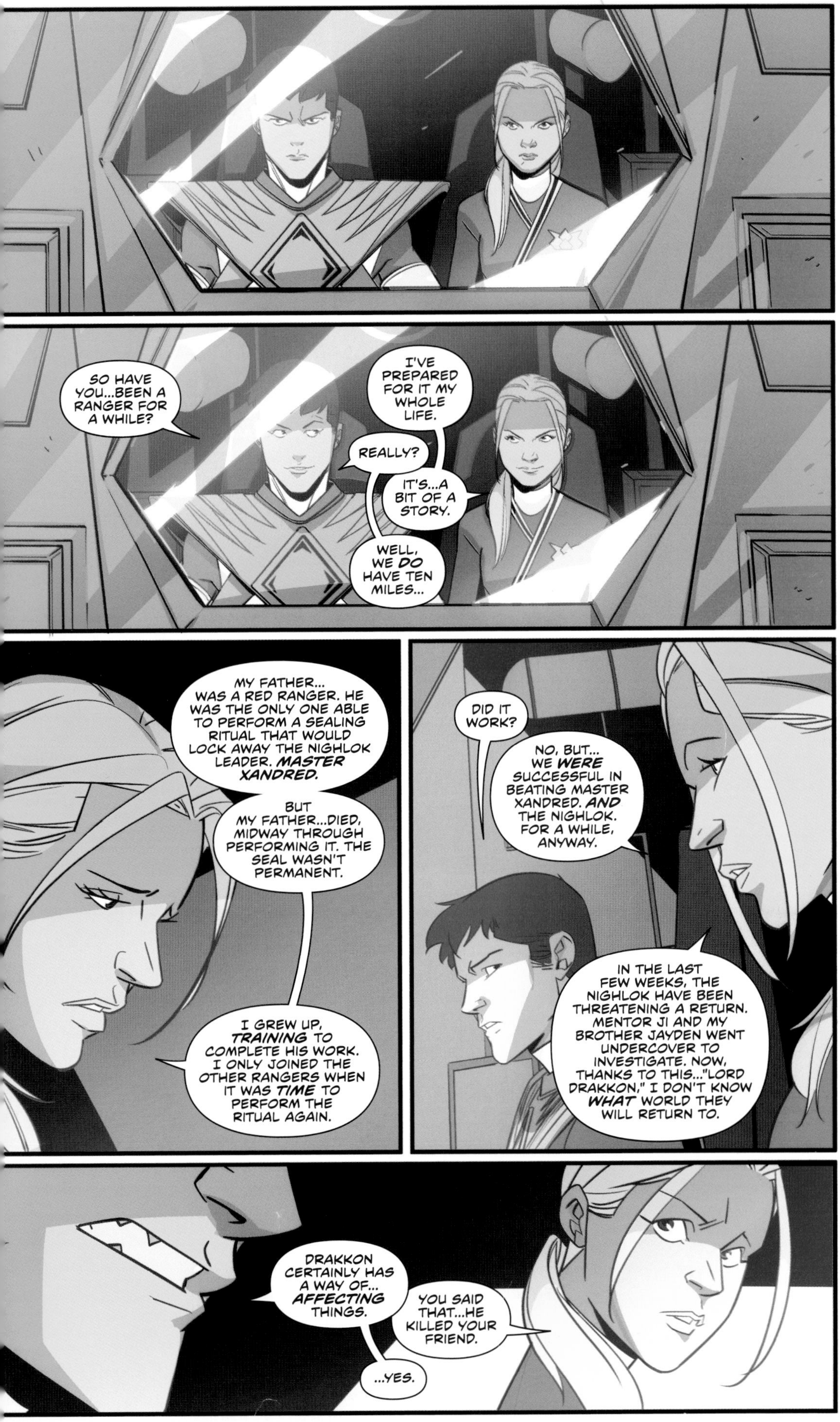
SO HAVE YOU...BEEN A RANGER FOR A WHILE?
I'VE PREPARED FOR IT MY WHOLE LIFE.
REALLY?
IT'S...A BIT OF A STORY.
WELL, WE *DO* HAVE TEN MILES...
MY FATHER... WAS A RED RANGER. HE WAS THE ONLY ONE ABLE TO PERFORM A SEALING RITUAL THAT WOULD LOCK AWAY THE NIGHLOK LEADER. ***MASTER XANDRED.***
BUT MY FATHER...DIED, MIDWAY THROUGH PERFORMING IT. THE SEAL WASN'T PERMANENT.
I GREW UP, ***TRAINING*** TO COMPLETE HIS WORK. I ONLY JOINED THE OTHER RANGERS WHEN IT WAS ***TIME*** TO PERFORM THE RITUAL AGAIN.
DID IT WORK?
NO, BUT... WE ***WERE*** SUCCESSFUL IN BEATING MASTER XANDRED. ***AND*** THE NIGHLOK. FOR A WHILE, ANYWAY.
IN THE LAST FEW WEEKS, THE NIGHLOK HAVE BEEN THREATENING A RETURN. MENTOR JI AND MY BROTHER JAYDEN WENT UNDERCOVER TO INVESTIGATE. NOW, THANKS TO THIS..."LORD DRAKKON," I DON'T KNOW ***WHAT*** WORLD THEY WILL RETURN TO.
DRAKKON CERTAINLY HAS A WAY OF... ***AFFECTING*** THINGS.
YOU SAID THAT...HE KILLED YOUR FRIEND.
...YES.

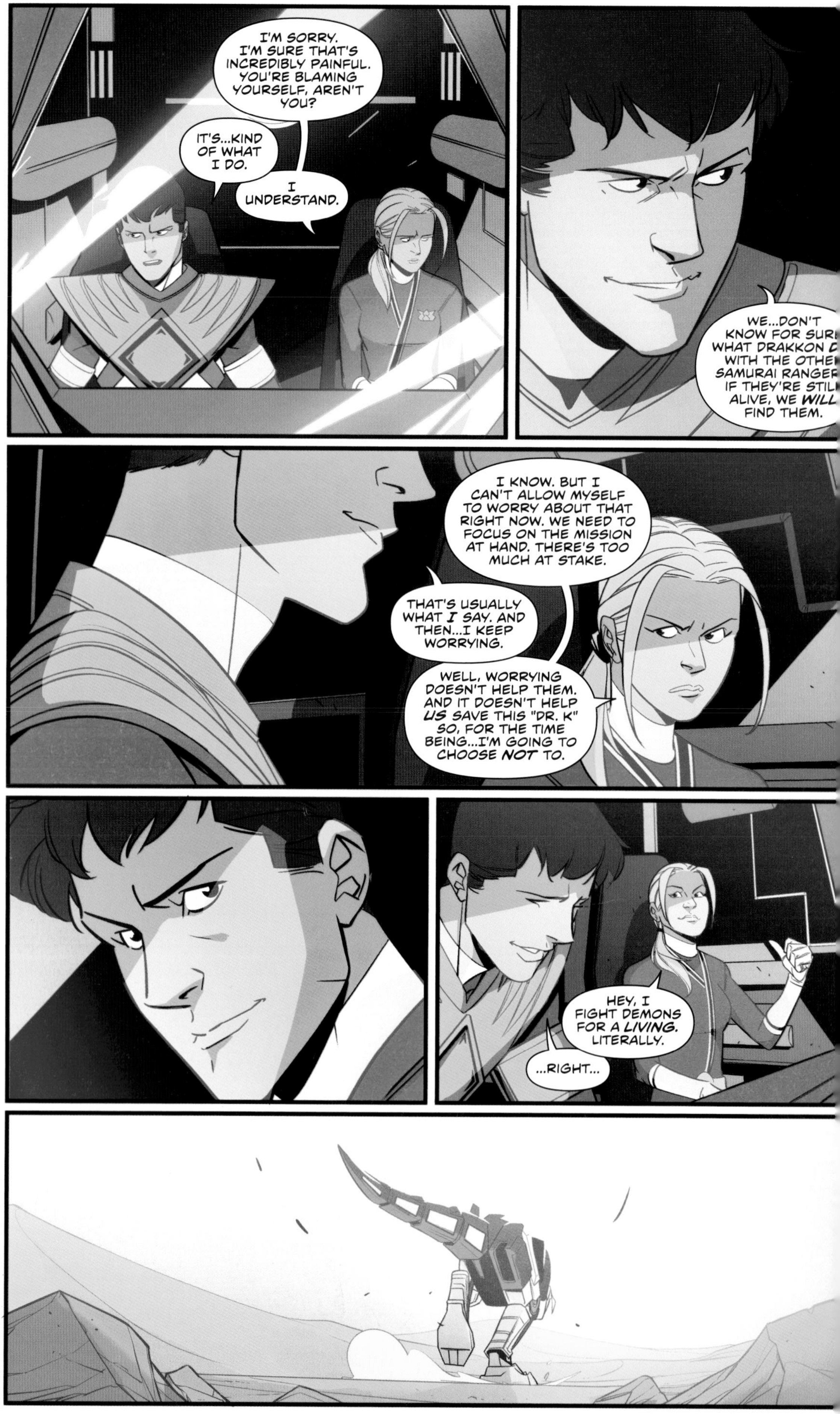
I'M SORRY. I'M SURE THAT'S INCREDIBLY PAINFUL. YOU'RE BLAMING YOURSELF, AREN'T YOU?
IT'S...KIND OF WHAT I DO.
I UNDERSTAND.
WE...DON'T KNOW FOR SUR
WHAT DRAKKON
WITH THE OTHE
SAMURAI RANGE
IF THEY'RE STIL
ALIVE, WE WILL
FIND THEM.
I KNOW. BUT I CAN'T ALLOW MYSELF TO WORRY ABOUT THAT RIGHT NOW. WE NEED TO FOCUS ON THE MISSION AT HAND. THERE'S TOO MUCH AT STAKE.
THAT'S USUALLY WHAT *I* SAY. AND THEN...I KEEP WORRYING.
WELL, WORRYING DOESN'T HELP THEM. AND IT DOESN'T HELP ***US*** SAVE THIS "DR. K" SO, FOR THE TIME BEING...I'M GOING TO CHOOSE ***NOT*** TO.
HEY, I FIGHT DEMONS FOR A *LIVING.* LITERALLY.
...RIGHT...

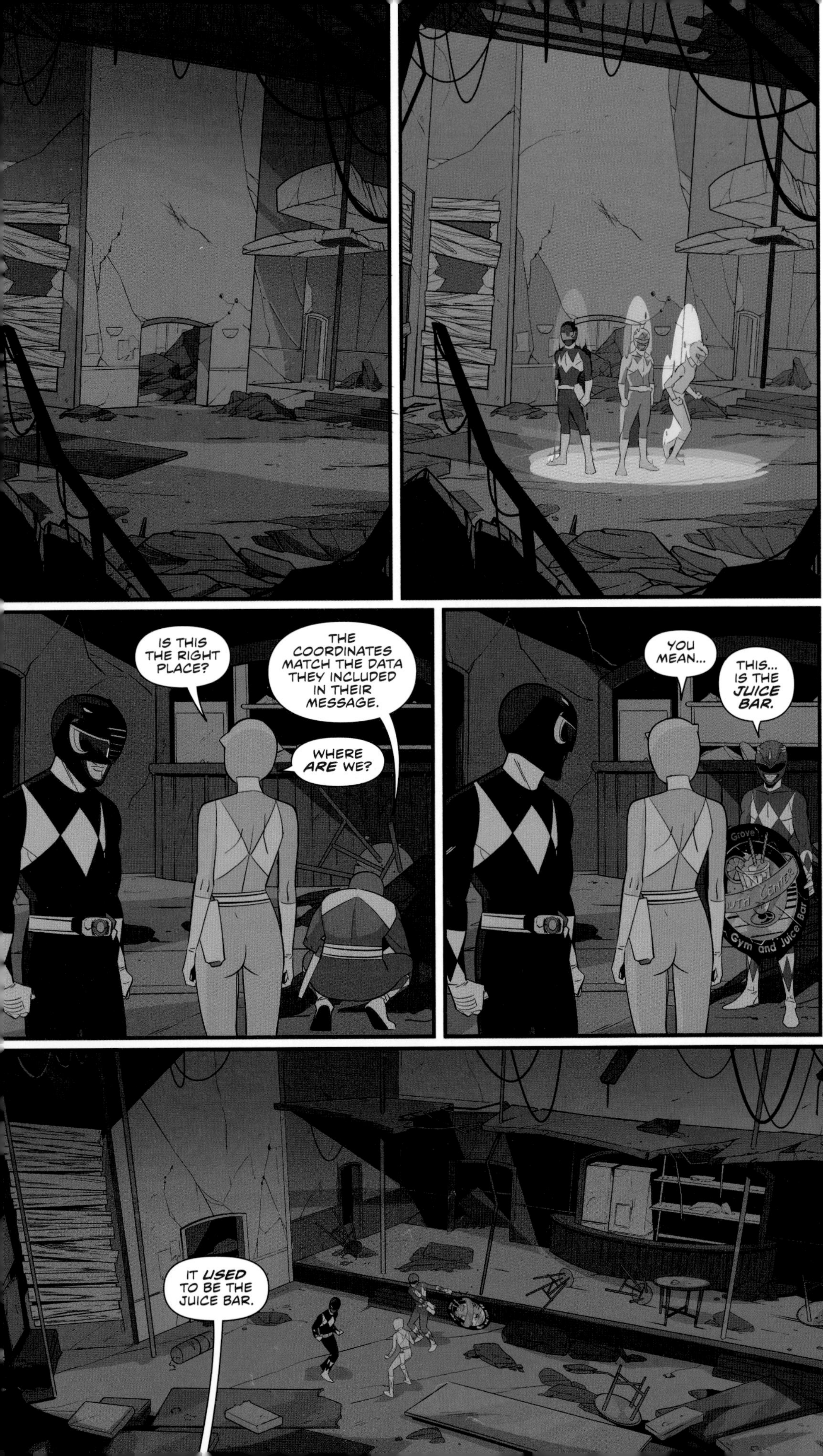

IS THIS THE RIGHT PLACE?
THE COORDINATES MATCH THE DATA THEY INCLUDED IN THEIR MESSAGE.
WHERE ARE WE?
YOU MEAN...
THIS... IS THE JUICE BAR.
Grove
Gym and Juice Bar
IT USED TO BE THE JUICE BAR.

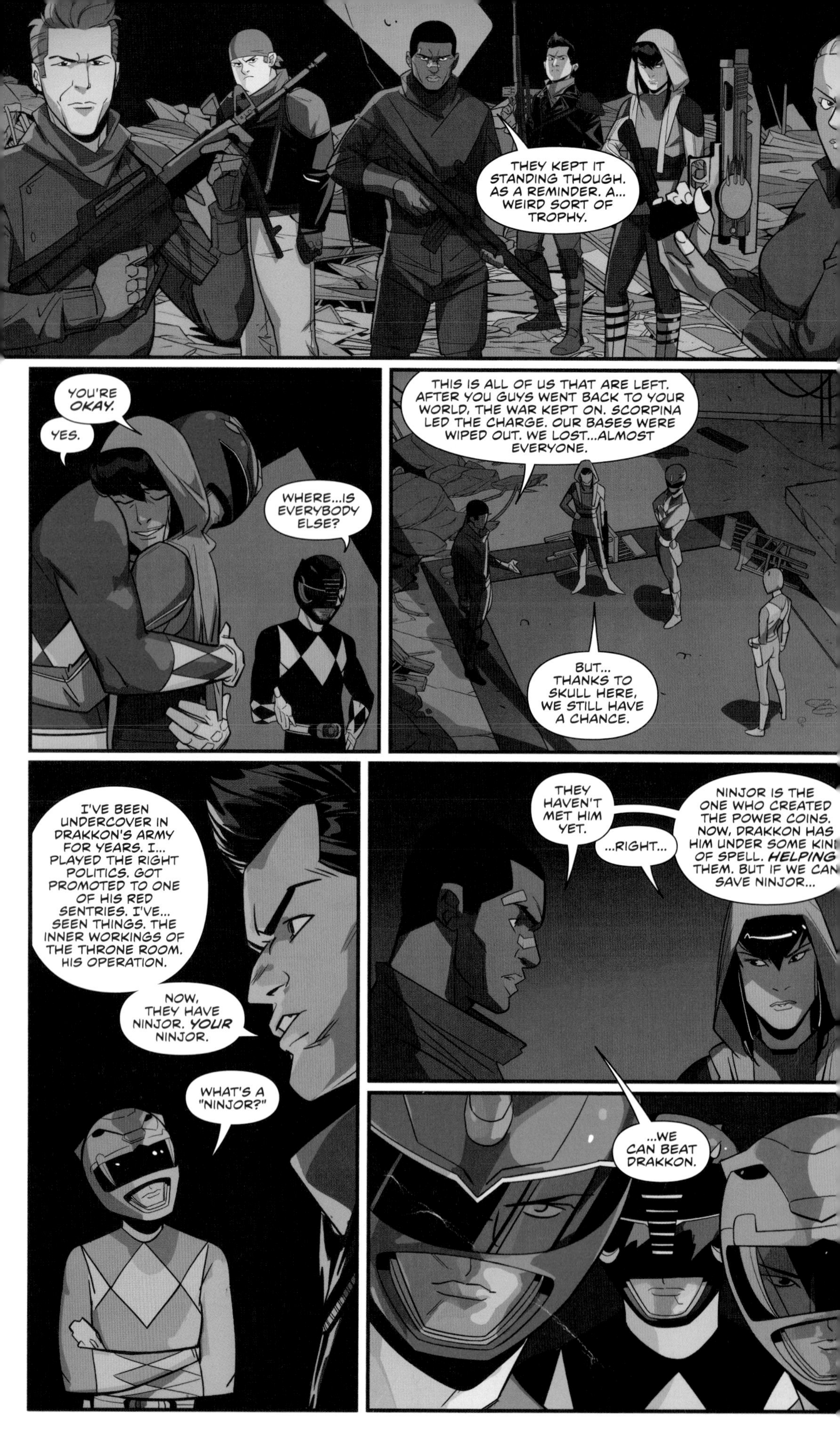
THEY KEPT IT STANDING THOUGH. AS A REMINDER. A... WEIRD SORT OF TROPHY.
YOU'RE *OKAY.*
YES.
WHERE...IS EVERYBODY ELSE?
THIS IS ALL OF US THAT ARE LEFT. AFTER YOU GUYS WENT BACK TO YOUR WORLD, THE WAR KEPT ON. SCORPINA LED THE CHARGE. OUR BASES WERE WIPED OUT. WE LOST...ALMOST EVERYONE.
BUT... THANKS TO SKULL HERE, WE STILL HAVE A CHANCE.
I'VE BEEN UNDERCOVER IN DRAKKON'S ARMY FOR YEARS. I... PLAYED THE RIGHT POLITICS. GOT PROMOTED TO ONE OF HIS RED SENTRIES. I'VE... SEEN THINGS. THE INNER WORKINGS OF THE THRONE ROOM. HIS OPERATION.
NOW, THEY HAVE NINJOR. *YOUR* NINJOR.
WHAT'S A "NINJOR?"
THEY HAVEN'T MET HIM YET.
...RIGHT...
NINJOR IS THE ONE WHO CREATED THE POWER COINS. NOW, DRAKKON HAS HIM UNDER SOME KIN OF SPELL. *HELPING* THEM. BUT IF WE CAN SAVE NINJOR...
...WE CAN BEAT DRAKKON.

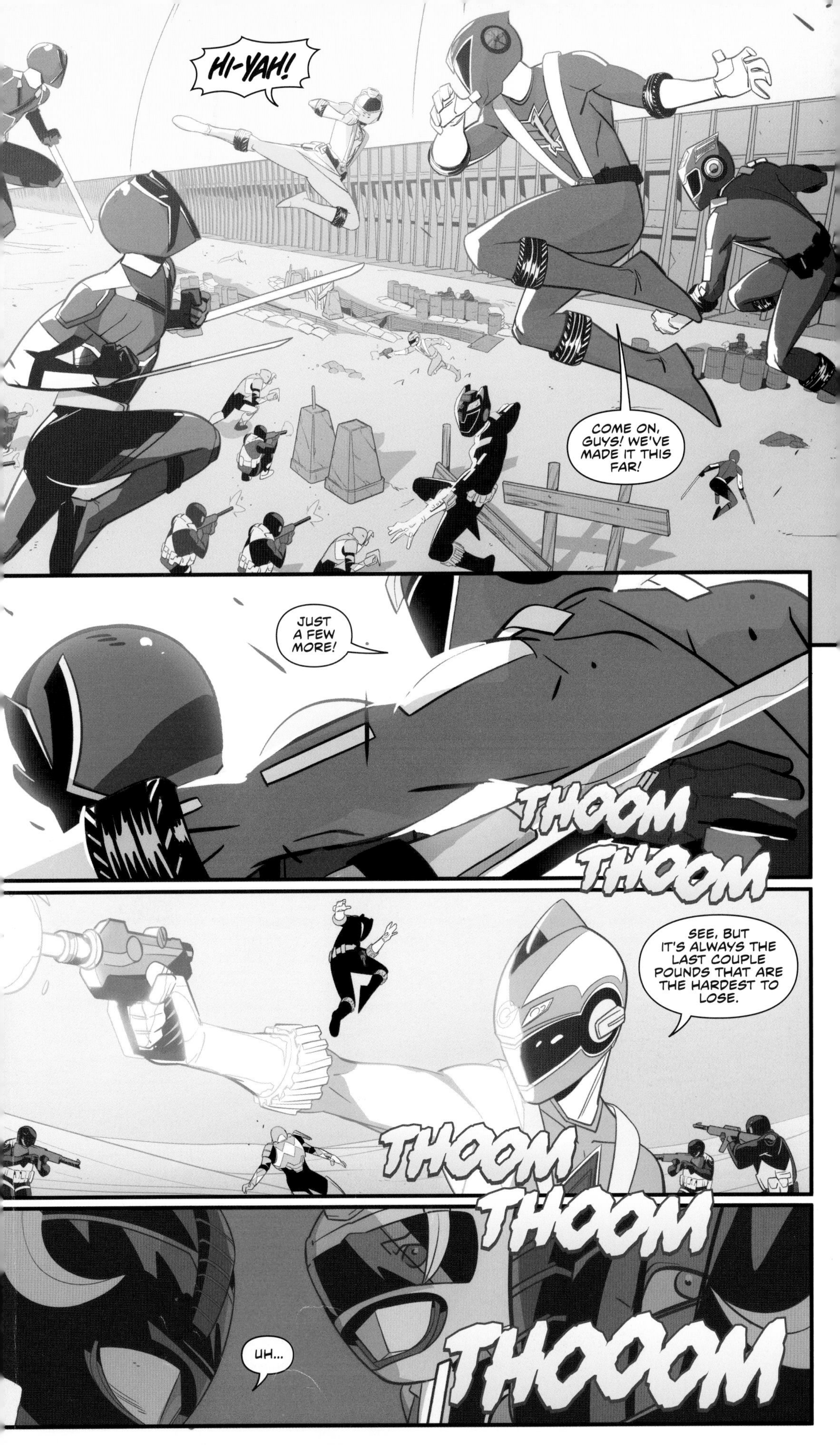
HI-YAH!
COME ON, GUYS! WE'VE MADE IT THIS FAR!
JUST A FEW MORE!
THOOM
THOOM
SEE, BUT IT'S ALWAYS THE LAST COUPLE POUNDS THAT ARE THE HARDEST TO LOSE.
THOOM
THOOM
UH...
THOOOM

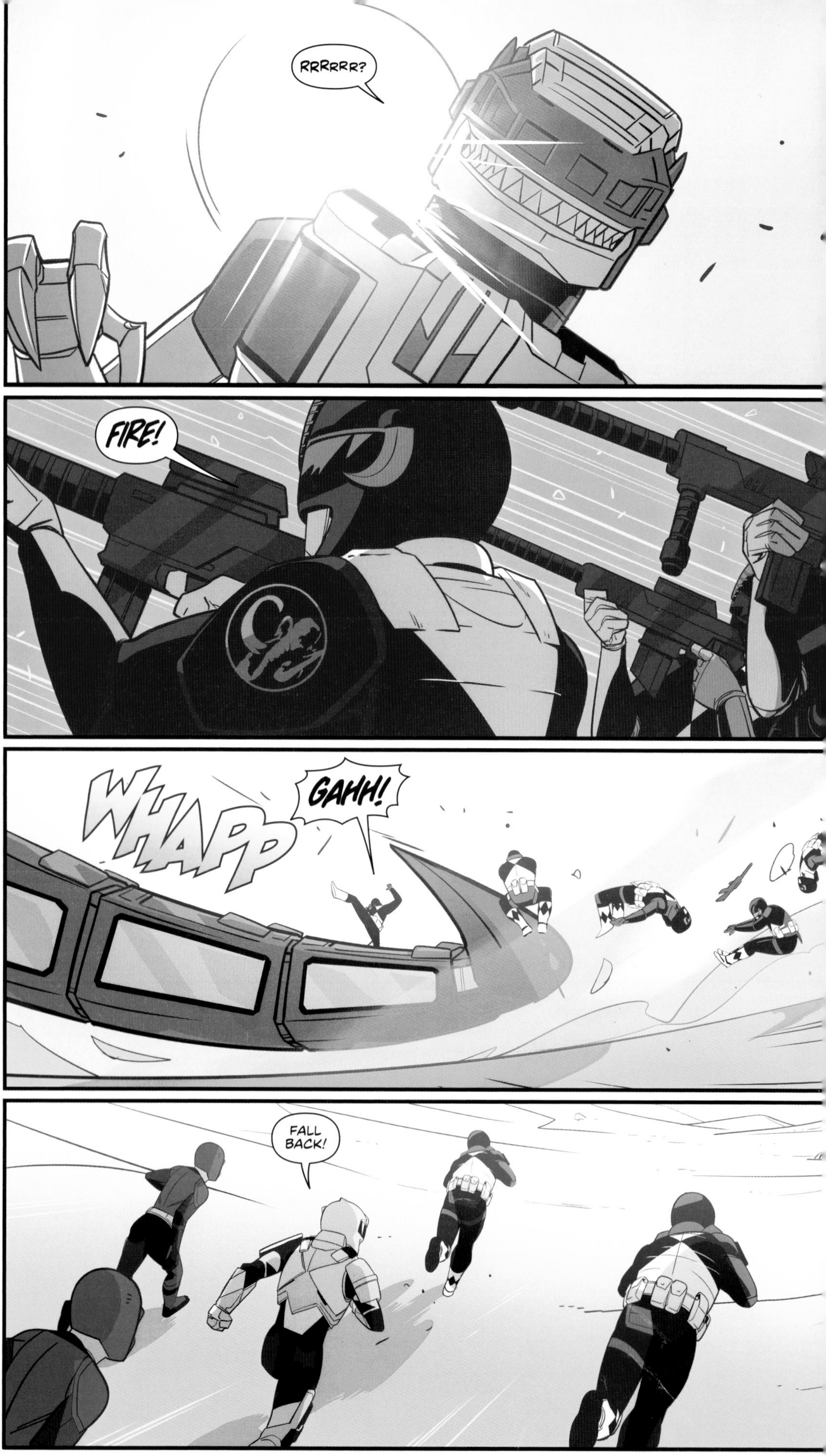
RRRRRR?
FIRE!
WHAPP
GAHH!
FALL BACK!

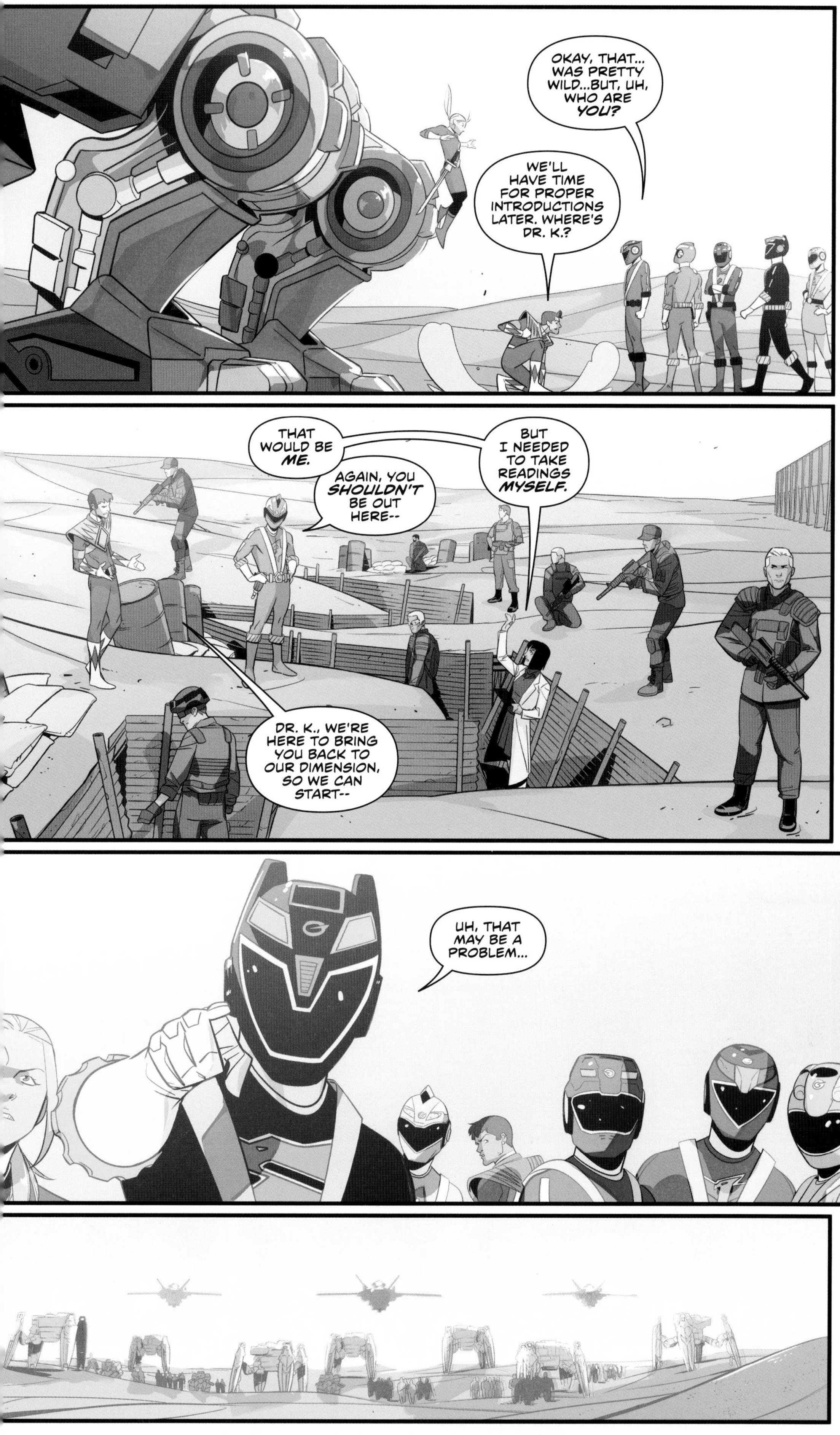
OKAY, THAT... WAS PRETTY WILD...BUT, UH, WHO ARE *YOU?*
WE'LL HAVE TIME FOR PROPER INTRODUCTIONS LATER. WHERE'S DR. K.?
THAT WOULD BE *ME.*
BUT I NEEDED TO TAKE READINGS *MYSELF.*
AGAIN, YOU *SHOULDN'T* BE OUT HERE--
DR. K., WE'RE HERE TO BRING YOU BACK TO OUR DIMENSION, SO WE CAN START--
UH, THAT MAY BE A PROBLEM...

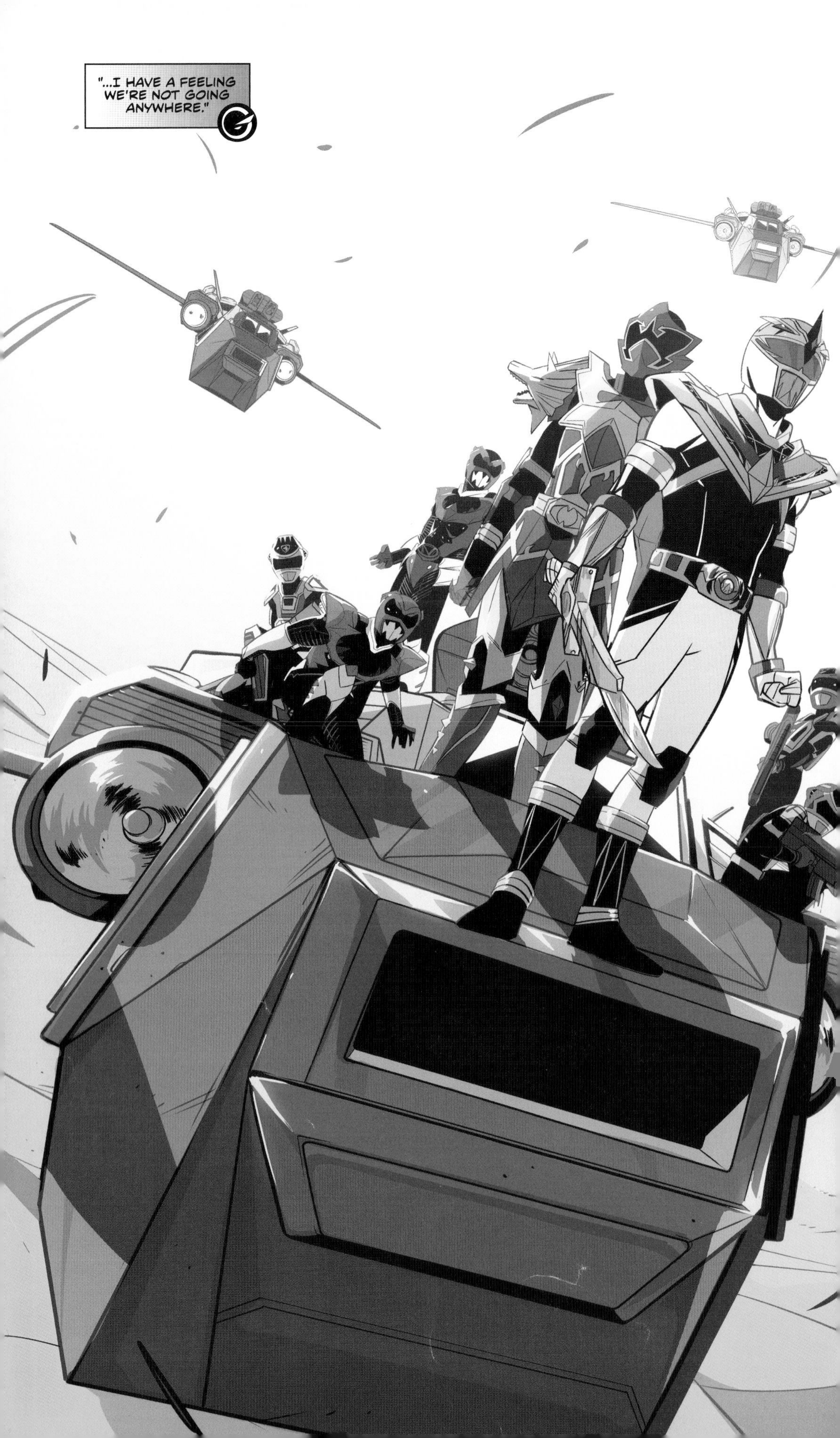
"...I HAVE A FEELING WE'RE NOT GOING ANYWHERE."

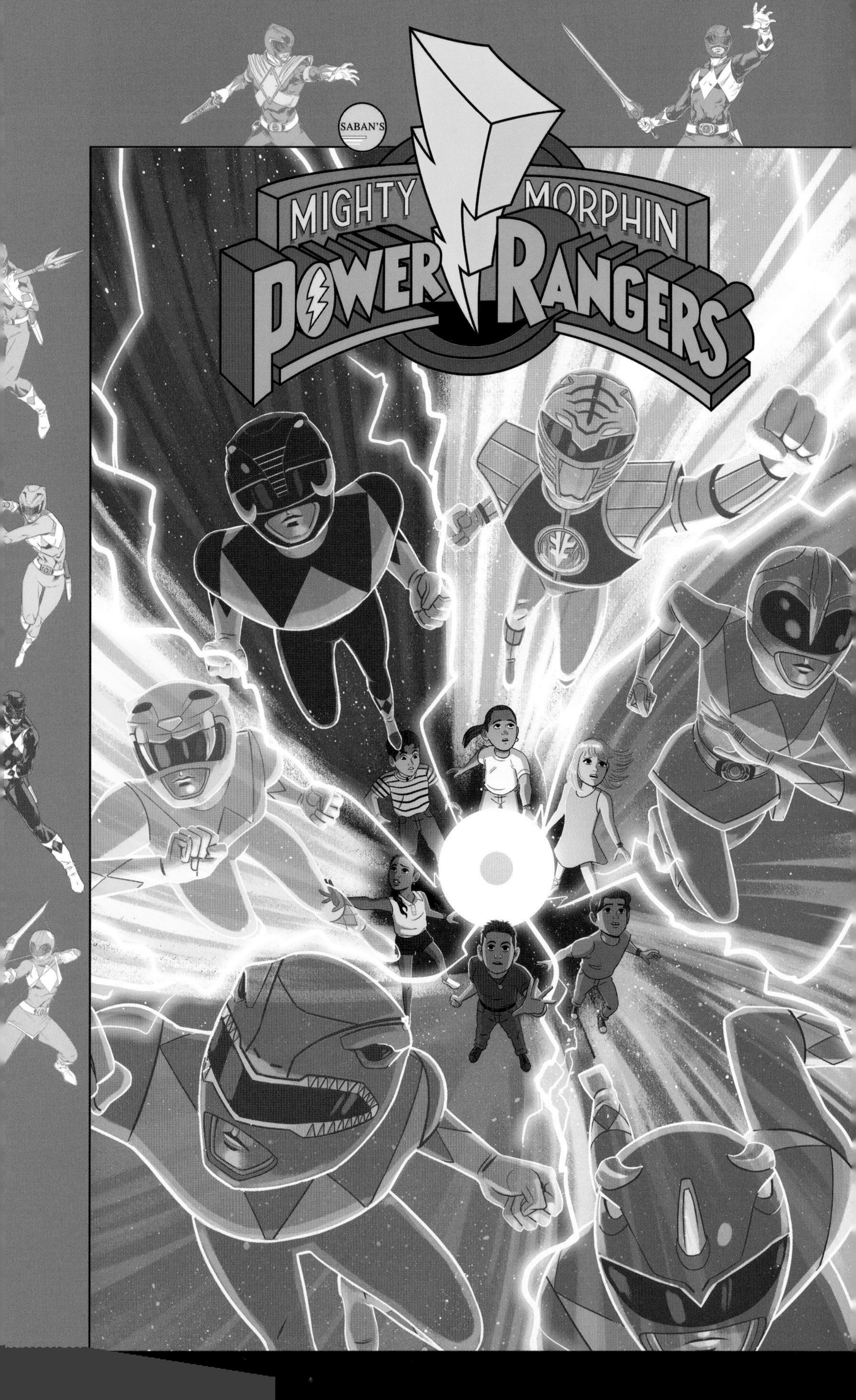
SABAN'S
MIGHTY MORPHIN
POWER RANGERS

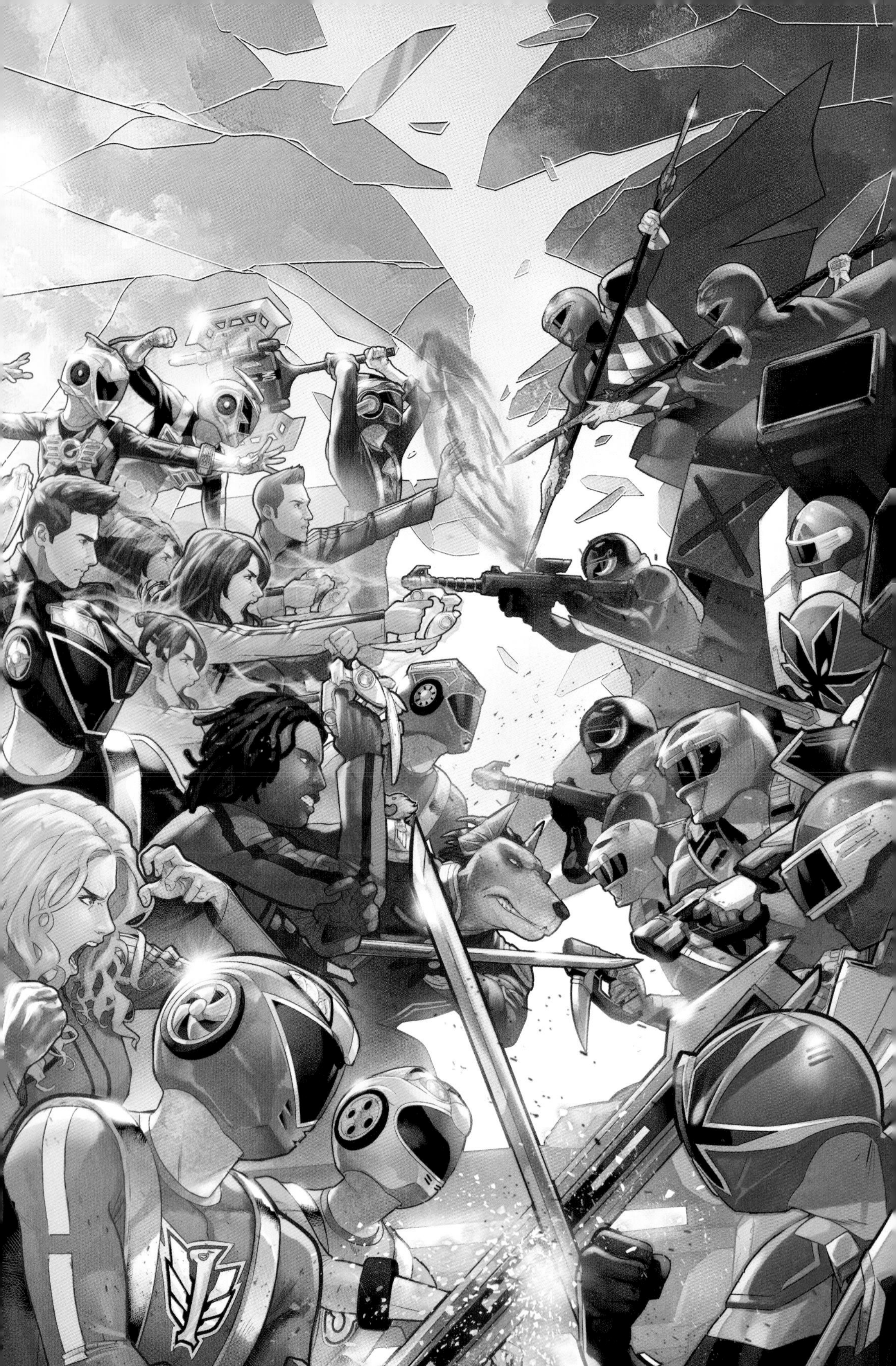

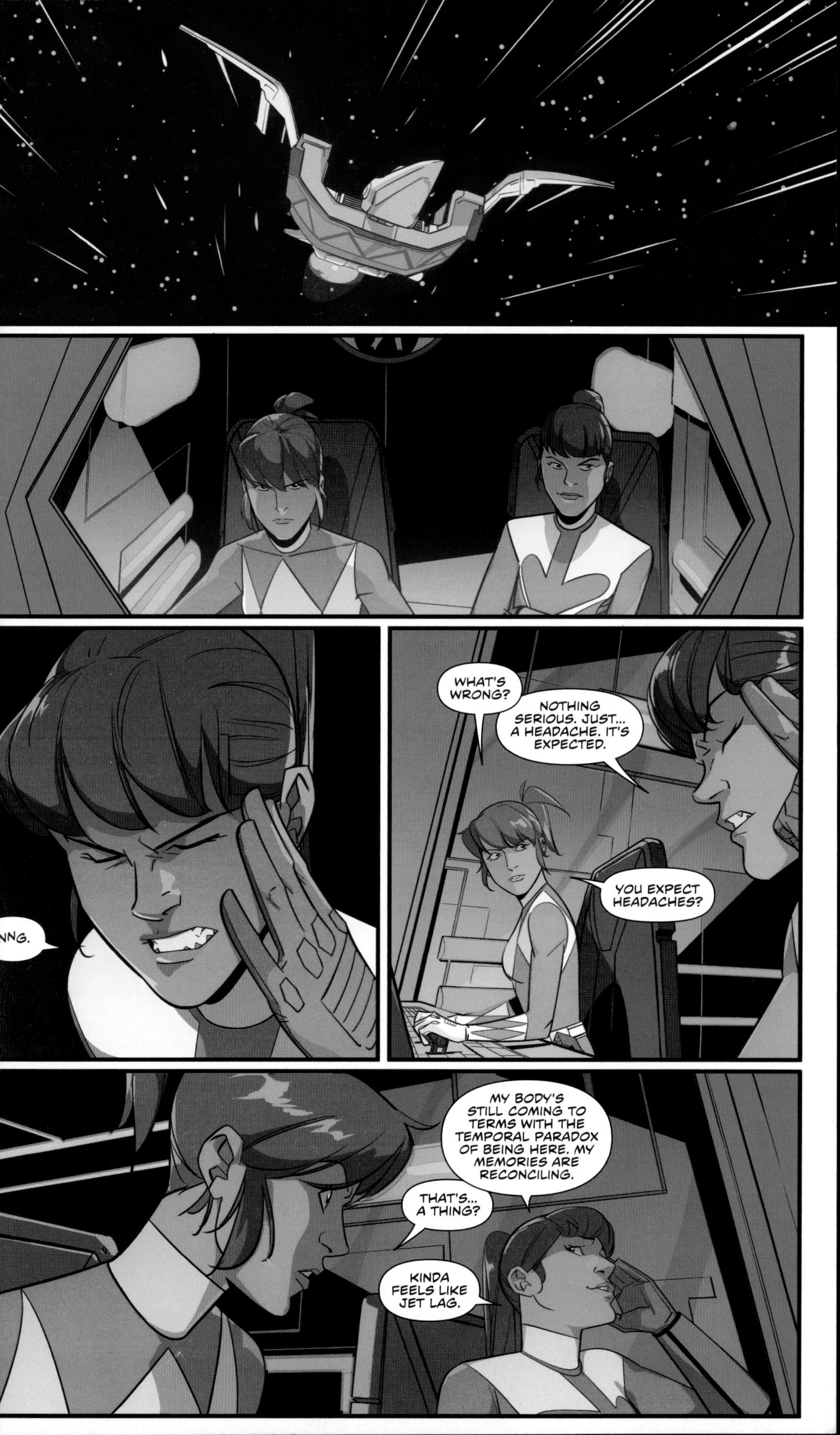
NNG.
WHAT'S WRONG?
NOTHING SERIOUS. JUST... A HEADACHE. IT'S EXPECTED.
YOU EXPECT HEADACHES?
MY BODY'S STILL COMING TO TERMS WITH THE TEMPORAL PARADOX OF BEING HERE. MY MEMORIES ARE RECONCILING.
THAT'S... A THING?
KINDA FEELS LIKE JET LAG.

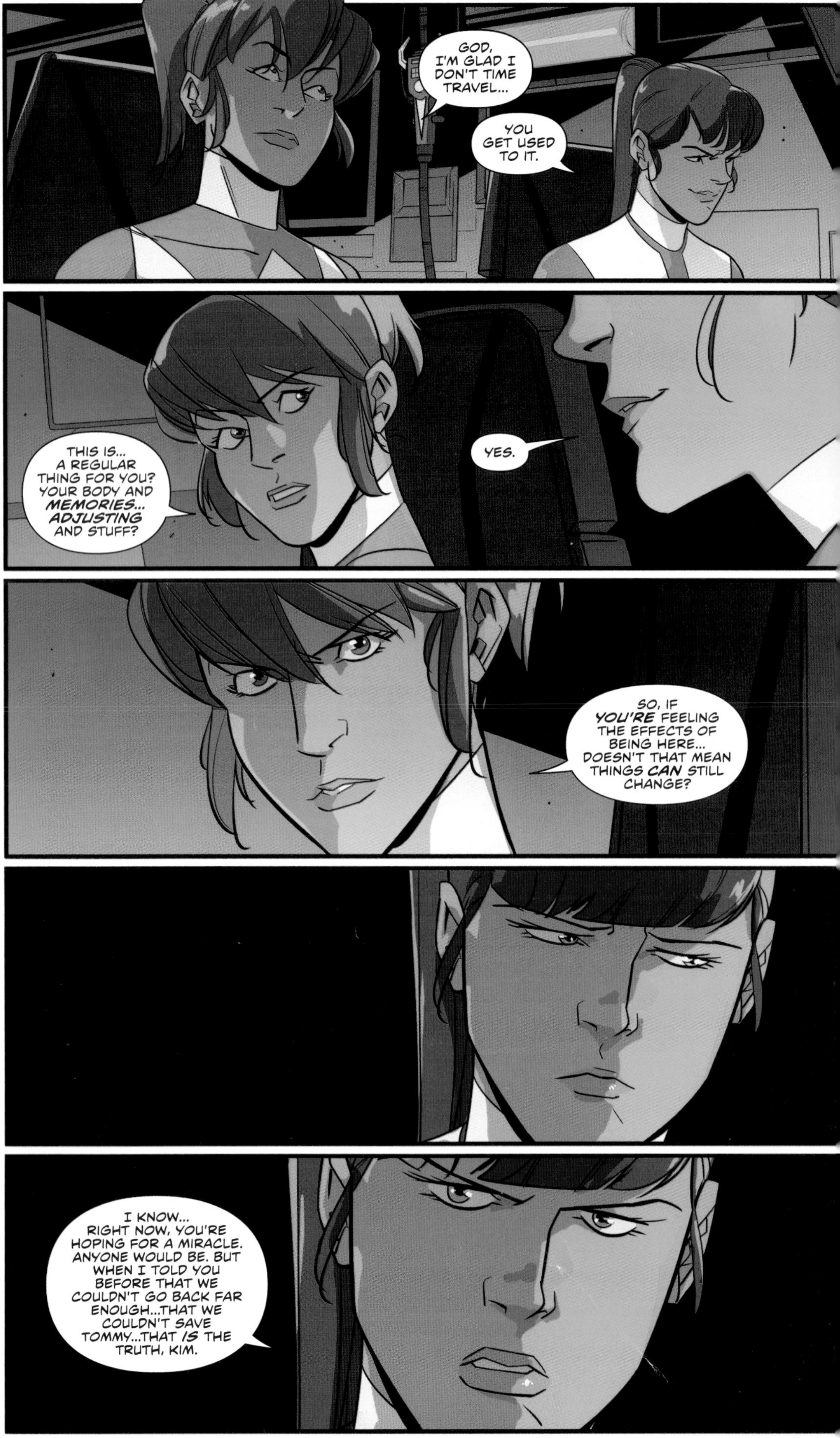
GOD, I'M GLAD I DON'T TIME TRAVEL...
YOU GET USED TO IT.
THIS IS... A REGULAR THING FOR YOU? YOUR BODY AND MEMORIES... ADJUSTING AND STUFF?
YES.
SO, IF YOU'RE FEELING THE EFFECTS OF BEING HERE... DOESN'T THAT MEAN THINGS CAN STILL CHANGE?
I KNOW... RIGHT NOW, YOU'RE HOPING FOR A MIRACLE. ANYONE WOULD BE. BUT WHEN I TOLD YOU BEFORE THAT WE COULDN'T GO BACK FAR ENOUGH...THAT WE COULDN'T SAVE TOMMY...THAT IS THE TRUTH, KIM.

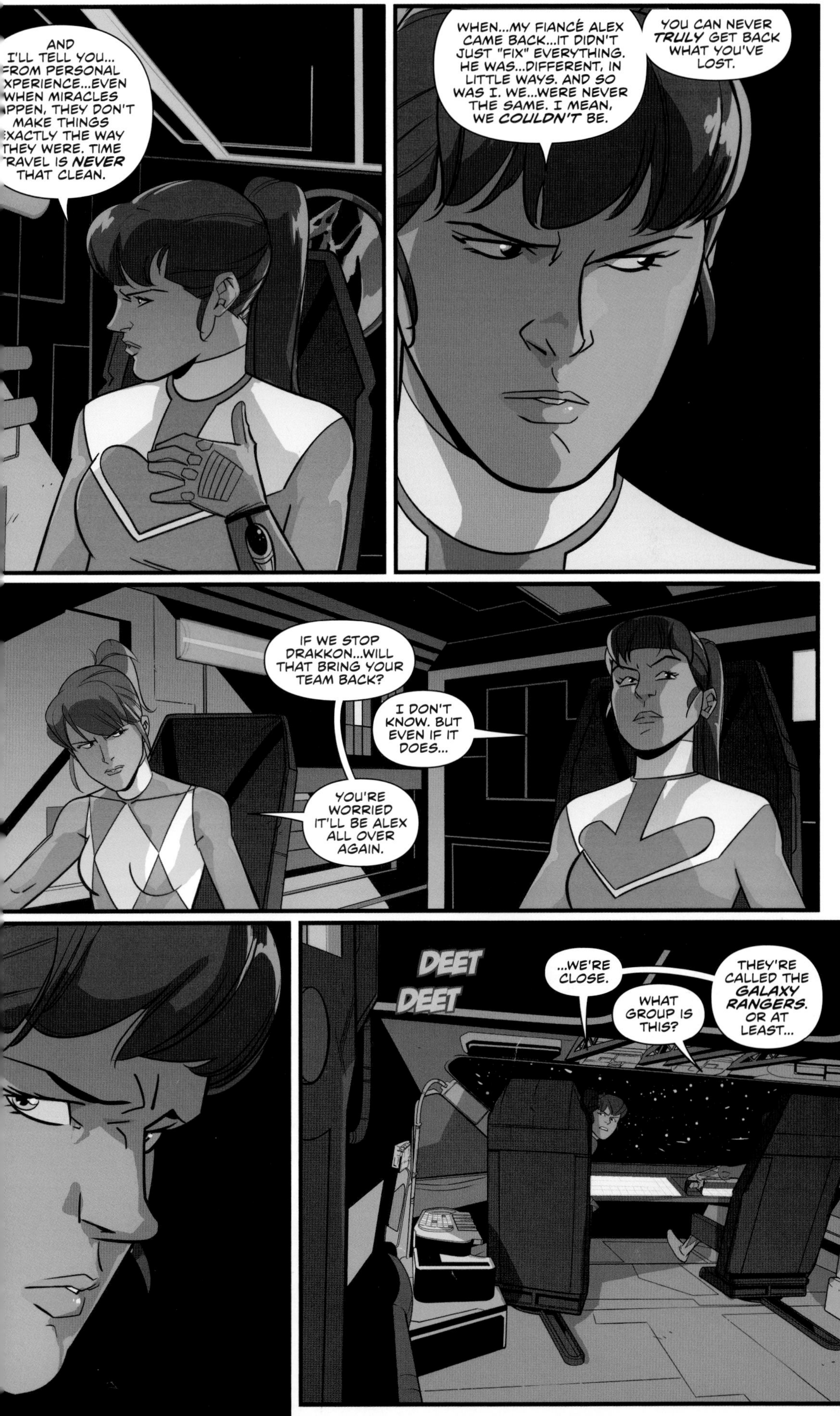

AND I'LL TELL YOU... FROM PERSONAL EXPERIENCE...EVEN WHEN MIRACLES HAPPEN, THEY DON'T MAKE THINGS EXACTLY THE WAY THEY WERE. TIME TRAVEL IS NEVER THAT CLEAN.
WHEN...MY FIANCÉ ALEX CAME BACK...IT DIDN'T JUST "FIX" EVERYTHING. HE WAS...DIFFERENT, IN LITTLE WAYS. AND SO WAS I. WE...WERE NEVER THE SAME. I MEAN, WE COULDN'T BE.
YOU CAN NEVER TRULY GET BACK WHAT YOU'VE LOST.
IF WE STOP DRAKKON...WILL THAT BRING YOUR TEAM BACK?
I DON'T KNOW. BUT EVEN IF IT DOES...
YOU'RE WORRIED IT'LL BE ALEX ALL OVER AGAIN.
DEET
DEET
...WE'RE CLOSE.
WHAT GROUP IS THIS?
THEY'RE CALLED THE GALAXY RANGERS. OR AT LEAST...

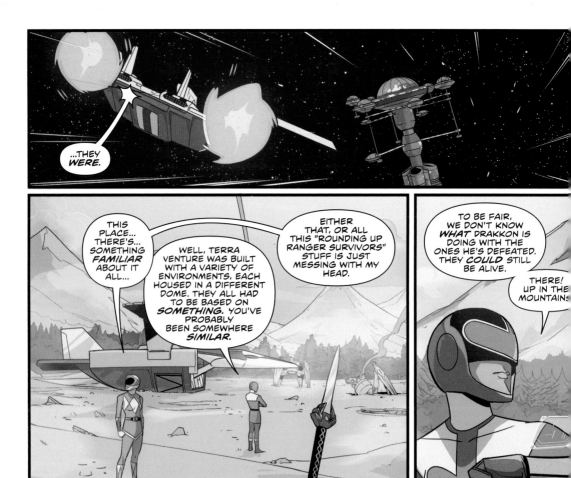

...THEY **WERE.**

THIS PLACE... THERE'S... SOMETHING **FAMILIAR** ABOUT IT ALL...

WELL, TERRA VENTURE WAS BUILT WITH A VARIETY OF ENVIRONMENTS, EACH HOUSED IN A DIFFERENT DOME. THEY ALL HAD TO BE BASED ON **SOMETHING.** YOU'VE PROBABLY BEEN SOMEWHERE **SIMILAR.**

EITHER THAT, OR ALL THIS "ROUNDING UP RANGER SURVIVORS" STUFF IS JUST MESSING WITH MY HEAD.

TO BE FAIR, WE DON'T KNOW **WHAT** DRAKKON IS DOING WITH THE ONES HE'S DEFEATED. THEY **COULD** STILL BE ALIVE.

THERE! UP IN THE MOUNTAIN!

HUH.

WHAT **NOW?**

THIS... ISN'T THE PINK RANGER I WAS EXPECTING.

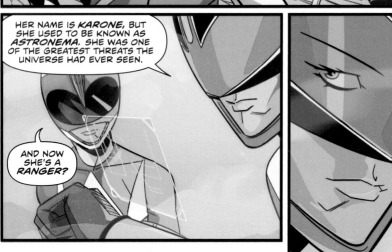

HER NAME IS **KARONE,** BUT SHE USED TO BE KNOWN AS **ASTRONEMA.** SHE WAS ONE OF THE GREATEST THREATS THE UNIVERSE HAD EVER SEEN.

AND NOW SHE'S A **RANGER?**

I GUESS THIS IS FURT... IN HER TIMELINE I THOUGHT. S ALREADY BE REFORMED. AN LITTLE QUIRK TIME TRAVE

HE HOW GOING THE

I MEAN, AS MUCH AS WE LOVE SITTING HERE INSIDE YOUR...THIS IS A DINOSAUR, RIGHT?

IT'S A PTERODACTYL.

THE BEST ZORD OF THE MIGHTY MORPHIN TEAM, OBVIOUSLY.

IT CAN FLY.

...YEAH, OKAY, WELL...YOU GUYS NEED A HAND OR ANYTHING?

I DEFINITELY APPRECIATE THE OFFER, CARTER--

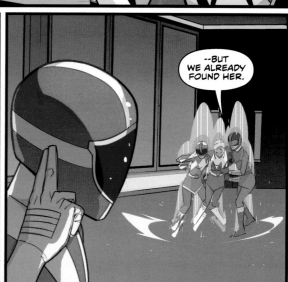

--BUT WE ALREADY FOUND HER.

SHE CAN PROBABLY USE A HAND, THOUGH, IF ANY OF YOU GUYS HAPPEN TO BE DOCTORS OR--

--FIREFIGHTER. HERE, LEMME TAKE A LOOK.

SHE WAS THE ONLY ONE LEFT?

I'M AFRAID SO.

KIM! JEN! ⇥KZZZT⇤ YOU ⇥KZZT⇤ HEAR ME?!

ALPHA? WE'RE HERE, BUT YOU'RE BREAKING UP--

LAUREN AND JASON ⇥KZZZT⇤ MADE IT TO CORINTH! THEY FOUND DR. K--

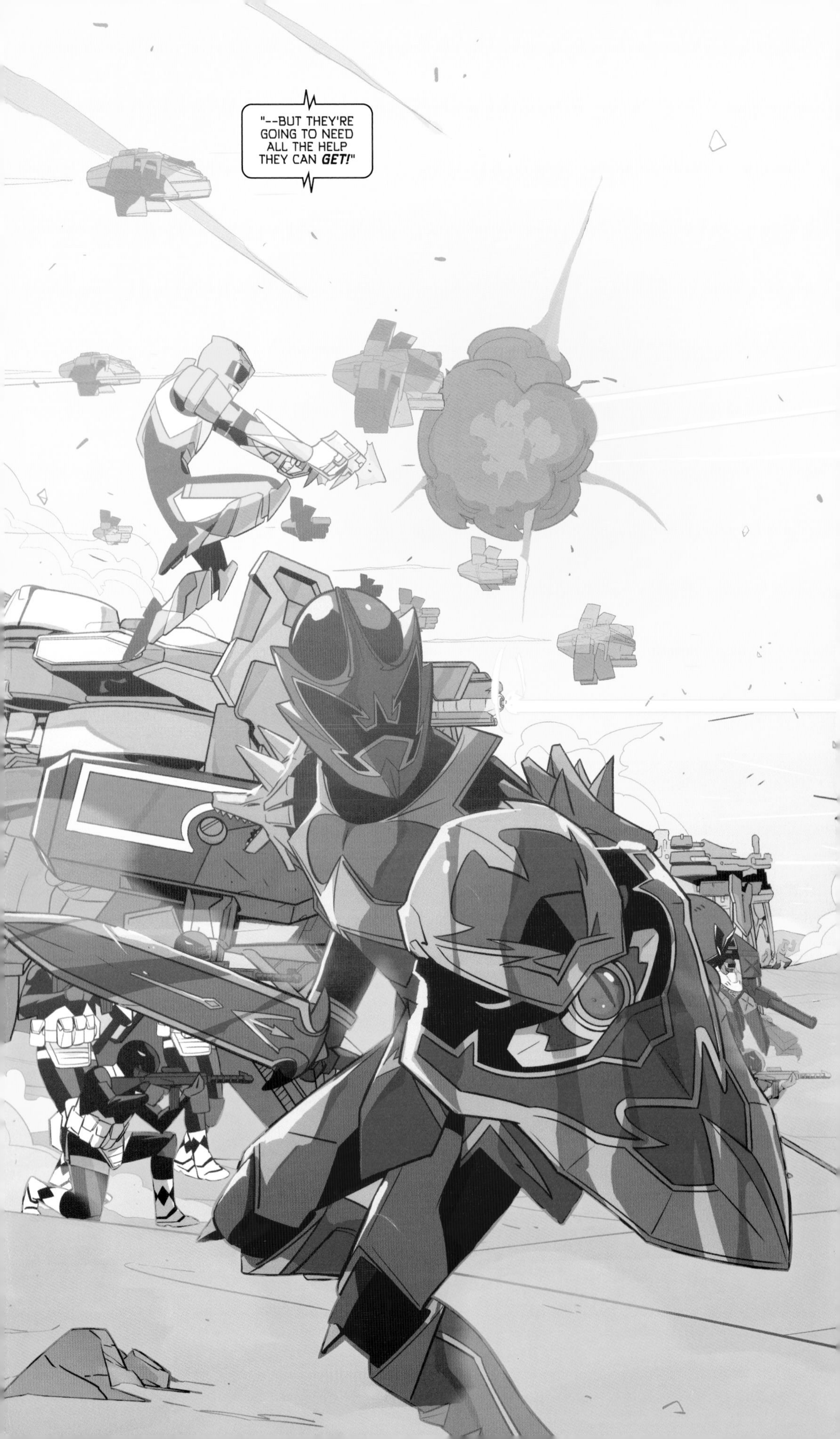
"--BUT THEY'RE GOING TO NEED ALL THE HELP THEY CAN *GET!*"

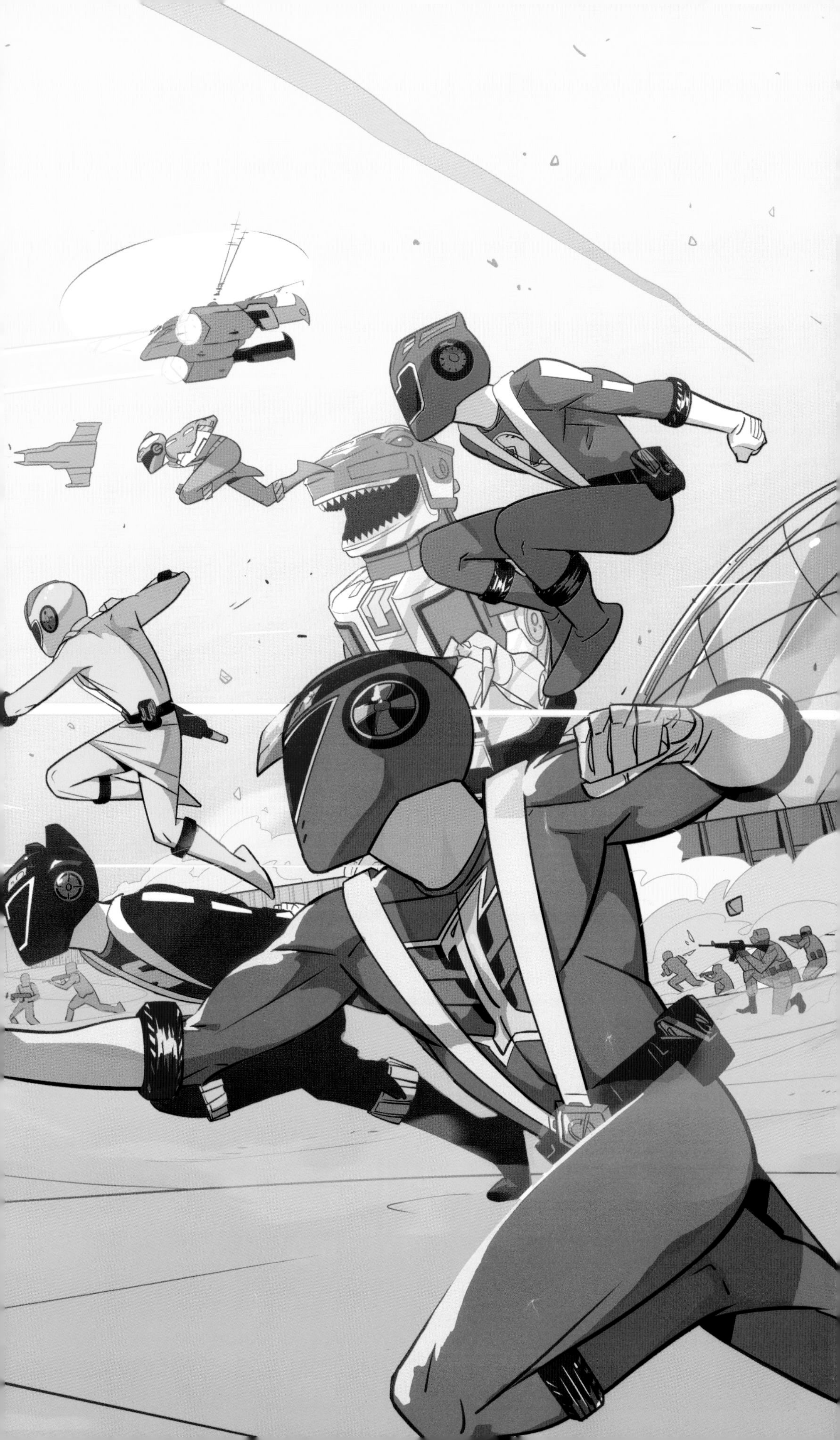

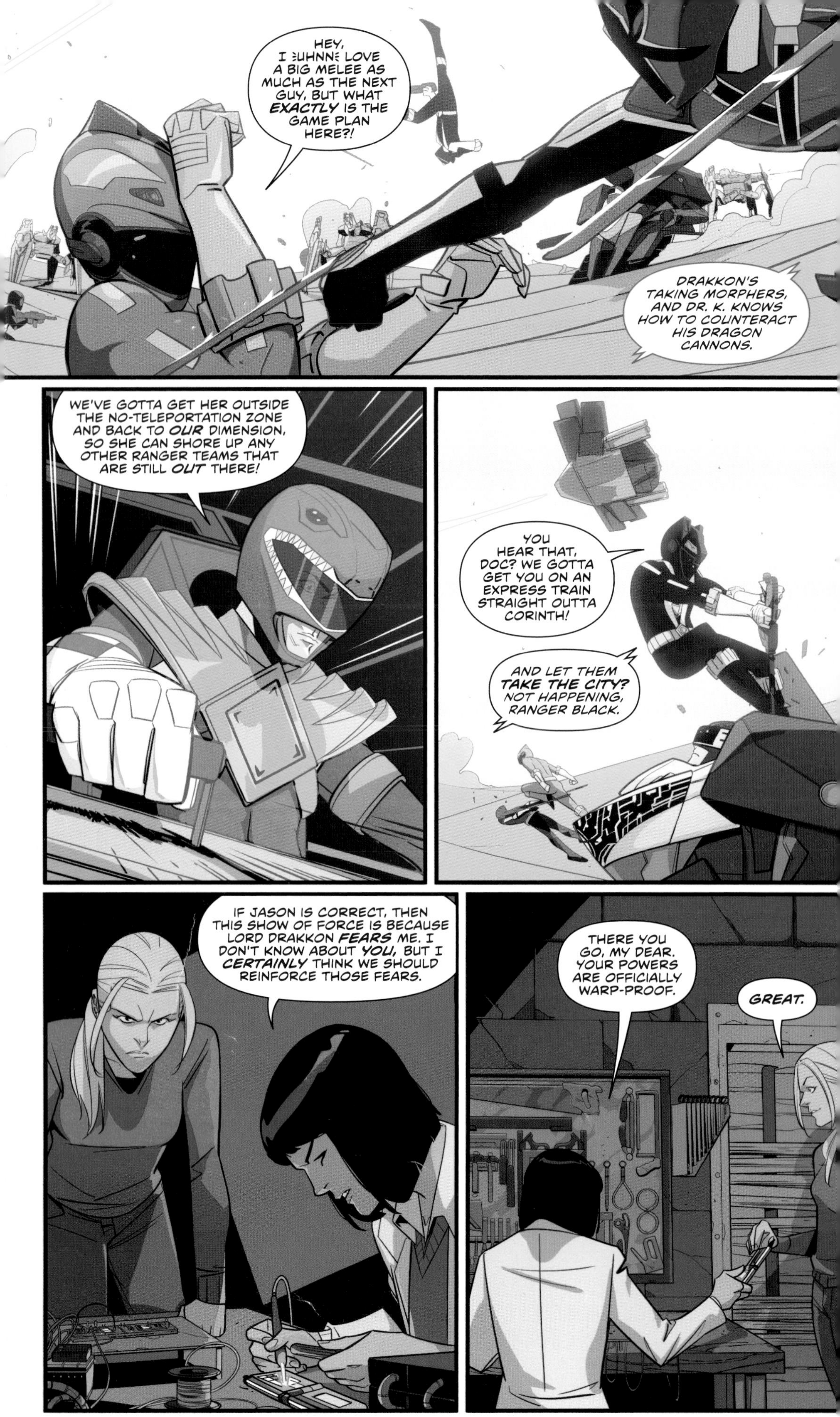
HEY, I UHNN LOVE A BIG MELEE AS MUCH AS THE NEXT GUY, BUT WHAT EXACTLY IS THE GAME PLAN HERE?!
DRAKKON'S TAKING MORPHERS, AND DR. K. KNOWS HOW TO COUNTERACT HIS DRAGON CANNONS.
WE'VE GOTTA GET HER OUTSIDE THE NO-TELEPORTATION ZONE AND BACK TO OUR DIMENSION, SO SHE CAN SHORE UP ANY OTHER RANGER TEAMS THAT ARE STILL OUT THERE!
YOU HEAR THAT, DOC? WE GOTTA GET YOU ON AN EXPRESS TRAIN STRAIGHT OUTTA CORINTH!
AND LET THEM TAKE THE CITY? NOT HAPPENING, RANGER BLACK.
IF JASON IS CORRECT, THEN THIS SHOW OF FORCE IS BECAUSE LORD DRAKKON FEARS ME. I DON'T KNOW ABOUT YOU, BUT I CERTAINLY THINK WE SHOULD REINFORCE THOSE FEARS.
THERE YOU GO, MY DEAR. YOUR POWERS ARE OFFICIALLY WARP-PROOF.
GREAT.

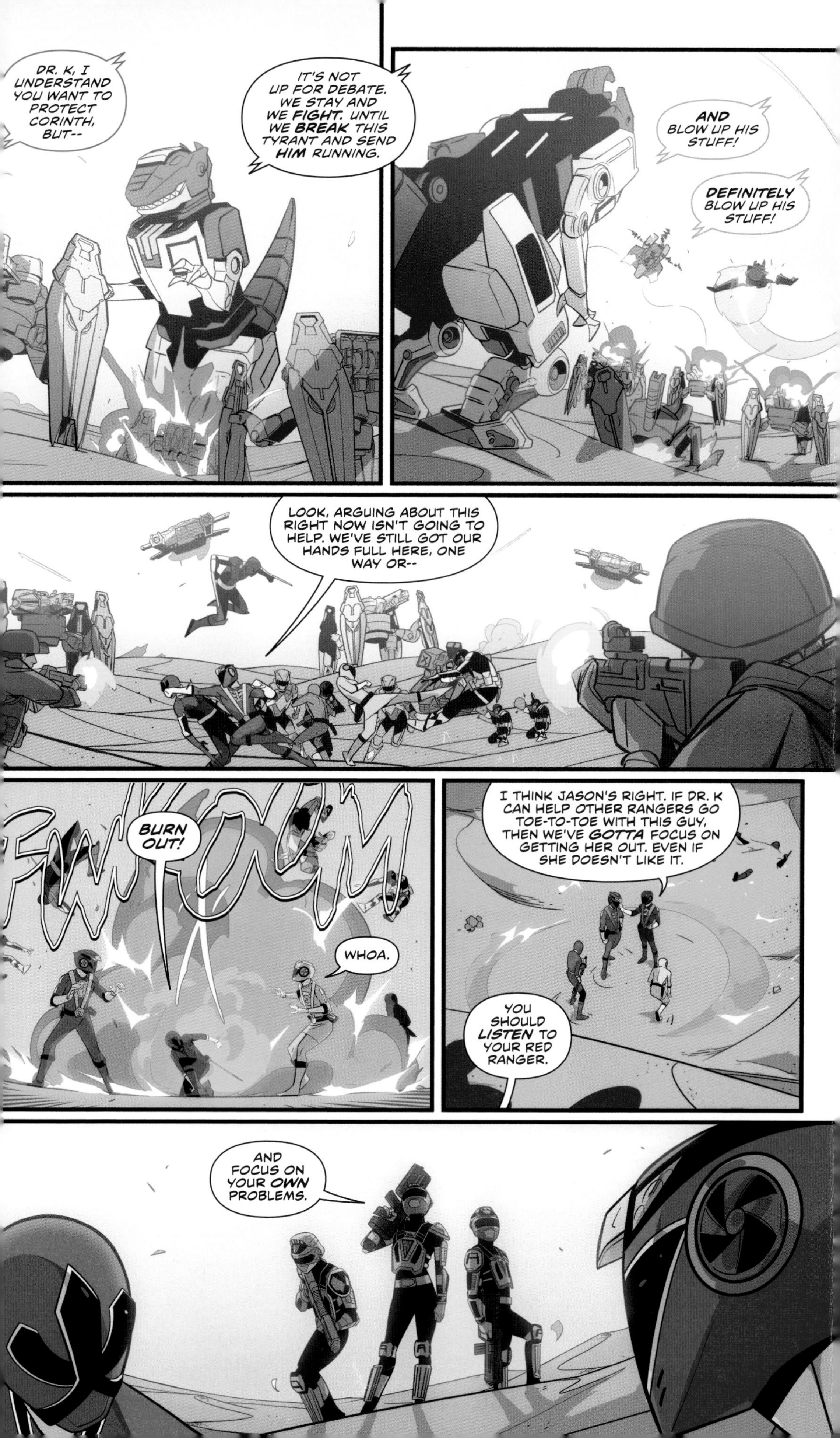
DR. K, I UNDERSTAND YOU WANT TO PROTECT CORINTH, BUT--
IT'S NOT UP FOR DEBATE. WE STAY AND WE FIGHT. UNTIL WE BREAK THIS TYRANT AND SEND HIM RUNNING.
AND BLOW UP HIS STUFF!
DEFINITELY BLOW UP HIS STUFF!
LOOK, ARGUING ABOUT THIS RIGHT NOW ISN'T GOING TO HELP. WE'VE STILL GOT OUR HANDS FULL HERE, ONE WAY OR--
FWOOM
BURN OUT!
WHOA.
I THINK JASON'S RIGHT. IF DR. K CAN HELP OTHER RANGERS GO TOE-TO-TOE WITH THIS GUY, THEN WE'VE GOTTA FOCUS ON GETTING HER OUT. EVEN IF SHE DOESN'T LIKE IT.
YOU SHOULD LISTEN TO YOUR RED RANGER.
AND FOCUS ON YOUR OWN PROBLEMS.

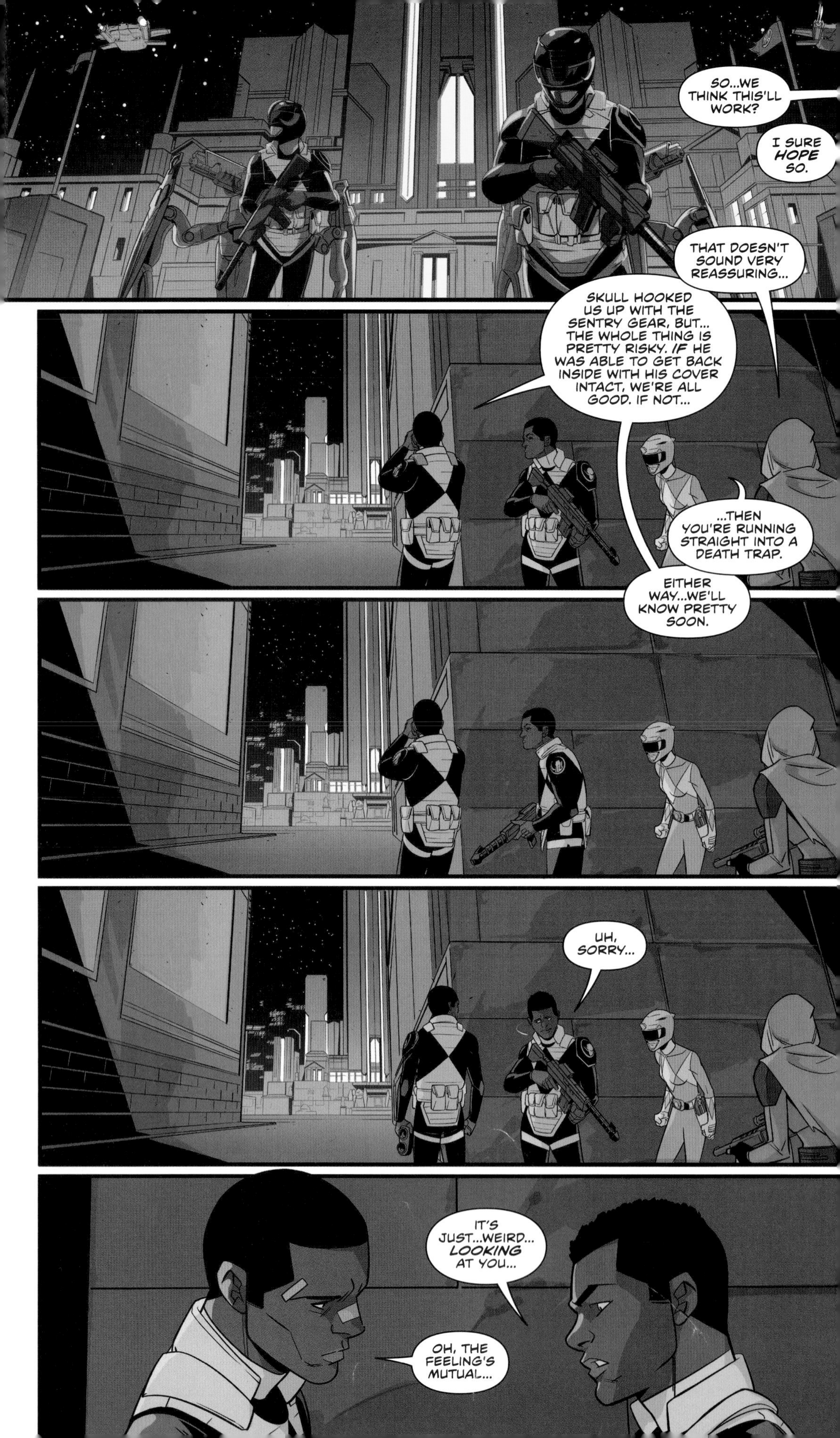
SO...WE THINK THIS'LL WORK?
I SURE HOPE SO.
THAT DOESN'T SOUND VERY REASSURING...
SKULL HOOKED US UP WITH THE SENTRY GEAR, BUT... THE WHOLE THING IS PRETTY RISKY. IF HE WAS ABLE TO GET BACK INSIDE WITH HIS COVER INTACT, WE'RE ALL GOOD. IF NOT...
...THEN YOU'RE RUNNING STRAIGHT INTO A DEATH TRAP.
EITHER WAY...WE'LL KNOW PRETTY SOON.
UH, SORRY...
IT'S JUST...WEIRD... LOOKING AT YOU...
OH, THE FEELING'S MUTUAL...

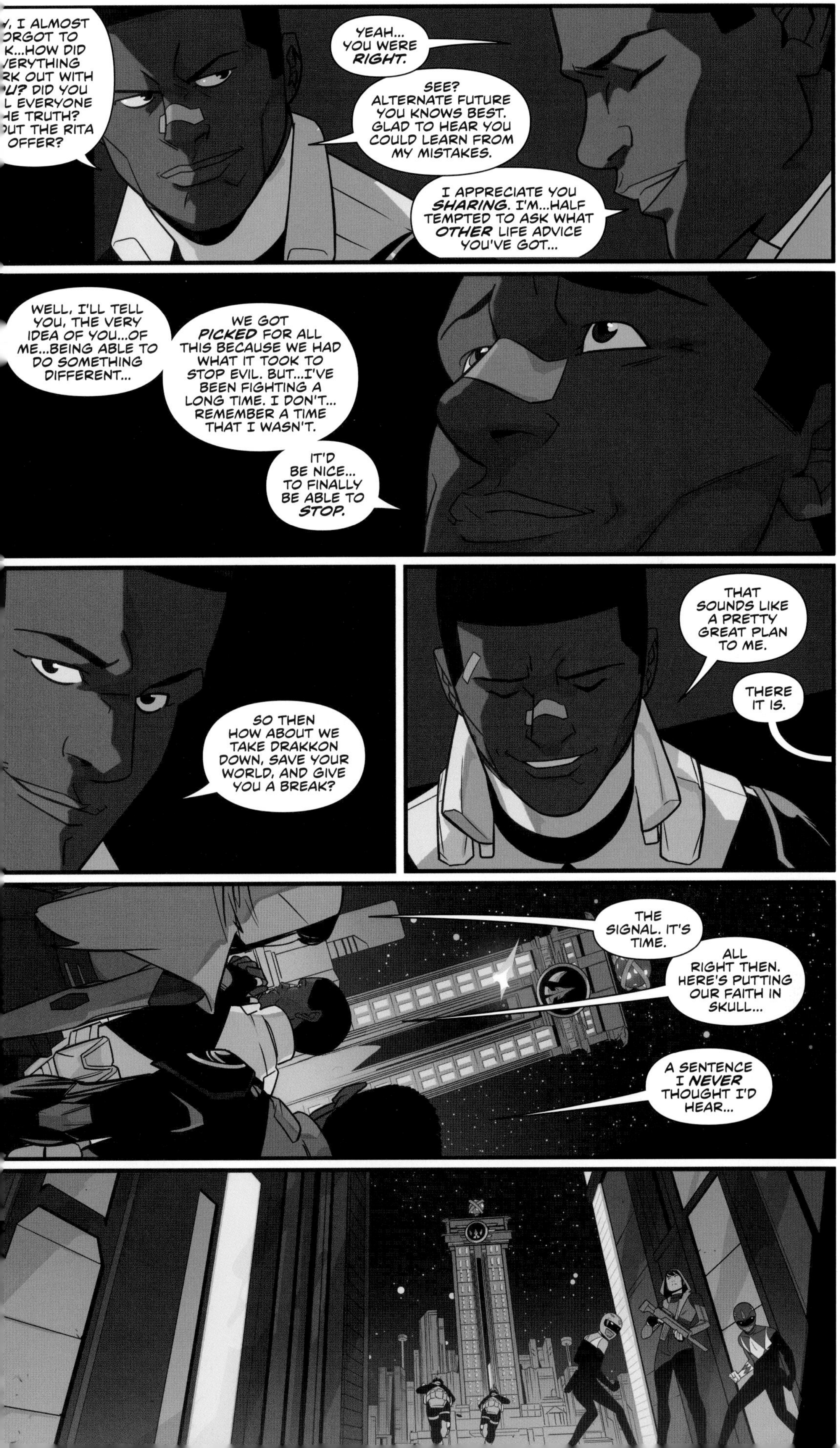

Y, I ALMOST ORGOT TO K...HOW DID VERYTHING RK OUT WITH U? DID YOU L EVERYONE HE TRUTH? UT THE RITA OFFER?
YEAH... YOU WERE RIGHT.
SEE? ALTERNATE FUTURE YOU KNOWS BEST. GLAD TO HEAR YOU COULD LEARN FROM MY MISTAKES.
I APPRECIATE YOU SHARING. I'M...HALF TEMPTED TO ASK WHAT OTHER LIFE ADVICE YOU'VE GOT...
WELL, I'LL TELL YOU, THE VERY IDEA OF YOU...OF ME...BEING ABLE TO DO SOMETHING DIFFERENT...
WE GOT PICKED FOR ALL THIS BECAUSE WE HAD WHAT IT TOOK TO STOP EVIL. BUT...I'VE BEEN FIGHTING A LONG TIME. I DON'T... REMEMBER A TIME THAT I WASN'T.
IT'D BE NICE... TO FINALLY BE ABLE TO STOP.
SO THEN HOW ABOUT WE TAKE DRAKKON DOWN, SAVE YOUR WORLD, AND GIVE YOU A BREAK?
THAT SOUNDS LIKE A PRETTY GREAT PLAN TO ME.
THERE IT IS.
THE SIGNAL. IT'S TIME.
ALL RIGHT THEN. HERE'S PUTTING OUR FAITH IN SKULL...
A SENTENCE I NEVER THOUGHT I'D HEAR...

YOU ALL *REALLY* SCREWED UP. IF YOU WERE SMART, YOU'D KNEEL FOR LORD DRAKKON *IMMEDIATELY*.

NAH, THAT SHIP HAS *SAILED* FOR THEM. THEIR BEST MOVE NOW IS A QUICK *END*.

BEFORE THIS GETS TOO PAINFUL.

THAT ƎHNƎ ISN'T HAPPENING!

YOU GOT *AWAY*.

YOU SHOULD HAVE CONSIDERED YOURSELF *LUCKY*.

OOO, I DIBS O BLUE

HIS DRAGON CANNONS WON'T WORK ON US! *TAKE* HIM HARD AND--

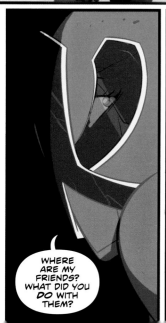

WHERE ARE MY FRIENDS? WHAT DID YOU *DO* WITH THEM?

DO YOU *REALLY* WANT TO KNOW?

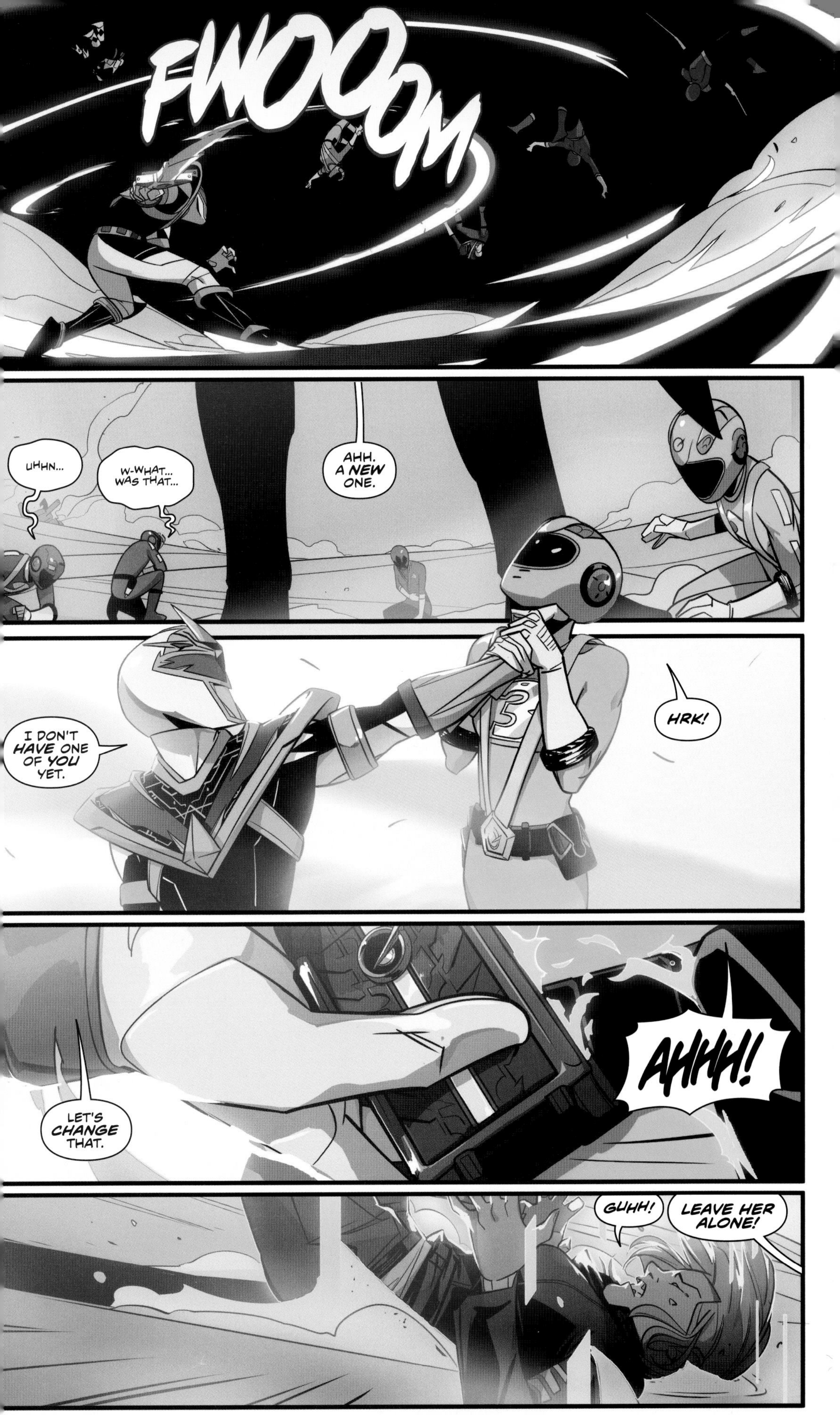
FWOOOOM
UHHN...
W-WHAT... WAS THAT...
AHH. A NEW ONE.
I DON'T HAVE ONE OF YOU YET.
HRK!
LET'S CHANGE THAT.
AHHH!
GUHH!
LEAVE HER ALONE!

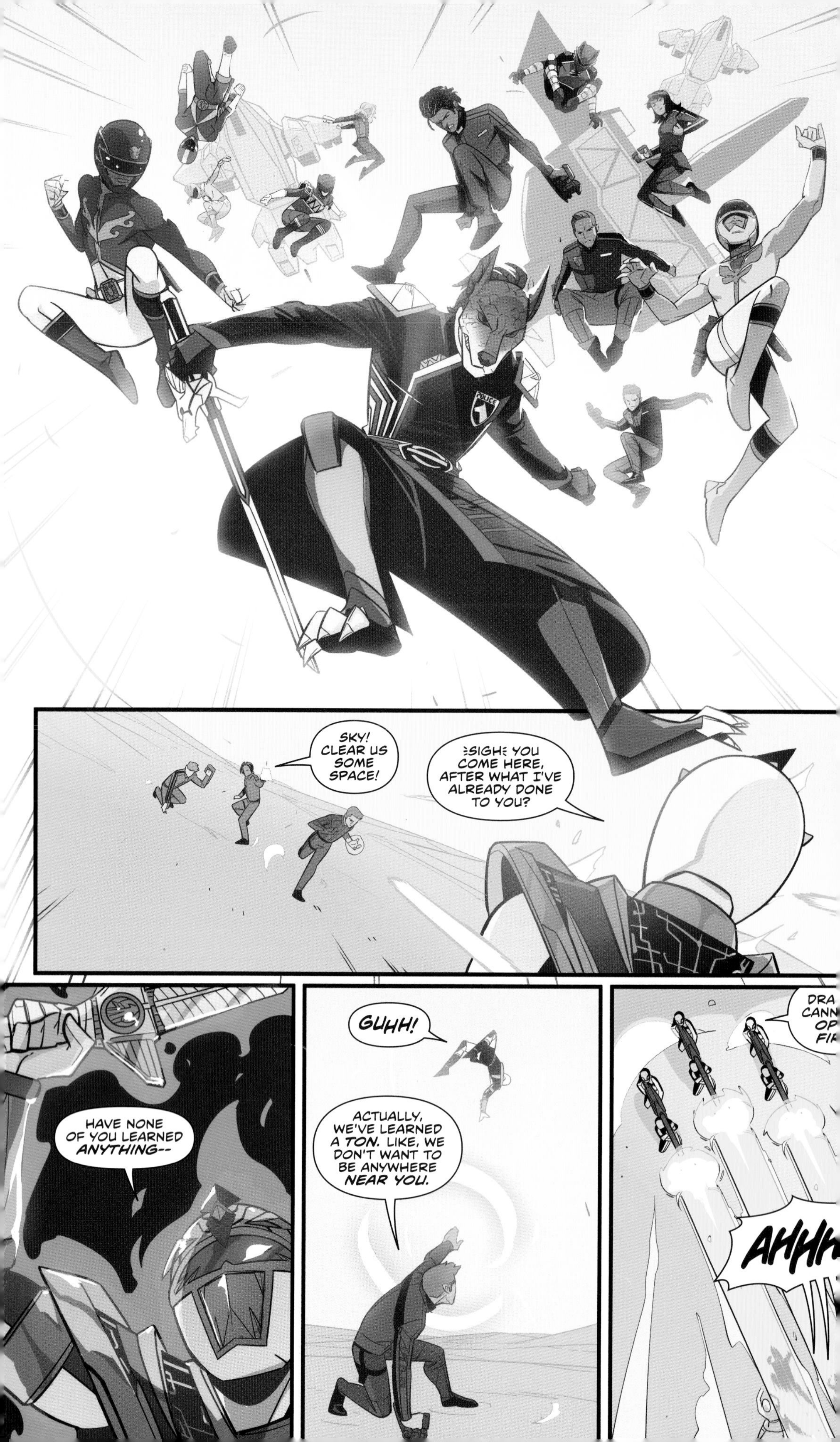
SKY! CLEAR US SOME SPACE!
SIGH YOU COME HERE, AFTER WHAT I'VE ALREADY DONE TO YOU?
HAVE NONE OF YOU LEARNED ANYTHING--
GUHH!
ACTUALLY, WE'VE LEARNED A TON. LIKE, WE DON'T WANT TO BE ANYWHERE NEAR YOU.

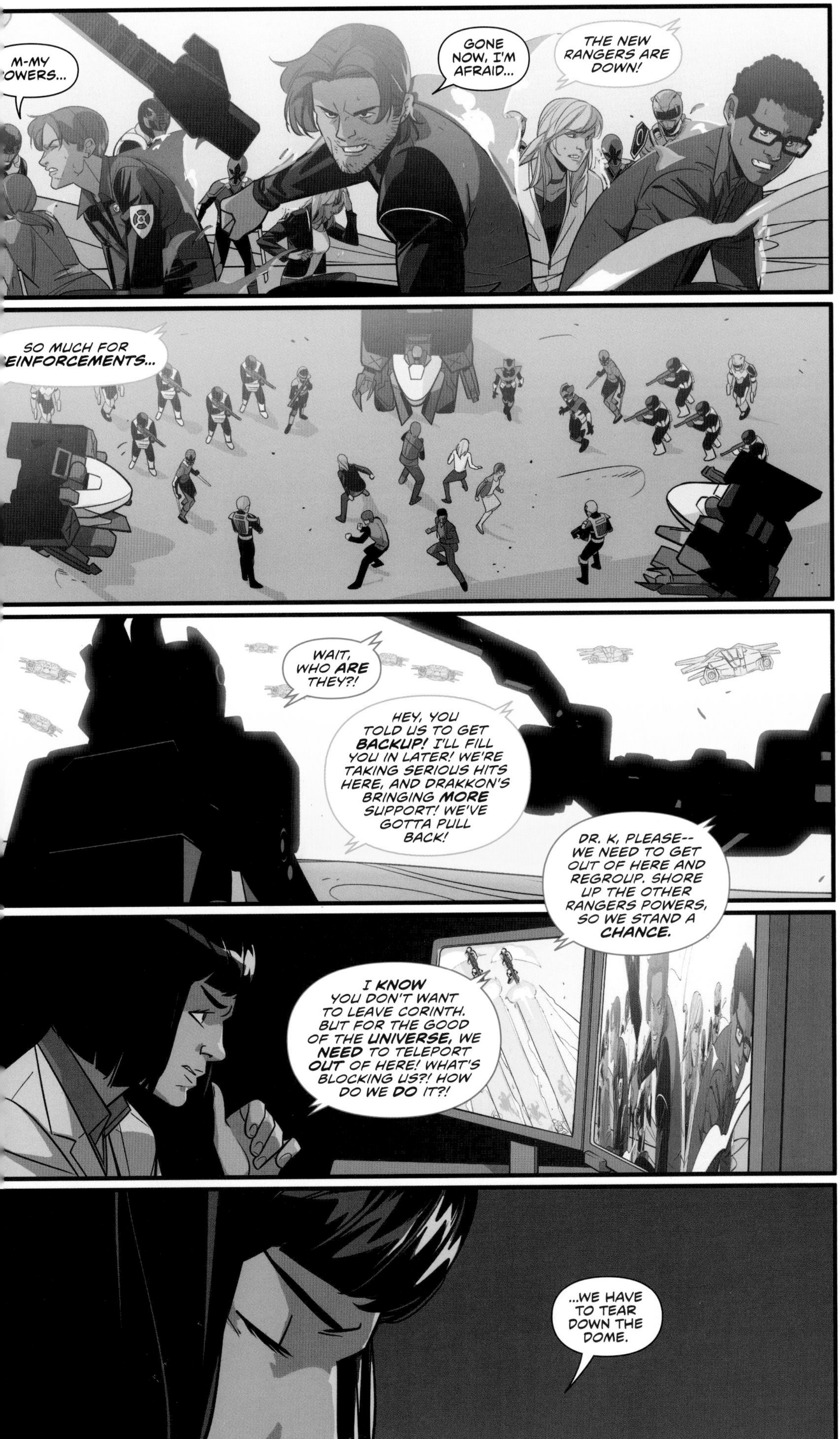
M-MY
OWERS...
GONE
NOW, I'M
AFRAID...
THE NEW
RANGERS ARE
DOWN!
SO MUCH FOR
EINFORCEMENTS...
WAIT,
WHO ARE
THEY?!
HEY, YOU
TOLD US TO GET
BACKUP! I'LL FILL
YOU IN LATER! WE'RE
TAKING SERIOUS HITS
HERE, AND DRAKKON'S
BRINGING MORE
SUPPORT! WE'VE
GOTTA PULL
BACK!
DR. K, PLEASE--
WE NEED TO GET
OUT OF HERE AND
REGROUP. SHORE
UP THE OTHER
RANGERS POWERS,
SO WE STAND A
CHANCE.
I KNOW
YOU DON'T WANT
TO LEAVE CORINTH.
BUT FOR THE GOOD
OF THE UNIVERSE, WE
NEED TO TELEPORT
OUT OF HERE! WHAT'S
BLOCKING US?! HOW
DO WE DO IT?!
...WE HAVE
TO TEAR
DOWN THE
DOME.

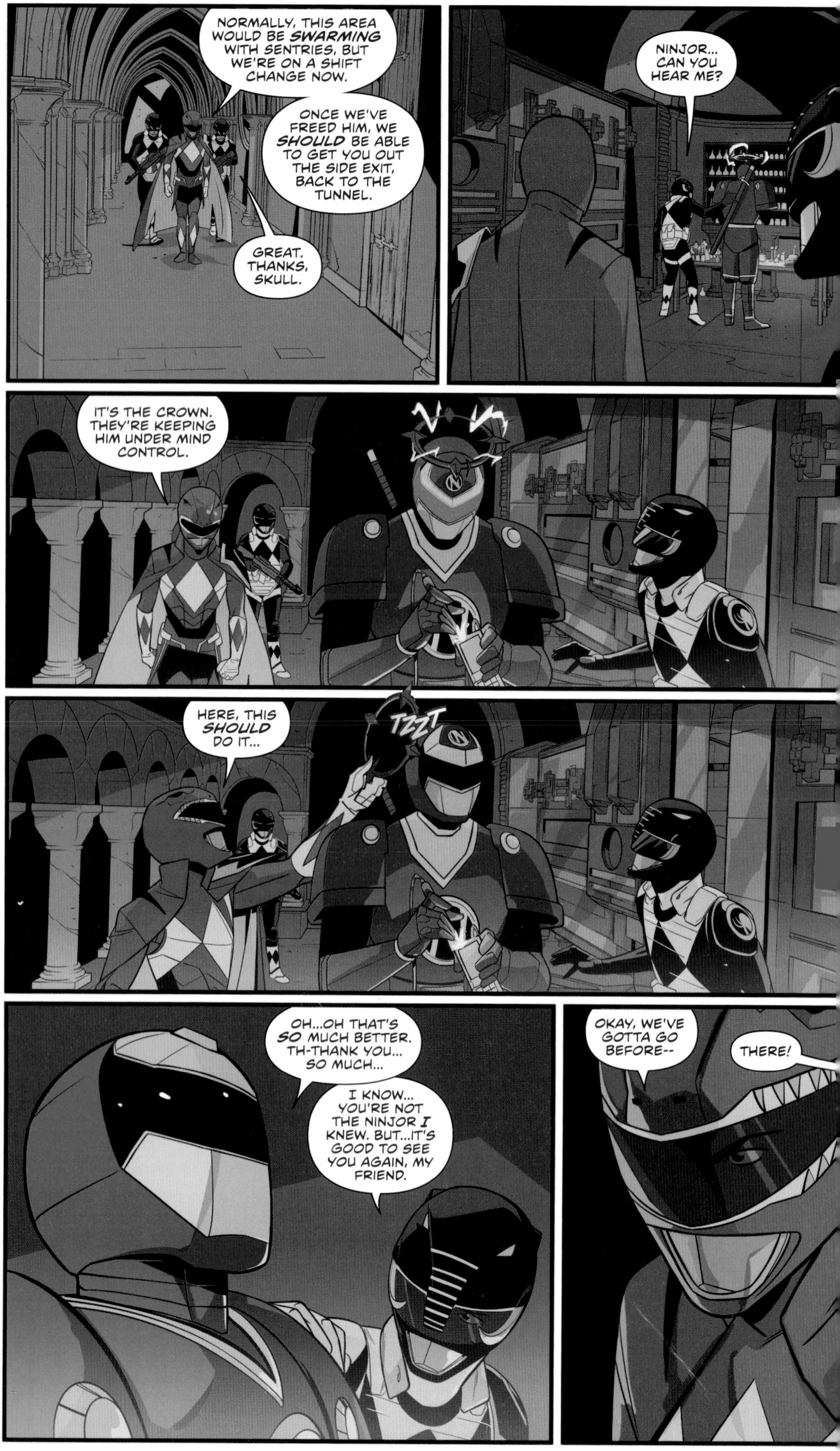
NORMALLY, THIS AREA WOULD BE SWARMING WITH SENTRIES, BUT WE'RE ON A SHIFT CHANGE NOW.
ONCE WE'VE FREED HIM, WE SHOULD BE ABLE TO GET YOU OUT THE SIDE EXIT, BACK TO THE TUNNEL.
GREAT. THANKS, SKULL.
NINJOR... CAN YOU HEAR ME?
IT'S THE CROWN. THEY'RE KEEPING HIM UNDER MIND CONTROL.
HERE, THIS SHOULD DO IT...
TZZT
OH...OH THAT'S SO MUCH BETTER. TH-THANK YOU... SO MUCH...
I KNOW... YOU'RE NOT THE NINJOR I KNEW. BUT...IT'S GOOD TO SEE YOU AGAIN, MY FRIEND.
OKAY, WE'VE GOTTA GO BEFORE--
THERE!

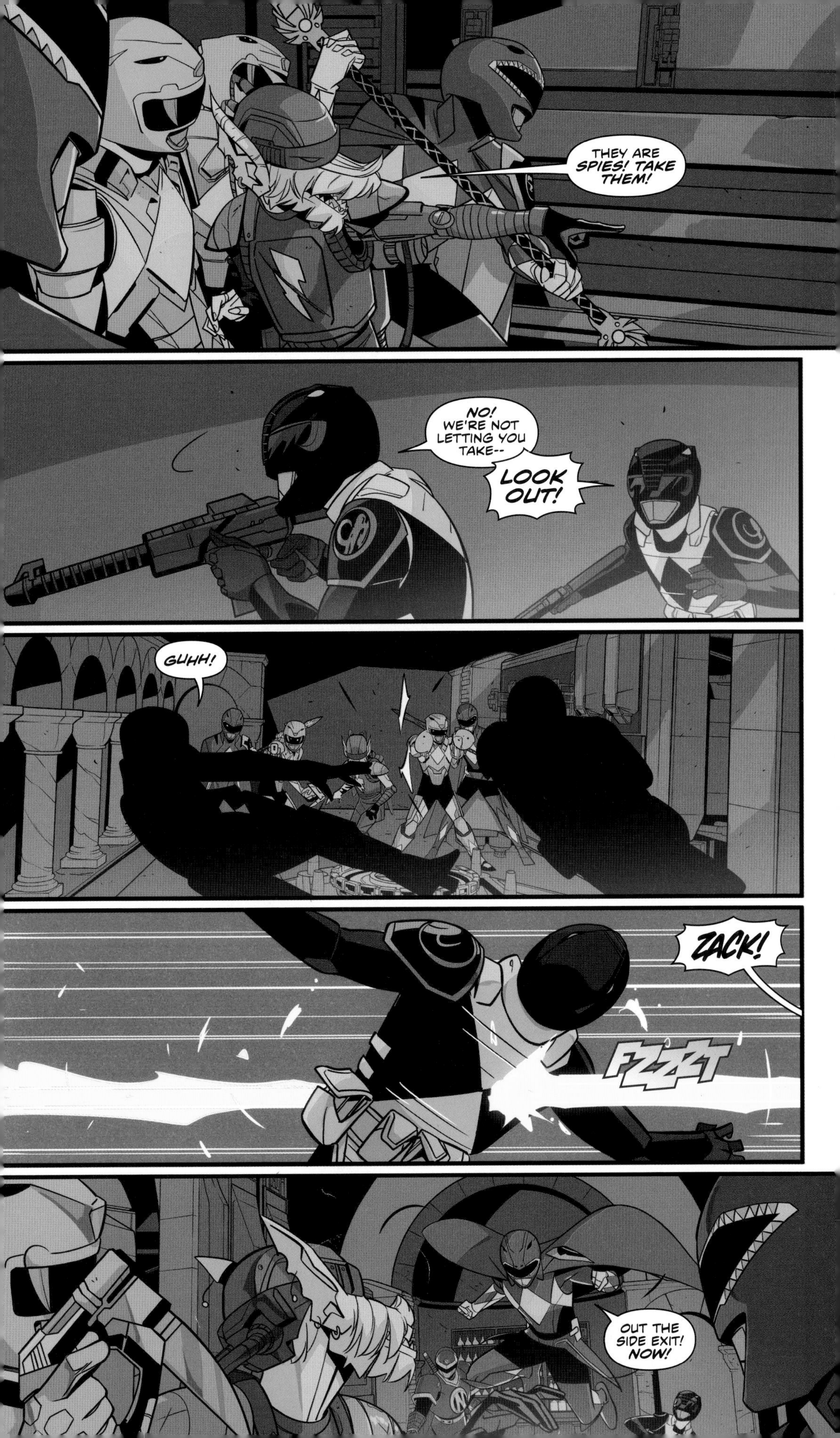
THEY ARE SPIES! TAKE THEM!
NO! WE'RE NOT LETTING YOU TAKE--
LOOK OUT!
GUHH!
ZACK!
FZZZT
OUT THE SIDE EXIT! NOW!

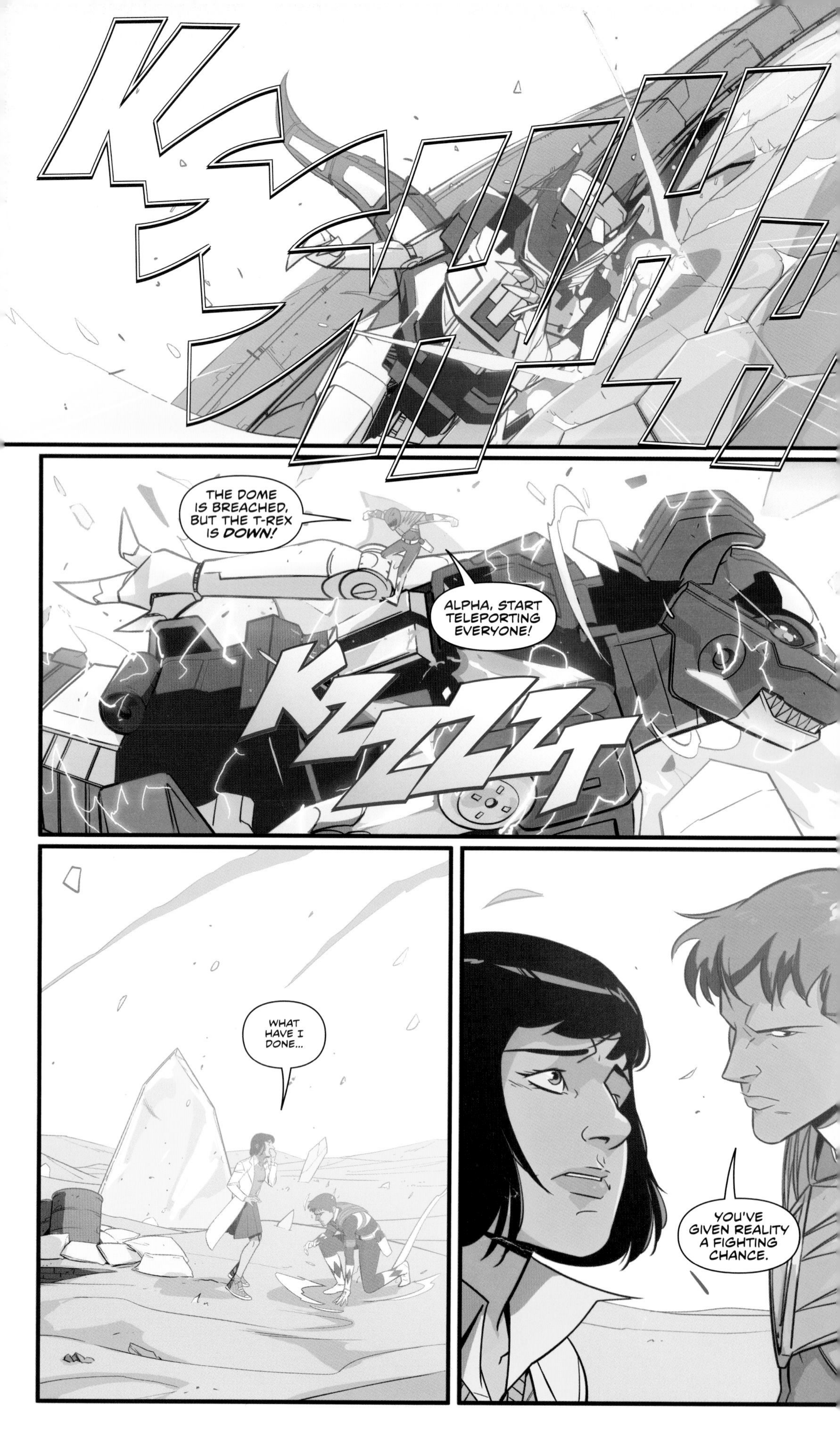

KSHUNNK
THE DOME IS BREACHED, BUT THE T-REX IS DOWN!
ALPHA, START TELEPORTING EVERYONE!
KZZZZT
WHAT HAVE I DONE...
YOU'VE GIVEN REALITY A FIGHTING CHANCE.

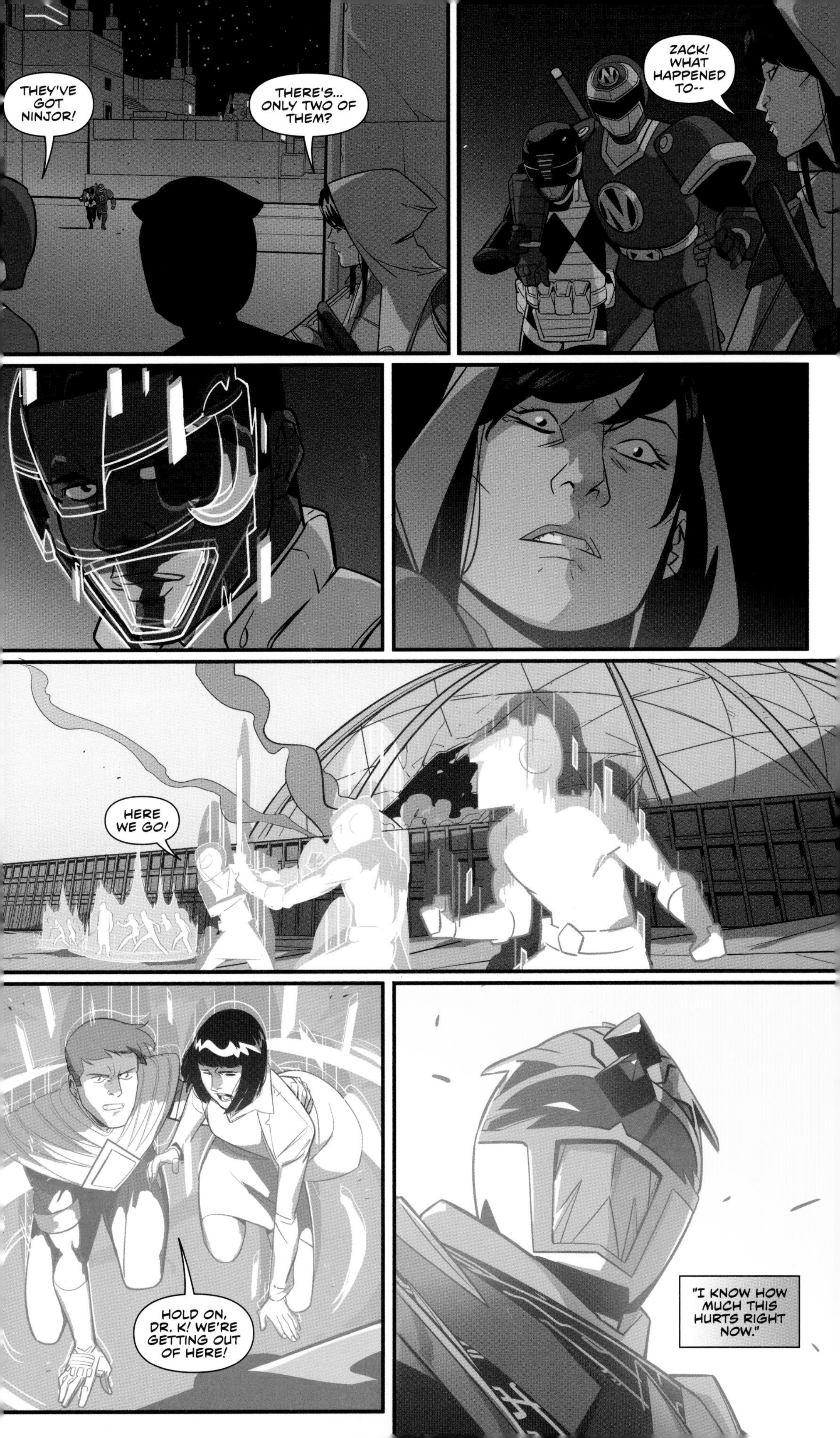
THEY'VE GOT NINJOR!
THERE'S... ONLY TWO OF THEM?
ZACK! WHAT HAPPENED TO--
HERE WE GO!
HOLD ON, DR. K! WE'RE GETTING OUT OF HERE!
"I KNOW HOW MUCH THIS HURTS RIGHT NOW."

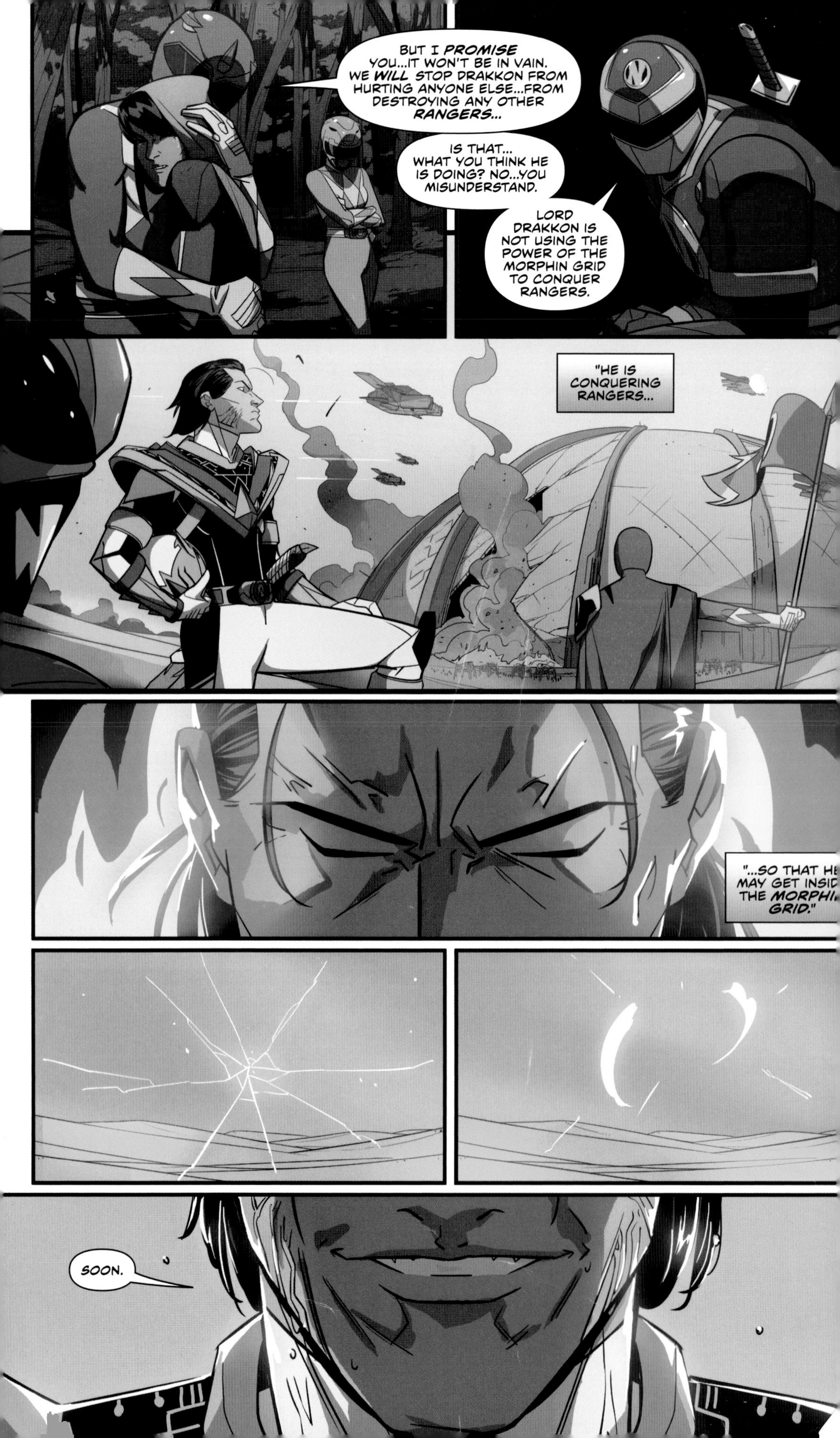

BUT I PROMISE YOU...IT WON'T BE IN VAIN. WE WILL STOP DRAKKON FROM HURTING ANYONE ELSE...FROM DESTROYING ANY OTHER RANGERS...
IS THAT... WHAT YOU THINK HE IS DOING? NO...YOU MISUNDERSTAND.
LORD DRAKKON IS NOT USING THE POWER OF THE MORPHIN GRID TO CONQUER RANGERS.
"HE IS CONQUERING RANGERS...
"...SO THAT HE MAY GET INSIDE THE MORPHIN GRID."
SOON.

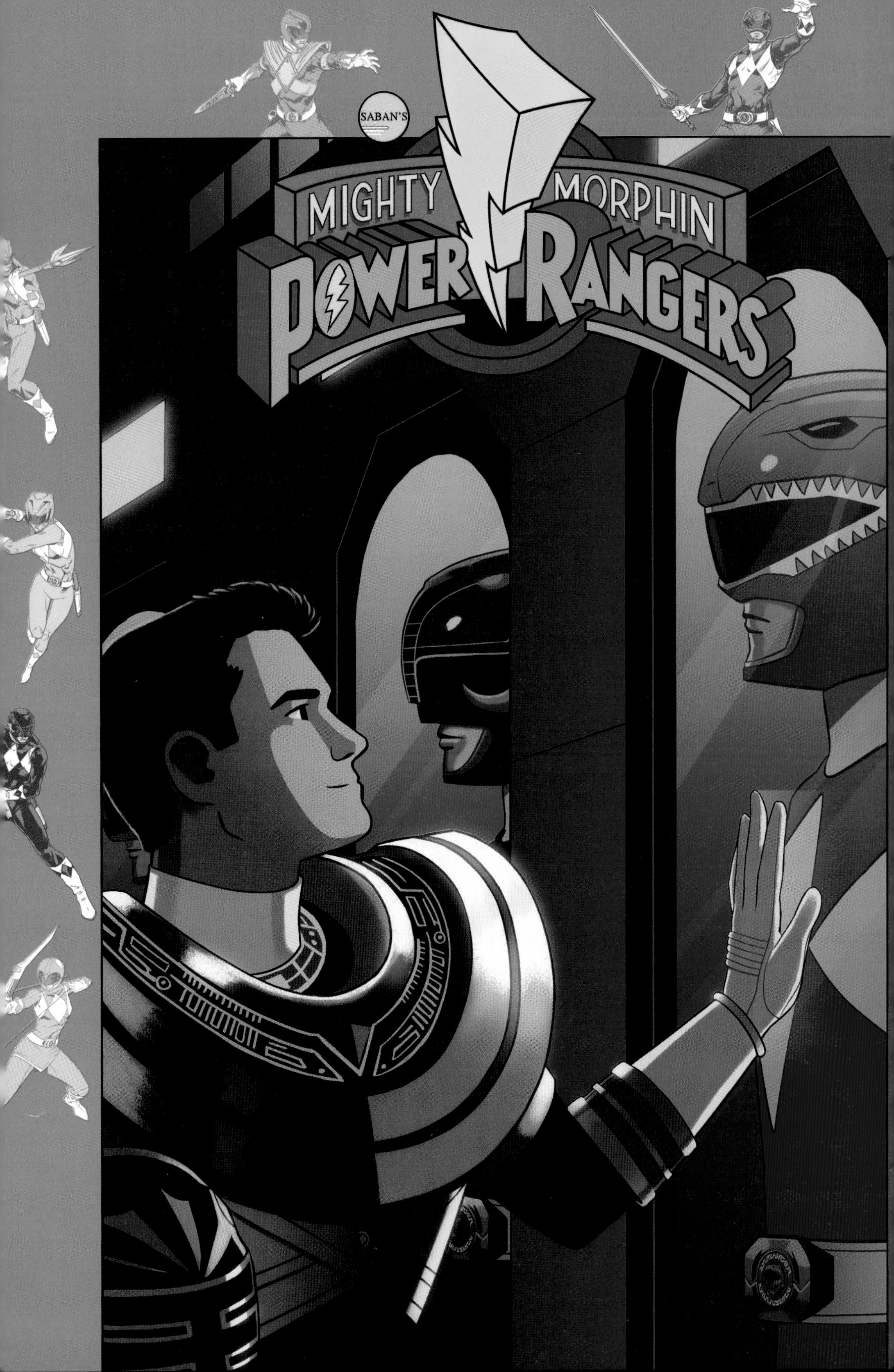
SABAN'S
MIGHTY MORPHIN
POWER RANGERS

CHAPTER **TWENTY-EIGHT**

JORDAN GIBSON ISSUE TWENTY-EIGHT SUBSCRIPTION COVER

THE NEW ADVENTURES OF
BLUE SENTURION & NINJOR

WRITTEN BY
RYAN FERRIER

ILLUSTRATED BY
BACHAN

COLORS BY
JEREMY LAWSON

LETTERS BY
JIM CAMPBELL

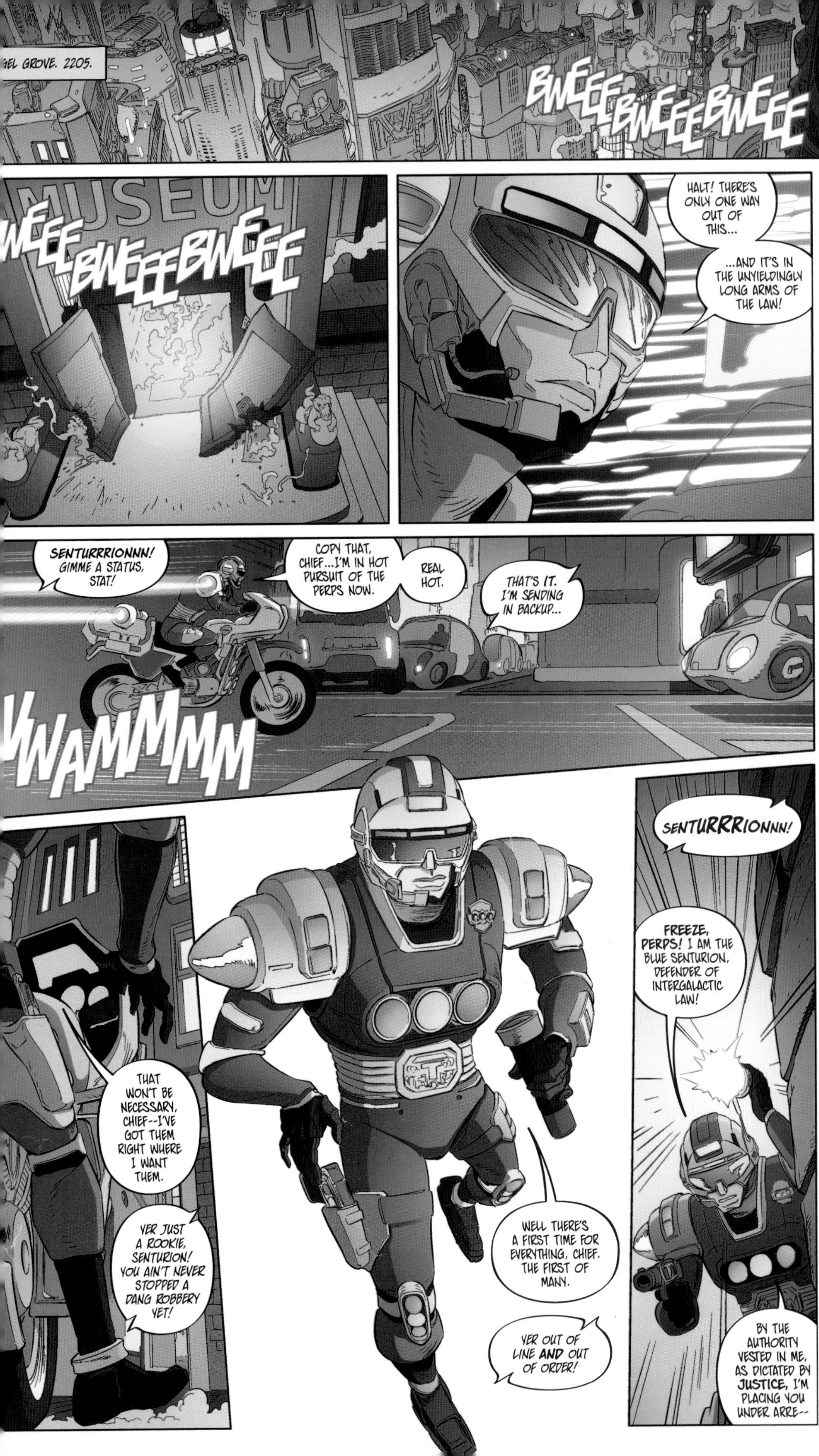

GEL GROVE. 2205.
BWEEEBWEEEBWEEE
MUSEUM
BWEEEBWEEEBWEEE
HALT! THERE'S ONLY ONE WAY OUT OF THIS...
...AND IT'S IN THE UNYIELDINGLY LONG ARMS OF THE LAW!
SENTURRRIONNN! GIMME A STATUS, STAT!
COPY THAT, CHIEF...I'M IN HOT PURSUIT OF THE PERPS NOW.
REAL HOT.
THAT'S IT. I'M SENDING IN BACKUP...
VWAMMMM
THAT WON'T BE NECESSARY, CHIEF--I'VE GOT THEM RIGHT WHERE I WANT THEM.
YER JUST A ROOKIE, SENTURION! YOU AIN'T NEVER STOPPED A DANG ROBBERY YET!
WELL THERE'S A FIRST TIME FOR EVERYTHING, CHIEF. THE FIRST OF MANY.
YER OUT OF LINE AND OUT OF ORDER!
SENTURRRIONNN!
FREEZE, PERPS! I AM THE BLUE SENTURION, DEFENDER OF INTERGALACTIC LAW!
BY THE AUTHORITY VESTED IN ME, AS DICTATED BY JUSTICE, I'M PLACING YOU UNDER ARRE--

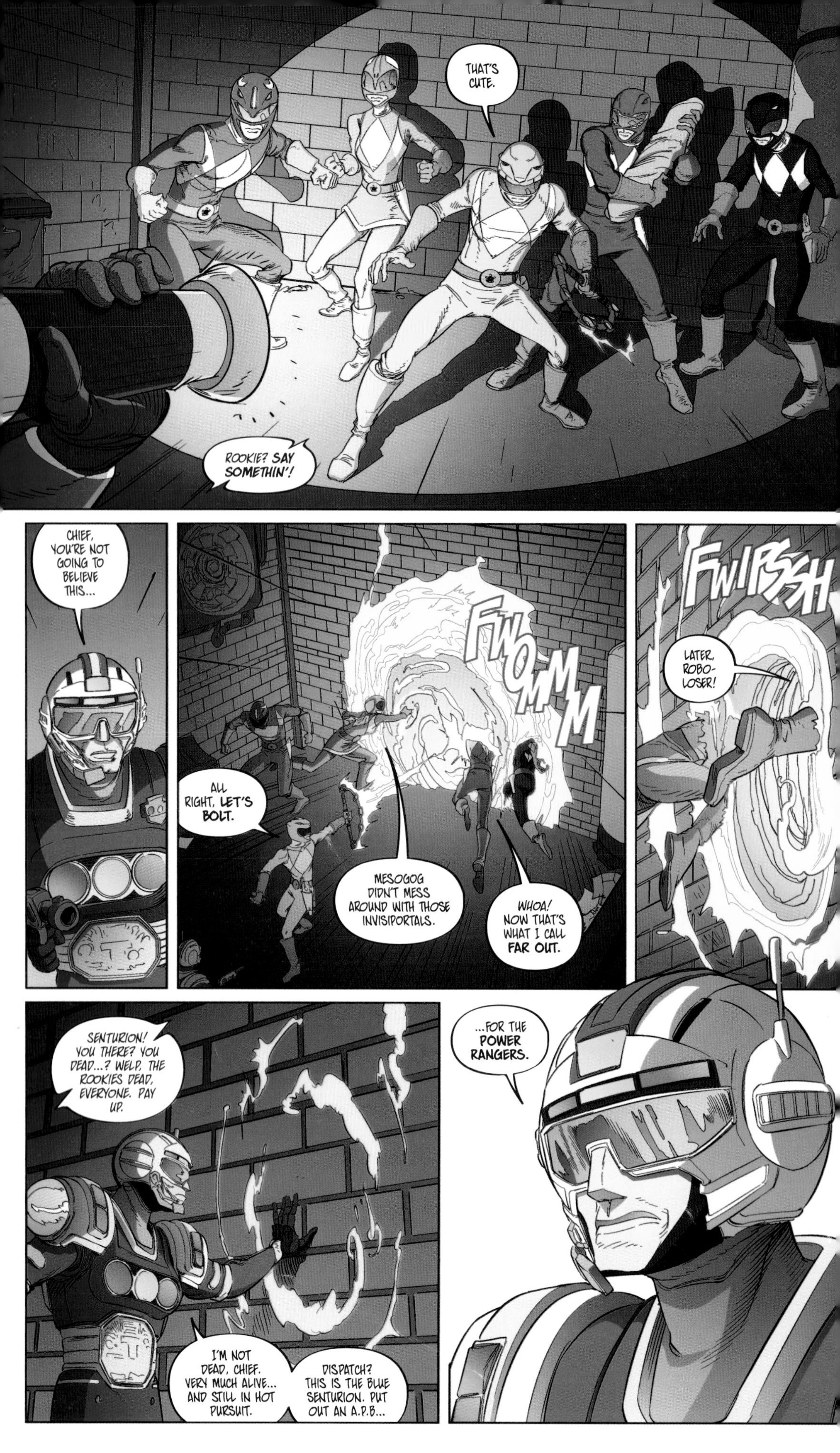
THAT'S CUTE.
ROOKIE? SAY SOMETHIN'!
CHIEF, YOU'RE NOT GOING TO BELIEVE THIS...
FWOMMM
ALL RIGHT, LET'S BOLT.
MESOGOG DIDN'T MESS AROUND WITH THOSE INVISIPORTALS.
WHOA! NOW THAT'S WHAT I CALL FAR OUT.
FWIPSSH
LATER, ROBO-LOSER!
SENTURION! YOU THERE? YOU DEAD...? WELP, THE ROOKIES DEAD, EVERYONE. PAY UP.
I'M NOT DEAD, CHIEF. VERY MUCH ALIVE... AND STILL IN HOT PURSUIT.
DISPATCH? THIS IS THE BLUE SENTURION. PUT OUT AN A.P.B...
...FOR THE POWER RANGERS.

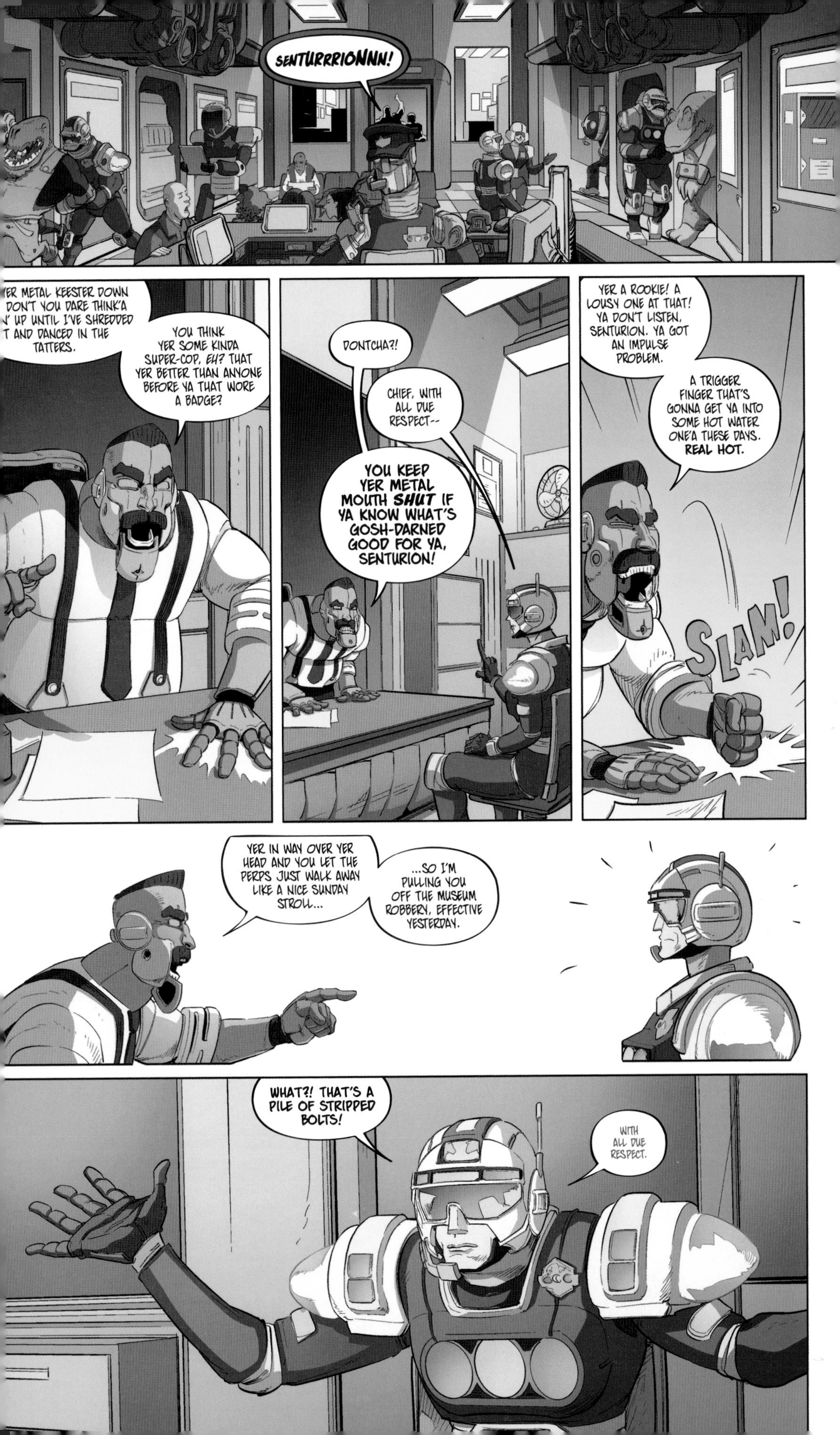
SENTURRRIONNN!
YER METAL KEESTER DOWN
DON'T YOU DARE THINK'A
N' UP UNTIL I'VE SHREDDED
T AND DANCED IN THE
TATTERS.
YOU THINK YER SOME KINDA SUPER-COP, EH? THAT YER BETTER THAN ANYONE BEFORE YA THAT WORE A BADGE?
DONTCHA?!
CHIEF, WITH ALL DUE RESPECT--
YOU KEEP YER METAL MOUTH SHUT IF YA KNOW WHAT'S GOSH-DARNED GOOD FOR YA, SENTURION!
YER A ROOKIE! A LOUSY ONE AT THAT! YA DON'T LISTEN, SENTURION. YA GOT AN IMPULSE PROBLEM.
A TRIGGER FINGER THAT'S GONNA GET YA INTO SOME HOT WATER ONE'A THESE DAYS. REAL HOT.
SLAM!
YER IN WAY OVER YER HEAD AND YOU LET THE PERPS JUST WALK AWAY LIKE A NICE SUNDAY STROLL...
...SO I'M PULLING YOU OFF THE MUSEUM ROBBERY, EFFECTIVE YESTERDAY.
WHAT?! THAT'S A PILE OF STRIPPED BOLTS!
WITH ALL DUE RESPECT.

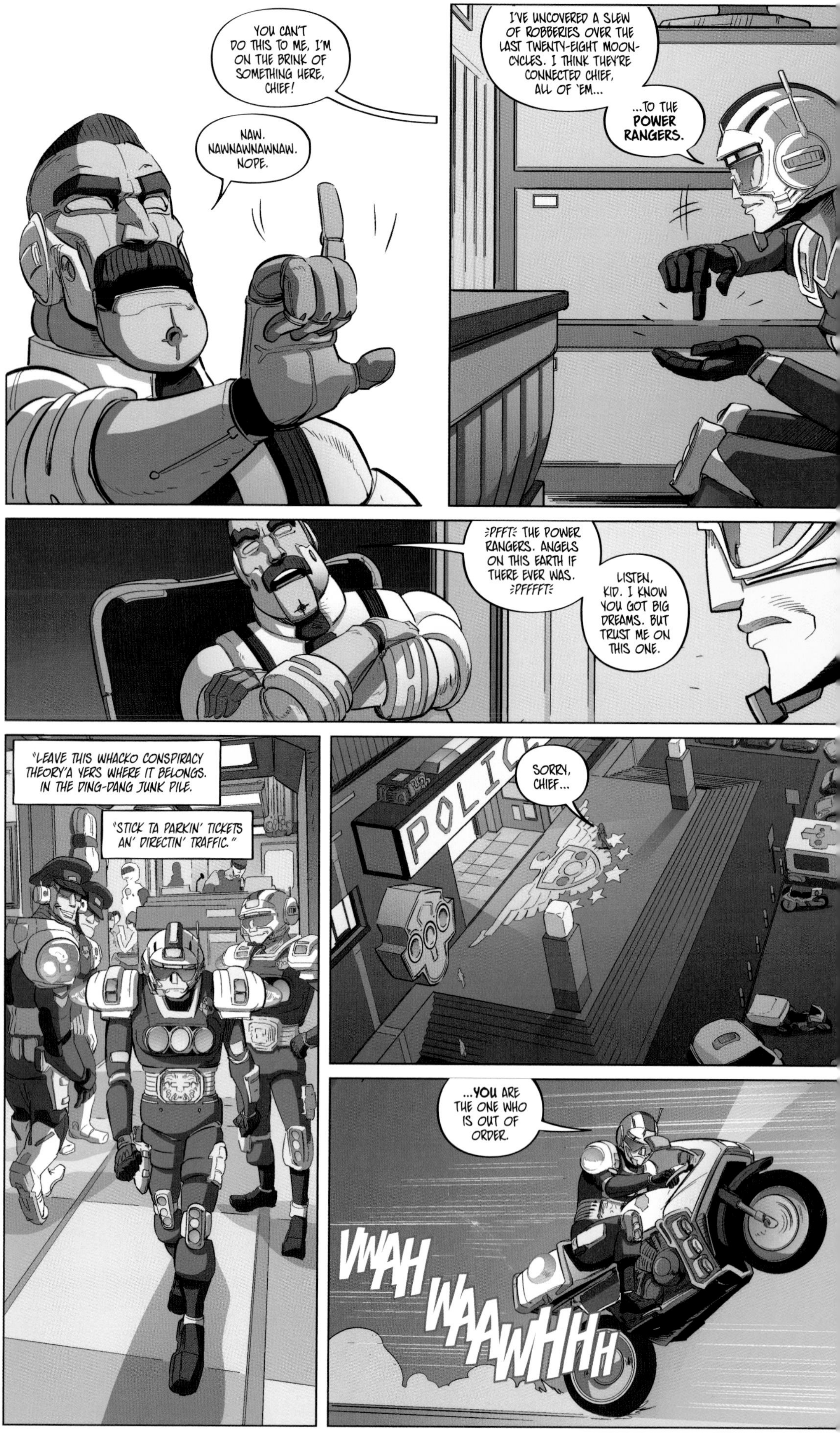
YOU CAN'T DO THIS TO ME, I'M ON THE BRINK OF SOMETHING HERE, CHIEF!
NAW. NAWNAWNAWNAW. NOPE.
I'VE UNCOVERED A SLEW OF ROBBERIES OVER THE LAST TWENTY-EIGHT MOON-CYCLES. I THINK THEY'RE CONNECTED CHIEF, ALL OF 'EM...
...TO THE **POWER RANGERS.**
=PFFT= THE POWER RANGERS. ANGELS ON THIS EARTH IF THERE EVER WAS. =PFFFFT=
LISTEN, KID. I KNOW YOU GOT BIG DREAMS. BUT TRUST ME ON THIS ONE.
"LEAVE THIS WHACKO CONSPIRACY THEORY'A YERS WHERE IT BELONGS. IN THE DING-DANG JUNK PILE.
"STICK TA PARKIN' TICKETS AN' DIRECTIN' TRAFFIC."
POLICE
SORRY, CHIEF...
...**YOU** ARE THE ONE WHO IS OUT OF ORDER.
VWAH WAAWHHHH

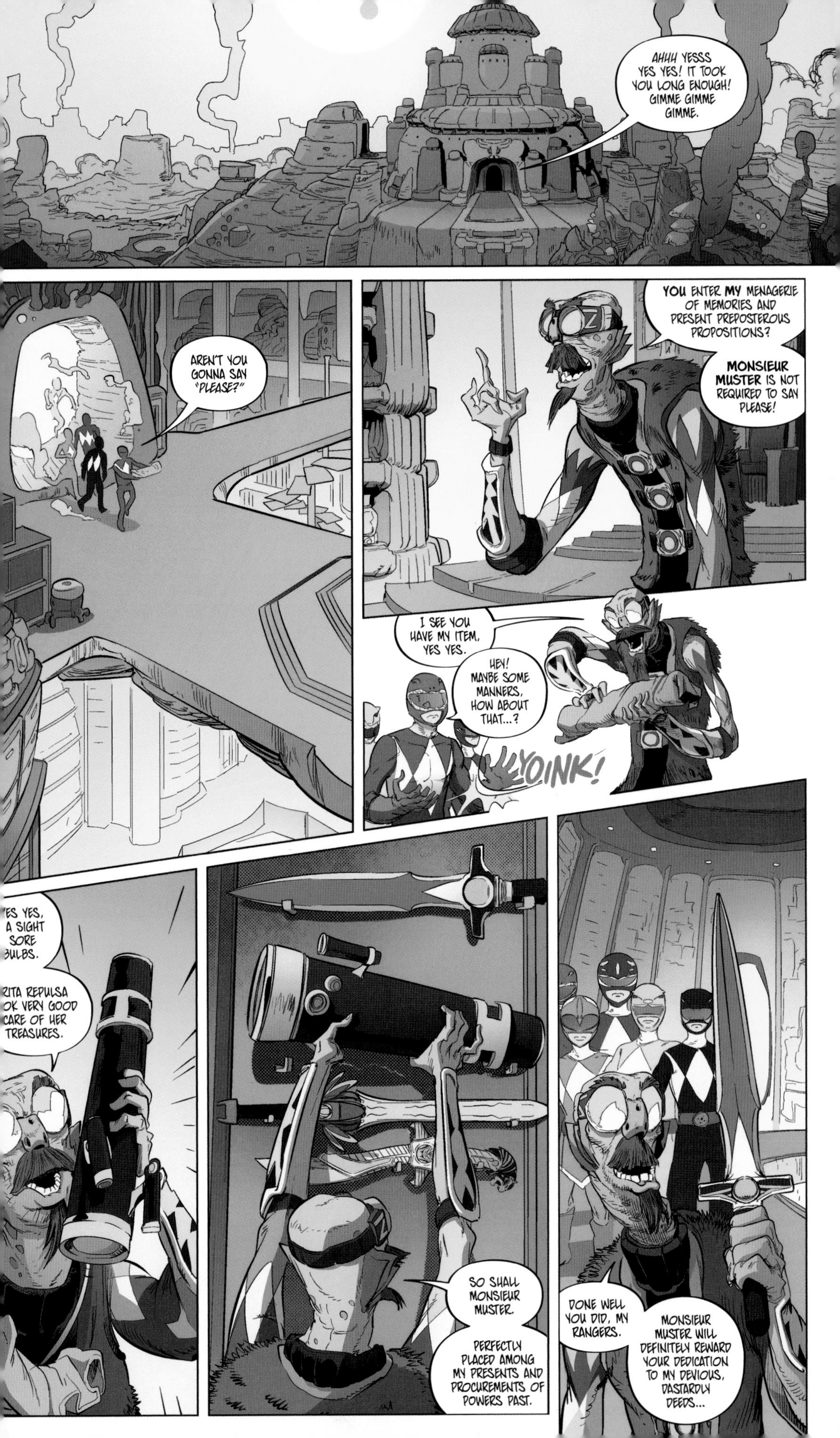

AHHH YESSS YES YES! IT TOOK YOU LONG ENOUGH! GIMME GIMME GIMME.
AREN'T YOU GONNA SAY "PLEASE?"
YOU ENTER **MY** MENAGERIE OF MEMORIES AND PRESENT PREPOSTEROUS PROPOSITIONS?
MONSIEUR MUSTER IS NOT REQUIRED TO SAY PLEASE!
I SEE YOU HAVE MY ITEM, YES YES.
HEY! MAYBE SOME MANNERS, HOW ABOUT THAT...?
YOINK!
YES YES, A SIGHT SORE BULBS.
RITA REPULSA OK VERY GOOD CARE OF HER TREASURES.
SO SHALL MONSIEUR MUSTER.
PERFECTLY PLACED AMONG MY PRESENTS AND PROCUREMENTS OF POWERS PAST.
DONE WELL YOU DID, MY RANGERS.
MONSIEUR MUSTER WILL DEFINITELY REWARD YOUR DEDICATION TO MY DEVIOUS, DASTARDLY DEEDS...

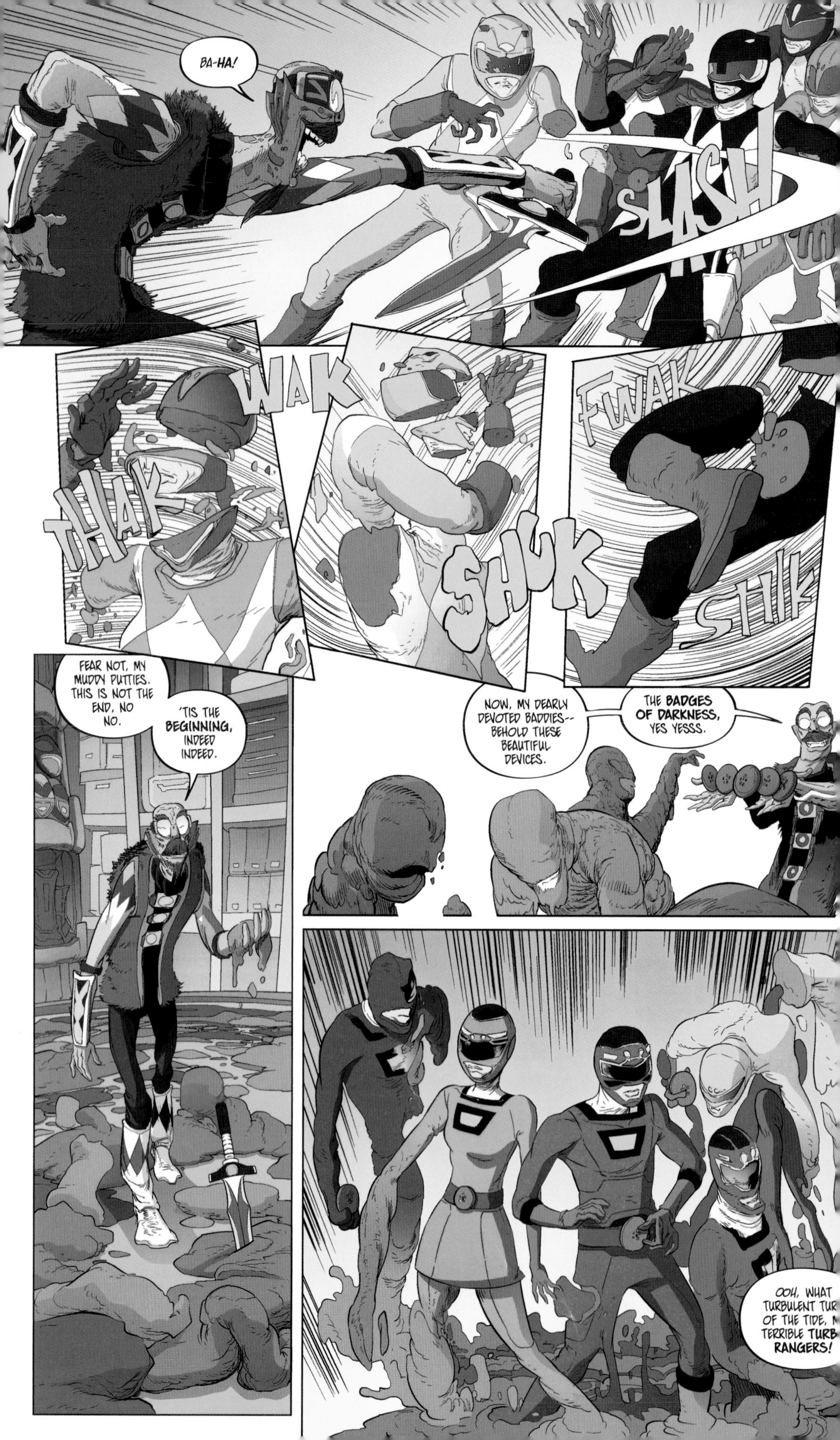

BA-HA!
SLASH
WAK
THAK
FWAK
SHUK
SHIK
FEAR NOT, MY MUDDY PUTTIES. THIS IS NOT THE END, NO NO.
'TIS THE BEGINNING, INDEED INDEED.
NOW, MY DEARLY DEVOTED BADDIES-- BEHOLD THESE BEAUTIFUL DEVICES.
THE BADGES OF DARKNESS, YES YESSS.
OOH, WHAT TURBULENT TUR OF THE TIDE, M TERRIBLE TURB RANGERS!

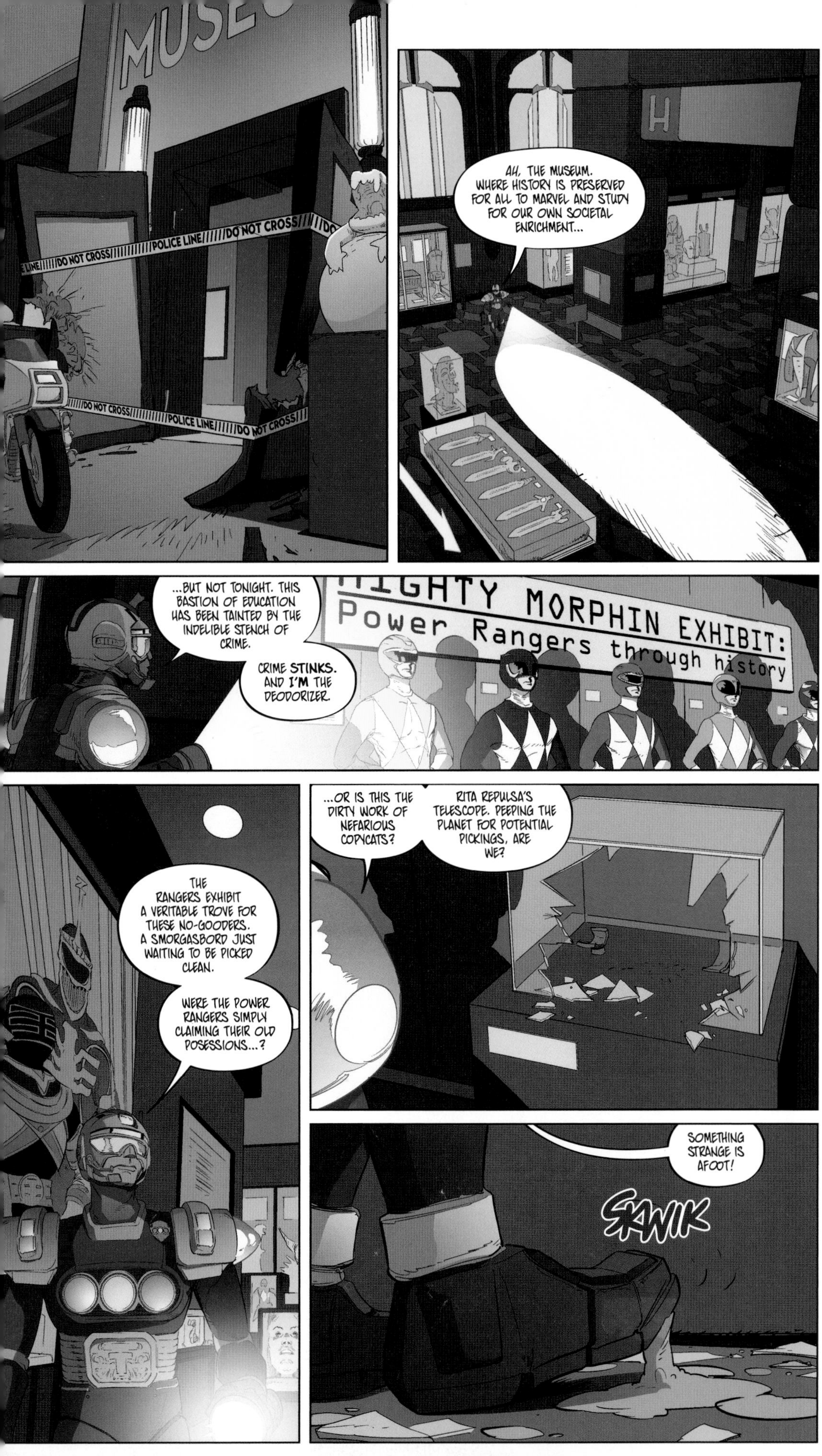

DO NOT CROSS
POLICE LINE
DO NOT CROSS
DO NOT CROSS
POLICE LINE
DO NOT CROSS
AH, THE MUSEUM. WHERE HISTORY IS PRESERVED FOR ALL TO MARVEL AND STUDY FOR OUR OWN SOCIETAL ENRICHMENT...
...BUT NOT TONIGHT. THIS BASTION OF EDUCATION HAS BEEN TAINTED BY THE INDELIBLE STENCH OF CRIME.
CRIME **STINKS.** AND **I'M** THE DEODORIZER.
MIGHTY MORPHIN EXHIBIT:
Power Rangers through history
THE RANGERS EXHIBIT A VERITABLE TROVE FOR THESE NO-GOODERS. A SMORGASBORD JUST WAITING TO BE PICKED CLEAN.
WERE THE POWER RANGERS SIMPLY CLAIMING THEIR OLD POSESSIONS...?
...OR IS THIS THE DIRTY WORK OF NEFARIOUS COPYCATS?
RITA REPULSA'S TELESCOPE. PEEPING THE PLANET FOR POTENTIAL PICKINGS, ARE WE?
SOMETHING STRANGE IS AFOOT!
SKWIK

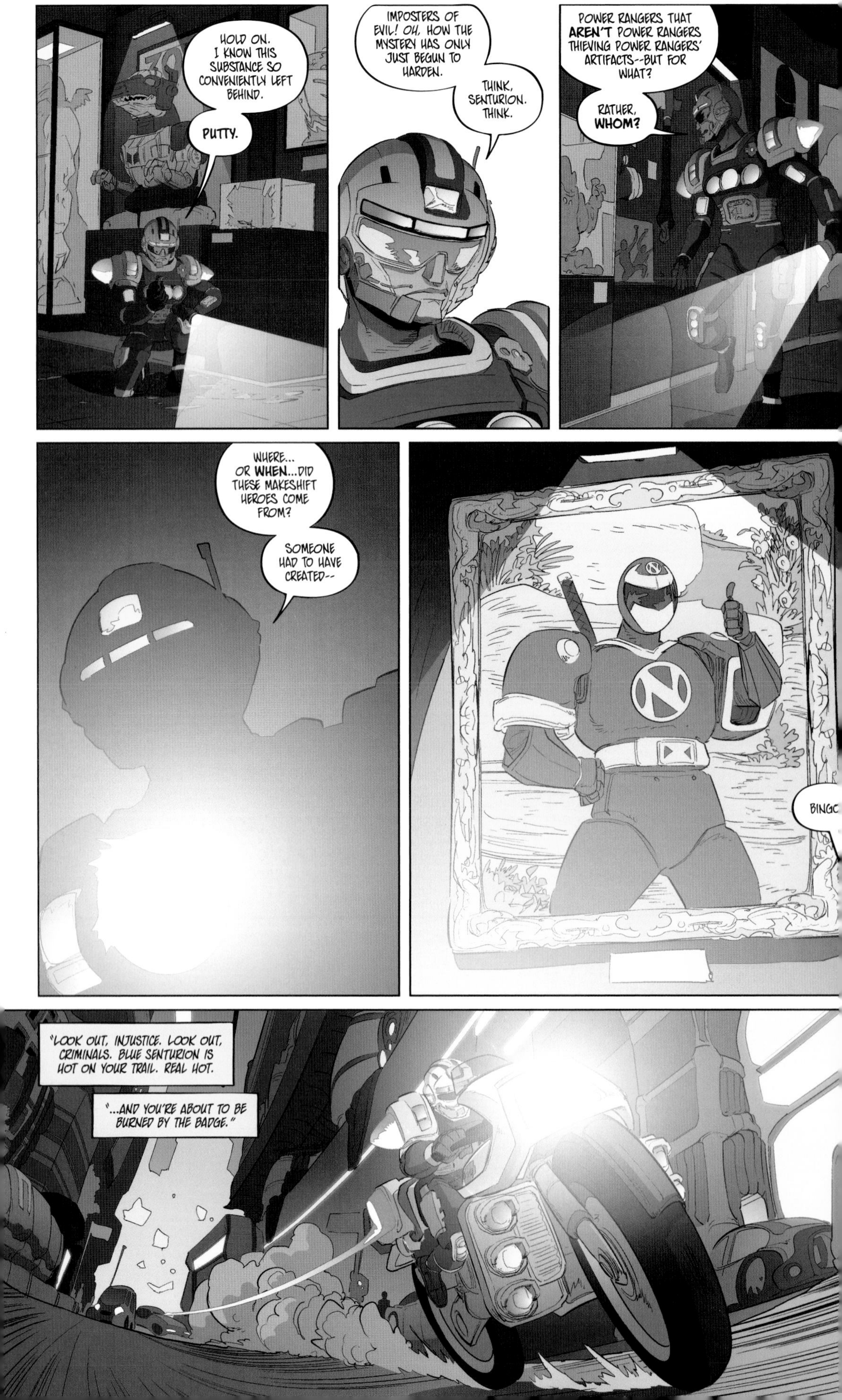
HOLD ON. I KNOW THIS SUBSTANCE SO CONVENIENTLY LEFT BEHIND.
PUTTY.
IMPOSTERS OF EVIL! OH, HOW THE MYSTERY HAS ONLY JUST BEGUN TO HARDEN.
THINK, SENTURION. THINK.
POWER RANGERS THAT AREN'T POWER RANGERS THIEVING POWER RANGERS' ARTIFACTS--BUT FOR WHAT?
RATHER, WHOM?
WHERE... OR WHEN...DID THESE MAKESHIFT HEROES COME FROM?
SOMEONE HAD TO HAVE CREATED--
BINGO
"LOOK OUT, INJUSTICE. LOOK OUT, CRIMINALS. BLUE SENTURION IS HOT ON YOUR TRAIL. REAL HOT.
"...AND YOU'RE ABOUT TO BE BURNED BY THE BADGE."

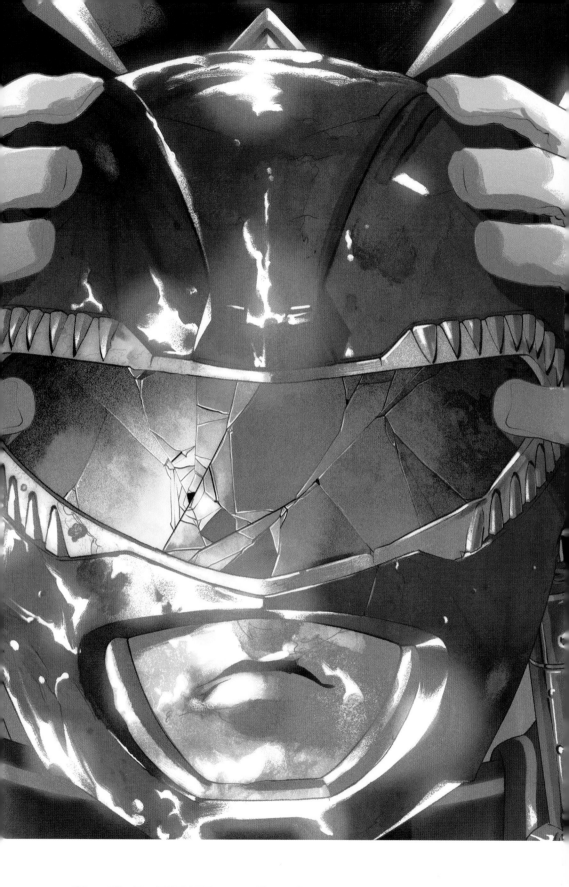

COVER GALLERY

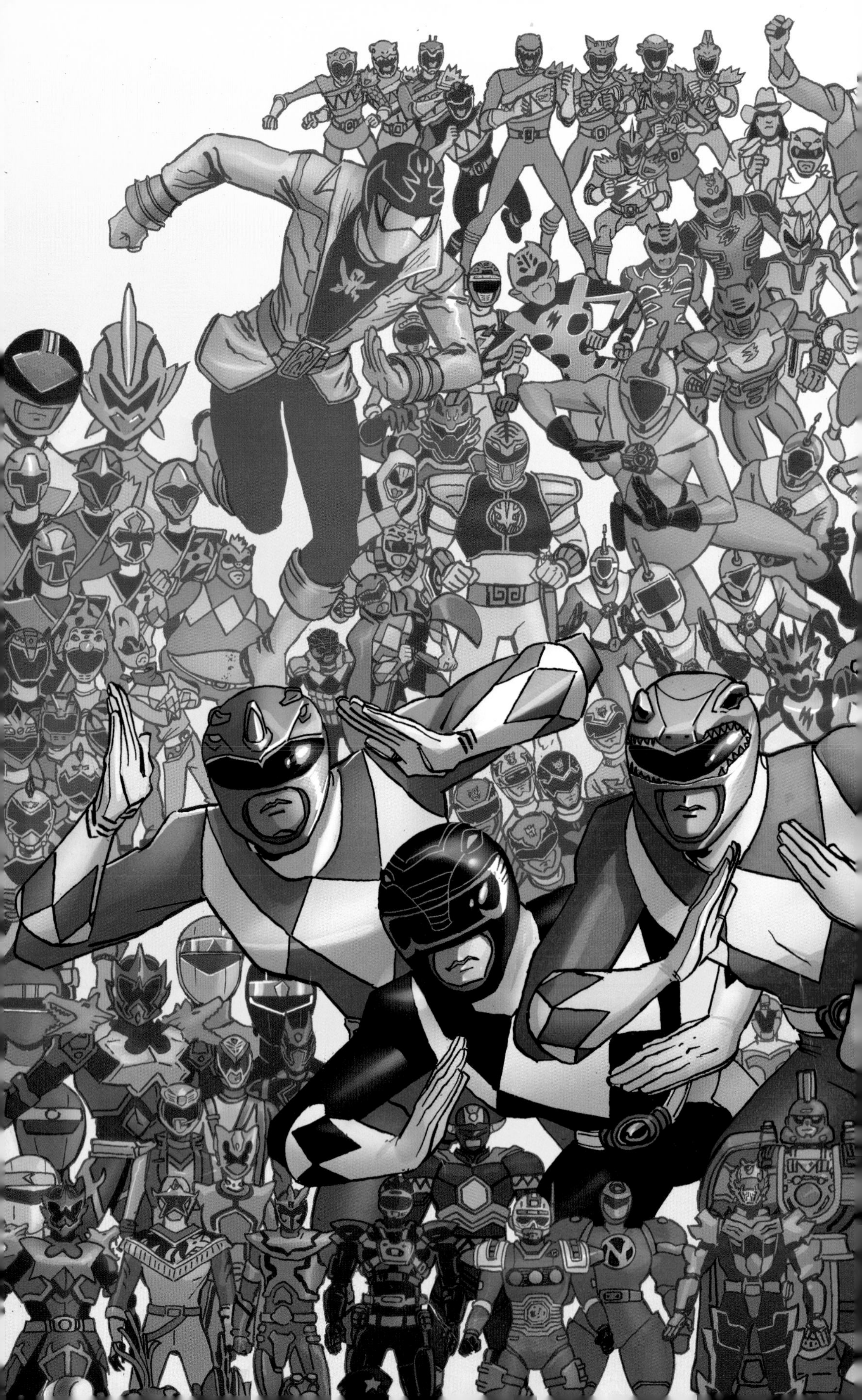

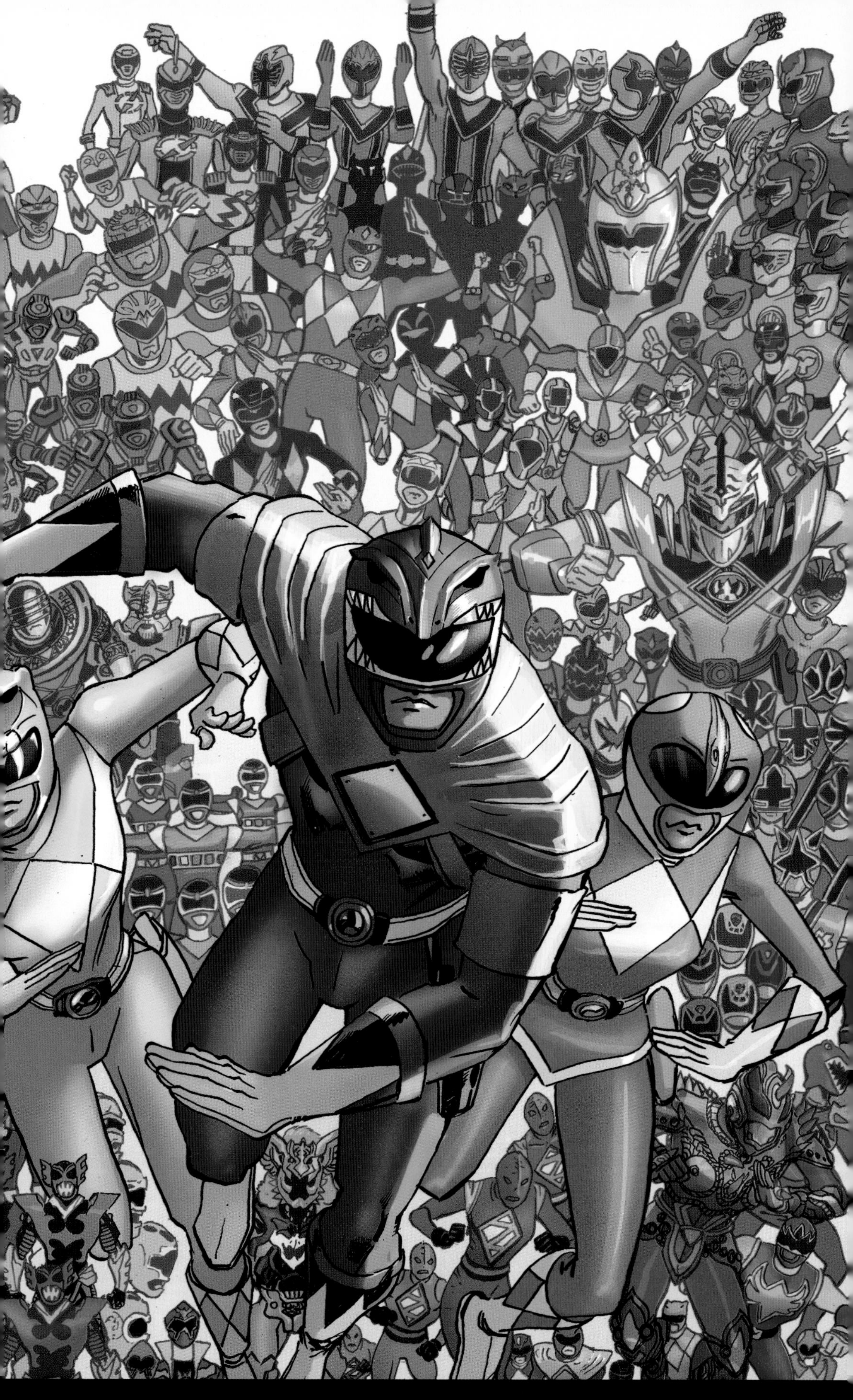

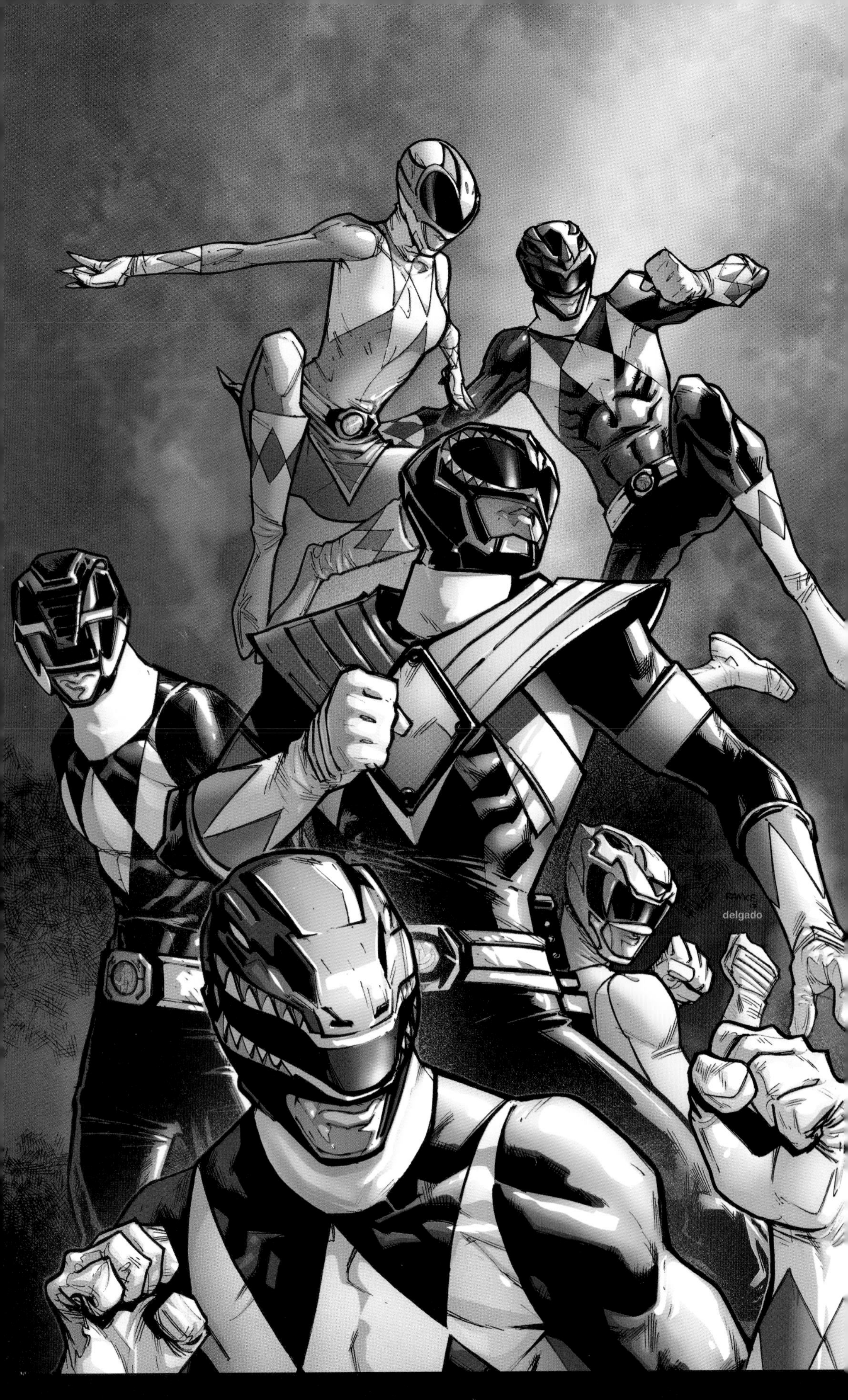
delgado

HUMBERTO RAMOS COLORS BY EDGAR DELGADO ISSUE TWENTY-FIVE ONE PER STORE VARIANT C

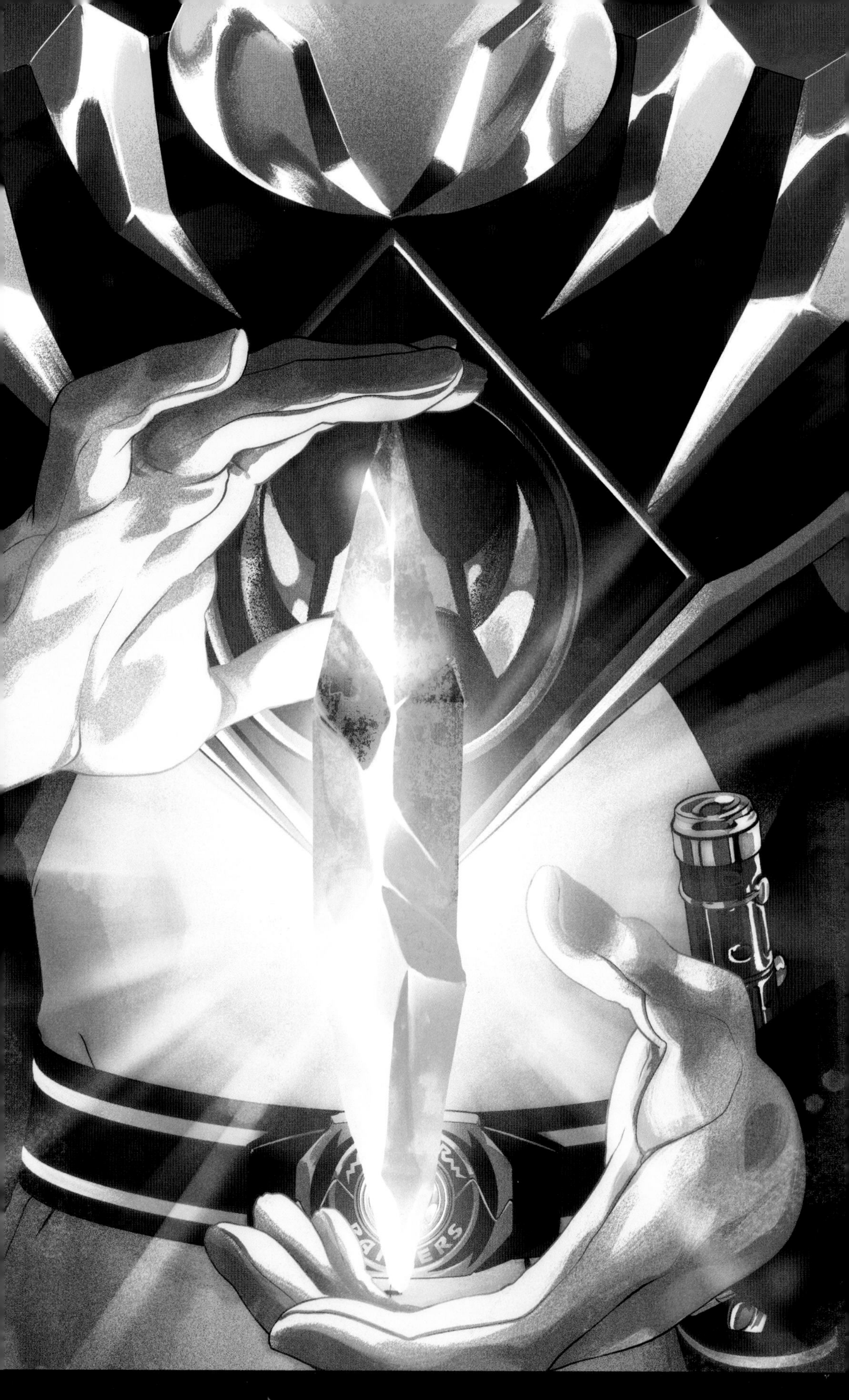

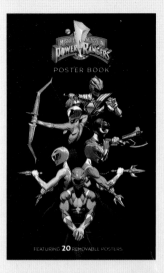